Against

the Wall

Israel's Barrier
to Peace

edited by **Michael Sorkin**

THE NEW PRESS

NEW YORK
LONDON

Requests for permission to reproduce selections from this book should be mailed to: Permissions Department, The New Press, 38 Greene Street, New York, NY 10013

Published in the United States by The New Press, New York, 2005
Distributed by W. W. Norton & Company, Inc., New York

LIBRARY OF CONGRESS CATALOGING-IN-PUBLICATION DATA
Against the wall: Israel's barrier to peace / edited by Michael Sorkin.
p. cm.
Includes biographical references.
ISBN 1-56584-990-6 (hc) — ISBN 1-56584-964-7 (pbk.)
1. Arab-Israeli conflict—1993- 2. Israeli West Bank Barrier. 3. Israeli West Bank Barrier—Social aspects.
4. Israel—Boundaries. 5. West Bank—Boundaries. I. Sorkin, Michael.

DS119.76.A385 2005
956.05'3—dc22   200504932

The New Press was established in 1990 as a not-for-profit alternative to the large, commercial publishing houses currently dominating the book publishing industry. The New Press operates in the public interest rather than for private gain, and is committed to publishing, in innovative ways, works of educational, cultural, and community value that are often deemed insufficiently profitable.

www.thenewpress.com

Book design by Distant Station Ltd and Isaac Gertman
This book was set in Akzidenz-Grotesk BQ

Special thanks to Britta Degn

Printed in Canada

10 9 8 7 6 5 4 3 2 1

Contents

Introduction: Up Against the Wall

Michael Sorkin

This book is frankly polemical, a collective protest against the "security wall" being built by Israel to physically separate itself from Palestine, a Palestine the wall seeks to define. While this volume is full of nightmarish images of life behind the wall, of its terrible effects, the sight of a 30-foot-high concrete barrier slashing through urban neighborhoods, while shocking, is also ordinary. The wall is both horrendous and familiar-looking, like an acoustic barrier along a highway—more "civil" engineering. Where it functions strictly as a wall—an uncrossable physical barrier—it joins a repertoire of "wallings"—from Berlin to Nicosia to Kashmir to the 38th parallel in Korea to the U.S./Mexican border—that is an indelible part of the everyday landscape of the modern world. Each of these barriers has been touted as providing security for one side or the other, but each clearly marks failed politics and aggressive intransigence.

Because such walls are so commonplace, *Against the Wall* includes discussions of a number of other barriers that are similarly exclusionary and aggrandizing, including the southern U.S. border fortifications, the historic spatial arrangements of apartheid, and the more flexible and instantaneous policing of virtual space. The book also holds essays that extrapolate the idea of boundary to the larger workings of global capital and that discuss this system in the context of the internal U.S. political division between "progressive" blue and "reactionary" red states, and that examine the idea of separation in its foundational, anthropological depth. These pieces, I hope, extend the analysis beyond its Middle Eastern context to situate it in the space of the global everyday. The truly invidious character of the Israeli wall can only be unpacked in this larger context. Indeed, arguing the singularity (and provisionality) of this wall has been a weapon of its partisans.

The wall ossifies a social physics that holds that two national bodies cannot share the same space at the same time. Although justice is not reducible to a just apportionment of space, the primary expression of the Middle East conflict has played out in spatial terms. The territorial division marked by the wall, however, is not just physical. The wall—only a small portion of which is comprised of the mammoth concrete barrier familiar from media coverage—is a template for invisible digital and electronic barriers, a system that girdles the earth. It is also part of a regime of walling that pervades almost every interaction between Palestinians and Israelis, expressed in discriminatory property regulations, in restrictions on marriage between Palestinians in Israel and those in the territories, in the semipermeable membrane of withheld employment, in floating bubbles of armed and dangerous sovereignty, and in the permanent mobility of all these boundaries.

Notwithstanding any larger implications for the shifting status of statehood, citizenship, and "rights," there are three principal claims against this particular wall. First, it makes life miserable and dangerous for Palestinians, cut off from family, jobs, property, medical care, and schools, severely restricted in movement, subjected to a gauntlet of daily humiliations, surveilled around the clock, and locked in ghettoes. Second, the wall is a very concrete proposition about the boundary between Israel and Palestine, supposedly still the subject of negotiation. Using the wall, Israel appropriates territory beyond the 1949 "green line" that amounts—nobody knows for sure—to something between 10 and 15 percent of the area of the West Bank. Such "provisional" facts on the ground easily become fixed. Finally, the wall—in its aggressivity and racism—contributes to narrowing the field of Palestinian aspirations, locking them deeper in a grim psychical space where every hope is blocked. The wall is designed to both contain and demean Palestinian aspirations.

The many architects and urbanists included in this volume reflect a special connection arising not simply from the territorial—geographic—nature of the dispute but also from the fact that the language of the conflict is often that of planning: the lingua franca of ordering space. Much of the battle against the wall to date has taken the form of legal actions pursued in Israeli courts, often in the format of environmental impact litigation—a planning staple—and there have been some reroutings as a result. This willingness to create occasional minor exceptions—culminating in the alignment approved by the Knesset in February 2005—has diluted focus on the wall as a comprehensive system of controls by cloaking it in a fantasy of give and take. Nevertheless, these modest results, as well as the numerous protests by peace groups, artists, and others, reinforce solidarity across the border and provide an arena for nonviolent, ethical activity, a model for this book.

An Everyday Wall

If the wall can be said to make a contribution to the science of obstacles, it is in the multiplicity of the registers—from physical to virtual—in which it operates. George W. Bush recently announced the "construction" of a virtual border to defend the United States from terror. This invisible yet ubiquitous border enables great elasticity in the territorial aspects of sovereignty. The law of nations becomes the law of the sea, a de facto shared space plied by tiny vessels of national sovereignty. By switching figure and the ground, national authority can be exercised anywhere on the globe. This wall not only protectively encloses citizens wherever they are but also draws the "line" of national territory around suspect noncitizens wherever they may be found. This is the space of assassination, of Giorgio Agamben's homo sacer, the "subject who is to be killed," perhaps by the blast of a Hellfire missile fired from a robot plane.

The dispersal of the body politic into bodies politic is part of a larger passage—described by Michel Foucault—from the idea of a "territorial state" to a "state of population," the transition from geopolitics to bio-politics. His idea elaborates Hannah Arendt's characterization of refugees as the "avant-garde of their people," an unsettling wave directed at the link between citizenship and rights, at the survival of the nation-state

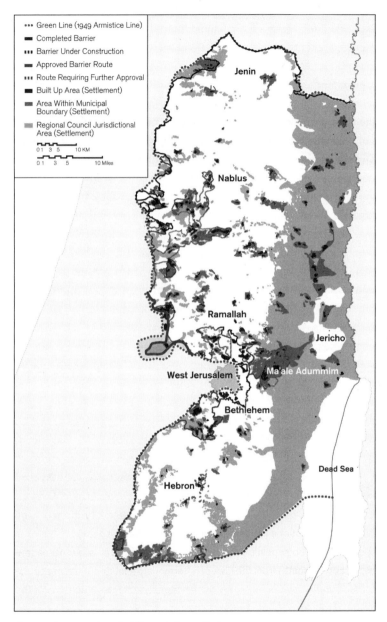

Legend:
- ••• Green Line (1949 Armistice Line)
- ▬ Completed Barrier
- ▬ Barrier Under Construction
- ▬ Approved Barrier Route
- ▬ Route Requiring Further Approval
- ▬ Built Up Area (Settlement)
- ▬ Area Within Municipal Boundary (Settlement)
- ▬ Regional Council Jurisdictional Area (Settlement)

0 1 3 5   10 KM
0 1   3   5   10 Miles

Jenin

Nablus

Ramallah

Jericho

West Jerusalem   Ma'ale Adummim

Bethlehem

Dead Sea

Hebron

Separation Barrier in the West Bank, May 2005. Source: B'tselem.

Introduction Michael Sorkin

itself. Setting aside the problem of constituting "peoples" as a category, the insight marks both a permanent state of displacement and the newly flexible enclosures that define life within it. For Jews—the historic diasporan citizens par excellence of such a "state of population"—the insistence on the Israeli nationality of the country's extraterritorial settlements has grim irony.

The physical wall is marked by its tortured geometry. It follows a remarkably serpentine path, designed not for defense—for which a straight line is more logical—but to reach into the West Bank and capture Israeli settlements for an expanded territory of Israel. Settlements too distant to fall on the "Israeli" side of the wall are brought into the system with their own autonomous walls that frame them as floating islands of Israeli territory. The wall is also articulated horizontally in a system of laminar segregations that compress Palestinian space along all axes, boxing Palestine in and allowing Israeli sovereignty to flow through it on every side, appropriating the subterranean aquifer and the airspace overhead. There is even a growing system of highway overpasses and underpasses that thread Israeli space above and below Palestinian territory, a political version of the "air rights" transfers of the real estate industry. Israeli settlers—subject only to Israeli law even when moving through nominally Palestinian space—are articulated as a set of fortified subjects, particles of Israeli territory ringed by their own conceptual walls wherever they go, gated communities of one.

The wall—in its relentless shrinking of the space of Palestinian inhabitation, mobility, and security—imposes the occupation as a form of house arrest, reducing Palestinians to the nationhood of their own bodies—a forced bio-politics and a perverse twist on the settler subject whose body confers nationality on any territory through which it passes. Israeli security forces are therefore free to invade the house of anyone under suspicion of resistance, to observe the movements of all inhabitants, and to listen in on their conversations. This control is reinforced by the preferred retribution for terrorism, the destruction of the house of the family of the terrorist, contaminated by association. The ultimate architecture of occupation is surely the "worming" of Israeli troops through the walls of houses to avoid circulating in the more dangerous public space of the street. In this regime of privacy degree zero, the police can appear from any direction, passing through any wall, at any time.

Singling out the family home is a particularly transgressive form of collective punishment, the occupation at the domestic scale. Just as Palestinian "rights" to live in their own homes are made contingent on unattainable forms of good behavior (as defined by the occupation authorities), so the rights of individuals to the peaceful enjoyment of their own homes and lands are trampled on the basis of someone else's bad behavior. Subject to violation at will, Palestinians are reduced to Agamben's "bare life," of complete disposability. Clearly, this line—these lines—cannot simply be redrawn: they must be withdrawn.

Indefensible Space

In a piece written for the *New York Times* in July 2004, former Israeli prime minister Benjamin Netanyahu responded to the just-delivered decision of the International Court of Justice, which had condemned the wall and demanded its removal, by stating bitterly that the ruling would be "cheered by the terrorists who would kill Israeli civilians." Implicit in this remark is the standard claim that the wall is simply and exclusively a matter of security. To this, Netanyahu added two more arguments intended to address the core of the legal case against the wall. The first was that Israel is not building the wall on "Palestinian land." Netanyahu argued that since the territory remains in dispute, Palestinians do not yet have any claim to it, although he failed to establish why Israelis do.

The second argument was that the fence is temporary and can always be moved. Netanyahu parried the claim that the fence has nonsecurity motives with a bold piece of sophistry. Because, he claimed, the fence is a matter of security, it must be drawn on a line that most efficiently puts the most Jews behind it. By annexing "less than" 12 percent of the West Bank, it "defends" 80 percent of the Jewish population while trapping "only 1 percent" of the Palestinians. At the same time, covering all his bets, Netanyahu, cited the snaking, settlement-grabbing, route of the wall—which he established as motivated by the needs of efficient colonization—as evidence of the supposed goodwill of Israel, marking the occasional willingness of the authorities to reroute it "to ease Palestinian daily life." What both these arguments obscure is that 100 percent of the Jewish population secured by the incursion of the fence lives on land that is, at best, "under dispute," an interpretation rejected by, among others, the United States, the European Union, and the United Nations.

This definition of security—the inclusion within a contiguous territory of the maximum number of Jews, wherever they may be—mocks Palestinian concerns about the can-tonment of their own territory, continuously redefining the "facts" by expanding Israel at the expense of Palestine. Netanyahu uses this security argument (it is not a sov-ereign territory that is to be defended but a sovereign people) in order to criticize those who say that the fence should run along the pre–June 1967 line, which he asserts "would have nothing to do with security and everything to do with politics." Like Bush's preemptive warfare, the claim suggests that there are no limits on state action taken in the name of "self-protection." The political origins of the need for self-protection are glossed over by defining the other's animosity as pure malevolence, unmotivated by anything but hatred.

By foregrounding what is allegedly a short-term concern—violence in the run-up to a permanent territorial solution—another nail is driven into the coffin of peace. The temporary situation has now lasted almost forty years, and it is hard to see how act after act that seeks to institutionalize the occupation of the West Bank and militarize the idea of security can lead to accommodation. Here, the 1949 boundary represents—precisely in its political dimension—the best source of security. But Netanyahu wants it both ways, claiming that the old boundary is political while the new one is not. This distinction works only by defining Israeli security as the protection of Israeli settlers wherever they are. The right of a legitimate national defense is willfully distorted by Netanyahu as a cover for getting away with murder. Even if the wall had the effect of enhancing the safety of Israel proper, the unanswered question is whether a different wall—one along the green line, for example—would also accomplish this aim.

Security from terrorism in Israel proper is the only argument for the construction of some wall offered by Netanyahu and the Israeli government that seems, at first blush, to have any authority. However much one factors in the inequality of mayhem, the far higher numbers of Palestinians killed by Israelis than of Israelis killed by Palestinians, the level of terror in Israel is appalling and indefensible. And it does appear that the corralling of the Palestinian population has contributed to Israeli security in the short term, although the lofting of rockets over the Gaza fence and the slaughter of tourists in the Sinai suggest that the locus of terror has simply shifted and that the desires of would-be terrorists are unaffected. Preventive detention—whatever its moral com-plexities—can work. The issue, both literally and figuratively, is where to draw the line.

No nation on earth has ever renounced the right of self-defense, and it is surely absurd to deny Israel this fundamental right of nationhood. One must, however, ask what the Israeli argument for self-defense actually defends. The question can be answered only by asking what other consequences the wall has. In a state with a large population of advocates for greater or lesser enlargement, this question is not academic: this wall is about much more than public safety, and the attempt to locate its meaning simply there is disingenuous.

Israeli expropriation of nonterritorial, supraterritorial, and "special" territorial assets (such as single horizontal laminations of space), including the aquifer, airspace, or even the olive groves hacked down in the name of "security," extends the wall by other means. As a legal matter, this concept provides a cover of ambiguity for Israeli claims, the same national "right" that putatively legitimates the American invasion of Iraq. Bush argued that continuation of the Saddamite regime imperiled the safety of the American nation to such a degree that it created the right of invasion, the same argument that Israel advances in defense of the extension of its wall beyond its acknowledged borders. The condominium of self-justification between Israel and the United States—now legitimated in the name of the global "war on terror"—has produced a frightening licentiousness, inuring both nations to the consequences of this murderous exercise in "self-defense," the state of exception that produces Guantánamo or the bulldozing of Jenin. This is intolerable.

Divided States

Whatever one thinks of the constitutive basis of Zionism, it surely meets the threshold of contemporary ideas of nationalism: it is not exceptional. Nor is the long-standing Palestinian aspiration to a statehood growing from a self-defined sense of nationality. These two facts, beyond any useful dispute, are at the heart of the conflict and are the reason that any other argument is ultimately insupportable as a practical matter. As Benedict Anderson observes, "Nation-ness is the most universally legitimate value in the political life of our time." Here is the irreducible core of the problem: On whom does the description—the authorization—of nationality rely? The conflict between Israel and Palestine is based on the insistence by one people that they can define the nationality of the other, whether in the famous (and fatuous) claim by Golda Meir that there is no Palestinian people or that of Hamas that Israel is illegitimate as a nation and must be expunged.

The solution of the Israel-Palestine dispute can yield only one state or two and there is a widespread consensus (admittedly not shared by all the contributors to this book) on the eventual format of two states on two territories. The perversities of the wall are produced by its own enforcement of a particular, willfully skewed, version of the two-state "solution" and most arguments against it are bound by this framework. But what about the idea of a single state? For exponents of a greater Israel or Palestine, the presence of the wall is either an obstacle or a stepping-stone to greater claims. For those in favor of any one-state solution—whether predicated in visions of harmony or domination—the wall concretizes an impossible and irrelevant division. For all others, the wall—in its clear physicalization of a specific two-ness—represents a de facto partition along a very particular line.

The fantasy of a single state presents both the possibility of alternative hege-monies—the demographic domination of Jews or Palestinians—and the appealing idea of a single state of exemplary tolerance in which cooperation is enabled by the flourishing of a secular civil space. Edward Said spoke eloquently for this idea: "The essence of that vision is coexistence and sharing in ways that require an innovative, daring, and theoretical willingness to get beyond the arid stalemate of assertion, exclusivism, and rejection. Once the initial acknowledgement of the Other as equal is made, I believe the way forward becomes not only possible but attractive."

While I admire the romance of the position and its interesting implications for the relationship of citizenship and space, I am certain of the consequences of a one-state solution in the obliteration of the Zionist project, for which it amounts to altruistic suicide. As Martin Buber asked of the Palestinians in 1948, "What nation will allow itself to be demoted from the position of a majority to that a minority without a fight?" Given such resistance, I am uncertain why a single state "of all its citizens" is superior to two such states. The persuasive arguments of Azmi Bishara and others for an Israeli civil society that offers equal rights to all of its citizens does not necessarily contradict the claims of separate nationality, even of nationality that foregrounds a predominantly Jewish or Arab flavor. In any event, the debate is crucial to advancing the shared claims of advocates for democracy on all sides and of deepening cooperation among them and the vision must persist as a background to whatever formal styles of accommodation eventually emerge. More, this "nightmare scenario" for the Israeli Right has already helped push it in the direc-tion of accepting plans and realities they might previously have rejected out of hand.

This idea of a single state of all its citizens also ramifies ineluctably in the practicalities of two states sharing a very small territory with limited resources and a variety of special human and natural ecologies that have little to do with political boundaries. In any territorial split, the idea of a single "entity" will pervade many decisions. Systems of economy, transportation, infrastructure, and public services in the two states cannot be totally disengaged, and it would be costly and foolish to try to do so, whatever the benefits to the sense of national autonomy. Sharing natural resources, especially water, green space, habitat, and airspace, is crucial to the ultimate viability of both states.

This necessity for sharing is made especially clear in Jerusalem—the omphalos of the crisis—where the issue is dramatically forced and where the fence assumes its most horrific visuality and complexity. The paradigm of the "open city" remains valuable to both sides for reasons both symbolic and practical: the city (two municipalities or no) cannot be shared—if only at the level of daily exchange—if its internal borders are not open to all. The implications for the two states that adjoin the city are also clear and beg the question of some condominium that exceeds nationalist pieties. Without open borders to the city two states claim as capital, the viability of the city itself fails.

Such a condominium would form a "third state" defined as the territory of cooperation between Israel and Palestine. This permeable border (as between the states in the United States or the European Union.) might lead to more logical planning and administration of the increasingly contiguous urban territories of Palestine and Israel, permitting the growth of a system of layered political authority embracing the contiguous urban region from Bethlehem to Jerusalem to Ramallah. In its working out, secure political autonomy for both sides could be enhanced while diluting the more atavistic aspects of the territorial struggle and creating a space for the return of many Palestinians to their former towns and villages. This shared space is not a proposition to be achieved all at once, but incremental advances toward it are already under way and must continue.

The right of nationality is aligned with (and often in conflict with) another prominent modern right: self-determination. This right includes freedom of association and dissociation both. Exclusion is necessary to nationalism: those who desire to constitute a nation must also define who will remain outside it. Such originary descriptions of a national subject are often far more complex than those that underlie the

Israeli-Palestinian struggle, where each side defines its constituency on the basis of a single characteristic. Indeed, contemporary democratic nationalism has as its predicate the idea that a nation can and must be a deliberately plural construction, not simply a matter of blood and soil.

The modern nation-state relies on the power of this abstract nationality to subsume the authority of the groups that comprise it—tribes, ethnicities, linguistic groups, etc.—resulting in their deference to the superior constitution of a collective, new, nationality. For much of its history, the United States has been a place where people fleeing the insecurities and depredations of their homelands could exchange a burdensome—or refused—nationality for one that offered relief. Citizens of a new nation of nationalities, their differences could be leveled by a hyphen. But such a marriage of relinquished identity is, to put it mildly, unrealistic in Israel/Palestine. Neither the utopia of a single state nor the dystopia of a bio-politicized planet offers much hope here: citizens of the world still enjoy very few rights. Only nations secure them.

Describing the turmoil following the breakup of the former Yugoslavia, Agamben writes that what happened was not "a re-emergence of the natural state of stuggle of all against all but rather the coming to light of the state of exception as the permanent structure of juridico-political de-localization and dis-location." For Agamben, the growth of this state of exception—progressing through states of siege and martial law, culminating in the concentration camp—is the new default for national organization, the raw form of bio-politics. Telling as critique, this despairing view offers little help for solving the situation "on the ground," where the idea of nationality— Anderson's "deep, horizontal, comradeship"—still structures aspiration. For the foreseeable future, the idea of nation remains closely tied to place and for democracy, the question of survival is centered not in displacement but sharing.

The perplexities and reflexive hostilities of the Israeli-Palestinian conflict are compounded by the fact that both peoples have been physically displaced, leading to a battle of claims, an argument about the authoritative relationship of place and time (buttressed by holy writ), the question of whether the tenure of displacement increases or decreases the authority of aspiration. What is seldom factored in by the Israeli side, however, is that it is deeply implicated in kicking out the Palestinians, a people who bear no responsibility for the historic displacement of the Jews. But these arguments from superior victimhood are fruitless. There is no equation that can solve the question of whether the Jewish claim of two thousand years of exile has a different weight than that of the much more recent displacement of Palestinians. What is clear is the admissibility of both claims. And this legitimacy is only susceptible to question from within the national body: the right of nationality is not one that can be ceded by another.

One of the least useful registers of the Middle East conflict is the frequent insistence that the key to its solution involves unreasonably exemplary behavior on one or both sides—the giving up of claims and desires that no other nation is called upon to surrender. This includes the endless Israeli refusal to negotiate, based on the incapacity of the Palestinian Authority to control violence while under occupation, and the same style of impossibility is reflected in Palestinians adamant for a total right of return that would overwhelm the Jewish character of Israel. This rhetoric of impossible expectations seems a further argument for a clarity of division in which neither nation risks having its dreamed-for character obliterated by the other.

What remains, then, is to locate equity in measurement, and we find ourselves back at the map, planning. Modern rights are predicated on the idea of equality and on a consequent distributive ideal of fairness and planning is the state's distributive geometry. The promise of even rudimentary equality of rights depends on the vigorous intervention of the state on behalf of those whose opportunities are constrained. In the United States., the results are clearly measurable: our growing income gap registers the ongoing failure of the state (or capital) to equalize opportunity, never mind rewards. Instead, the state persistently acts in favor of those who have already made the most of their opportunities, a policy the current administration gleefully exacerbates. Other states (one thinks of northern Europe, although the growing crisis of the foreign-born—Europe's own "Palestinians"—shows the limits of the equity of the welfare state) have achieved far more egalitarian results.

Despite these examples, and despite copious lip service, the global struggle against inequality has not made great progress. Sixty years of the mass production of nations continues to affirm the idea that national rights extend only over national territory and the process of nation creation inevitably involves the assignment of boundaries and the adjustment of territory. Here the argument seems entirely on the side of Palestine in resisting Israeli encroachment, whether by the settlements, the wall, racism, or electronic surveillance. A clear and contiguous territory is the minimum, a view shared by virtually every other nation on the planet.

While the fantasy of a "good" fence (producing good neighbors) might ratify an equi-table two-ness, any wall impedes another right—freedom of movement—that is thrown into particularly high relief by the character of the division of Israeli and Palestinian territorial states. Given the distribution of Palestinian Arabs on both sides of any foreseeable border, any impediment to their free circulation also impinges dra-matically on their fundamental rights of association. The division of families from each other and from their property that has been created by the wall is simply a more recent refinement of the primary division of 1948. After all, the production of nations doesn't simply displace, it "misplaces," or internally exiles, people, producing refugees, Arendt's characteristic citizenship of the age. Such misplacement can only be redeemed by the right to move and the right to a nationality that guarantees it.

Free association is foundational for democracy: the politics of free movement and association are its trenches. Cultures at peace welcome their neighbors. But this right to move and associate freely is not the same as either the "law of return" or the "right of return." These imply restoration both of property (whether the property of the "people" or that of individuals) and, presumably, of citizenship. The question for Israelis and Palestinians is what rights belonging to the other are infringed by the exercise of the general rights of movement and association, and whether the rights of return are sufficiently elastic ethically to support selective access to them. What is to be the relation between the right of the Jewish diaspora to return to Israel and that of the Palestinian diaspora to return to Palestine? Palestinians displaced by Israel are, at the minimum, entitled to restoration of property or compensation as well as citizenship in a Palestinian state, while Israelis—exiled 2,000 years ago by powers that no longer exist, are entitled, at the maximum, to nationhood within the territory defined in 1948.

Settlers returning to Palestine or Palestinians returning to Israel beg the question of how a nation might support, among its own enfranchised citizens, a population with-out citizenship and the right to participate in national life, a conundrum also legible in the problems of illegal aliens in the United States guest workers in Europe or the Persian Gulf, sex slaves in Southeast Asia, and myriad refugee populations. The idea of national citizenship defined territorially suggests either that a Palestinian right of return in the context of a two-state solution would offer a right to return to what is now Israel and to become Israeli or that citizenship and territory be disengaged. In the same way, any continued inhabitation of Israeli settlers in the Palestinian national territory should oblige them to assume and observe the legal status and burdens of Palestinians and Palestinians to agree either to afford them full rights or to institute a dual system. The idea of second-class citizenship—such as that held by Arab Israelis—will not solve the problem any more than would the erasure of one national project or the other. This is an interesting territory for negotiation in which extra-territorial citizenship might be exchanged (for every Israeli remaining on the West Bank, a Palestinian returns to Israel) or used as a bridge to a shared "third state."

Behind the Walls

Ours is the age both of the enclave, of withdrawal from the collectivity, and of the rise of such global alternatives as "netizenship." The communities of settlers on the West Bank, hilltop-smug in their buff stucco walls and Mediterranean tile roofs, look very much like the gated settlements of Southern California, also buttressed against the intrusion of an implacable Other. The criminals and anxious others against whom American gated communities are defended are, however, shadowy and imaginary, a generalized cultural fear fueled by both racism and the growing atmosphere of anxiety stoked by calculated paranoia of the administration. Media coverage of the bourgeois idyll of the settlements—with their manicured lawns, backyard pools, and well-coded apparatus of lifestyle tranquillity—begs us to see them as normal. These places are surely much less threatening than the squalor of the refugee camps that they are so instrumental in perpetuating. Indeed, the images portray the settlements as pioneering, carrying out a "mission civilitrice" in hostile, infidel ground.

This pattern of enclaves and slums is ringing the planet more and more densely as the war of the powerful against the poor accelerates. In this context, the comparison of the Israeli settlement and fortification policy to the apartheid regime in South Africa is completely apt. Even Likud stalwart Ehud Olmert now says that the Israeli war on the Palestinians has shifted from an Algerian-style conflict to a South African one. The continuing pressure for a Palestine of nonviable Bantustans—territorially discontinuous, economically dependent, and subject to draconian forms of internal interference by Israel—reflects precisely the desperate arrogance of the white regime in South Africa, searching with maniacal ingenuity to find forms to concretize the injustices of the system. This "internal" racism, directed at a minority within a perceived national space, is joined by the "external" racism of xenophobia, such as that of Islamic (or Christian or Jewish) fundamentalism.

The occupation degrades both the Palestinians who suffer its daily violence and humiliation and the Israelis who impose it. The national project that was intended once and for all to free Jews from the violence and humiliation of the ghetto has produced a political culture steeped in the practices of ghettoization, practices imposed on the Palestinians with reciprocal effects on Israel. It has led to the gilded ghettoes of the settlements, cut off from any productive intercourse with their neighbors and seething with anxiety and hostility and it has produced two nations, walled off behind impenetrable physical, cultural, and psychological barriers. These serve to perpetuate hostility and suspicion and to create the image of the other as irredeemably alien. For the Israeli government (and for the American), the violent rage of Palestinians (or Iraqis) under occupation can only be accounted for by moral defect.

The wall is a symptom of a larger failure of conciliation and justice and opposition to the wall opposes this. This book is not simply a plea to remove this wall but also to abandon the system of inequality and domination that produced it. The prescription is straightforward. However other issues—including the right to return and the right to remain—may be resolved, the division of this territory into an Israeli state and a Palestinian state is the sine qua non of any resolution. No amount of rhetorical point scoring, moralizing about the superiority of one cause or the other, or arcane historical claims can gainsay this most fundamental configuration of rights. And the citizens of these states should not be expected to reconcile only by becoming the vanguard of new, postnational, forms of association, realizing another alien utopia.

A frequently heard complaint from Israelis is that the Palestinians lack a leader of the stature of Nelson Mandela to pursue the peace. This absence of a Mandela is a problem shared by many nations, including Israel and the United States. Mandela is celebrated for his sense of justice and compassion, for his great human sacrifices, for his dedication to his people and his cause, for his wisdom. Perhaps most remarkable, though, has been Mandela's capacity to forgive. Few events compare with the public confession of the perpetrators of apartheid and their absolution by its victims in the amazing work of the South African Truth and Reconciliation Commission. Perhaps concealed in this complaint about incapacity is also a plea for forgiveness. Justice must be done but it can be very abstract, mired in legal precision and weighted calculation.

The escalating gyre of claims and counterclaims, of superior victimhood, of inflexible national and territorial "rights" reduces the possibility of reconciliation with every twist. What is missing is the will to peace and real peace always demands empathy and generosity.

Mr. Sharon, tear down this wall.

Miki Kratsman

Miki Kratsman (2)

Miki Kratsman

Dafna Kaplan (2)

Dafna Kaplan

Against the Wall

The Monster's Tail[1]

Ariella Azoulay and Adi Ophir

Dafna Kaplan

Although Israel has insisted that the wall is no more than a temporary shield against terrorist attacks, its critics claim that it is a major illegal geopolitical project that cuts into Palestinian lands and that de facto annexes large parts of them, bringing unjustifiable devastation to the Palestinians living along its route and to their environment. Others argue that the true role of the wall is to draw and ensure the future border between a larger Israel and a shrunken Palestine. Both critics and defenders present the wall as a new strategy, whether in the fight against terrorism or in the project of colonization and domination of the West Bank. Both judge or justify the wall by the presumed intentions behind its construction and by its direct effects (which are so far mostly predicted but not actually measured) on its surroundings. In what follows we shall question these assumptions. We shall argue that the wall is one among several instruments used by the Israeli ruling apparatus in the Occupied Territories whose function must be understood in the context of a structural and historical analysis of the modus operandi of this apparatus. We shall propose here an outline of such an analysis as the basis on which the wall's strategic significance will be examined. This immense project of construction and destruction, we shall argue, is part and effect—the most visible one, perhaps, but not the major one—of a phase of the occupation that is more than a decade old,[2] and which the second intifada has greatly intensified without altering its basic logic and structure.

The Economy of Violence

Since the beginning of the second Palestinian intifada, the Israeli-Palestinian conflict has become ever more violent and the violence has become ever more spectacular. Spectacular violence kills instantly, mostly innocent people, and spreads injuries and damage in concentric circles around the center of its eruption. Such eruptions take place on both sides when guns and bombs are used in a more or less indiscriminate manner against both civilians and combatants. Despite the many attempts to declare the violence of one side as justified and of the other as a barbarous expression of sheer cruelty, the very consistency and regularity of this series of spectacular scenes creates an impression of symmetry between the two parties and is easily captured rhetorically in such figures of speech as "cycle of violence" and "unending chain of revenge." These are misleading metaphors, no doubt, but not because the justice of one side and the cruelty of the other can be established and demonstrated. The symmetrical reading of violence is misleading not only because it ignores the context of almost four decades of colonization and dispossession, but because it takes into account only spectacular violence and ignores the fact that this kind of violence is but one aspect and one component of an entire economy of violence. In order to understand this economy, it is necessary to analyze the functional and structural relations between different forms and occurrences of violence and the overall patterns of its distribution among the parties to the conflict. Only on this basis is it possible to grasp the systematic production of chronic disaster in the Occupied Territories, which has brought the Palestinian population "to the verge of a humanitarian catastrophe."[3]

A short digression on the concept of violence is necessary at this point. Violence is usually associated with a more or less spectacular outburst of physical forces that tear apart bodies and objects. We call this kind of violence *spectacular* (even in cases when nobody watches, such as the case of robbery in a dark alley or a massacre in a desolated area, for there is always the occurrence of an event to be seen). But an action is violent even when the eruption of physical force is suspended and insinuation and deterrence take the place of material contact with the exposed body. We shall call this violence *suspended* (here there is hardly anything to be seen, even if the whole world watches). Violence is always exercised through the interplay between spectacular outburst and suspension, and its efficiency depends on maintaining a gap between these two poles.[4]

Political forms of society differ characteristically in the way this gap is structured and maintained. Differences between forms of governments and the structure of domination may be described in terms of patterns of suspension of violence and modes of deterrence, as well as the tendency to rely on recourse to spectacular violence. Modern liberal democracies, for example, are often presented as systems of power that strive to reduce spectacular violence, to replace it with suspended violence, and to make both as invisible as possible. In a liberal democracy, the transition from suspended to spectacular violence is supposed to be strictly supervised and controlled by the law, and it is supposed to take place only as a means of enforcing the law. When a government loses its legitimacy or fails to regain it, when a political rule is unilaterally enforced on those subjected to it and the memory of this enforcement is still fresh, suspended violence is not enough. But even in the most extreme situations, the two extreme forms of violence coexist and interact. If the outburst of force were to continue uninterrupted without any lull, the parties to the conflict would be destroyed in a struggle to the death.[5]

Since the outbreak of the second intifada, Israeli domination of the Occupied Territories has been characterized by an unstable balance between spectacular and suspended violence. A massive and extensive deployment of military forces has made possible a visible, intensified presence of suspended forces, shortened the time span required to let these forces loose, and rendered the moments of eruption more frequent, lethal, and destructive than ever before during the four decades of the occupation. Military forces are deployed everywhere, as in a state of war, but there is no war for war itself is being suspended. There are "only" numerous serial incursions, night raids, and targeted killings with their local "collateral damage"; suicide bombings; sporadic shootings; demolition of houses (as a way of punishment or a form of attack);

and intended and circumstantial destruction of infrastructure, along with numerous cases of detention and incarceration. Despite the sharp increase in the number, length, and scope of violent, well-planned attacks and clashes, especially in the Gaza Strip (which no doubt has its own cumulative impact), the majority of the soldiers that have been stationed in the Occupied Territories in the last decades, including the years of the second intifada, have not been fighting anyone. Their violence has been kept confined to their guns, clubs, or tanks; it has been insinuated at the checkpoint gate or by the anonymous voice declaring a curfew, and echoed in the rhythm of their marching or rolling patrols. This restraint in the use of force is precisely the way violence has most often been exercised. Anywhere this violence is present and may suddenly erupt—which means virtually everywhere, at any time—it constrains the Palestinians' movements and impacts their actions. The suspended violence is effective without bursting out because it forbids, deters, and delays, complicates simple actions, undermines preferences, undercuts daily schedules, drives people crazy, and sometimes even kills. Its impact is often more, not less, disastrous than that of spectacular violence.

However, the more intense the presence of suspended violence, the more blurred the distinction between its suspension and outburst. Recently (November–December 2004) a new wave of the occasional "moral questioning" and "soul searching" has appeared in the Israeli press. Once again the press has become attentive to "the immoral behavior" of Israeli soldiers in the territories and strives to describe the military operations there in accordance with certain moral rules that are supposed to regulate violence and legitimize it. Almost every week the press reveals some new incident in which suspended violence erupts and becomes spectacular and deadly in ways that have not been sanctioned by the rules. When talking about these supposedly exceptional and outrageous events, many tend to forget that it is the suspended violence involved in the very presence of Israeli troops in Palestinian territories that should be questioned, and that the rules allowing a transition from suspended to spectacular violence are subject to constant change. The presence of suspended violence and the change of rules that allows its eruption are governed by no rule. Too often suspended violence turns into spectacles of death and destruction in a "the unexpected is-always-to-be-expected" manner, while spectacles of violence congeal into the suspended, threatening presence of visible troops and invisible "special units," "instigators," and "terrorists."

In fact, the Occupied Territories have become "a zone of indistinction"[6] between these two forms of violence, in which the occupied body is constantly exposed to all sorts of dangers, forsaken and abandoned. The recent "moral outrage" at certain outbursts of violence may be interpreted as an attempt to maintain the important distinction between and the appearance of legitimacy of (and control over the transition from) one form of violence and another. This happens precisely at a time when the distinction between the two modes of violence and the controlled transition from one to the other, which are crucial for rationalizing the operation of the ruling apparatus, are threatened by new techniques of segregation and control of movement this same apparatus has recently implemented.[7]

But even now, after the recent array of reported "immoral incidents" and the sharp increase in the number and scope of armed clashes between Israeli troops and the Palestinians' scattered militias, most of the time and almost everywhere in the territories, the force stored away in the various instruments of violence does not flare up. The threshold of spectacular violence is not easily crossed.[8] Most of the time, the occupied prefer to obey, turn back, stop working, stand in line, undress, stand up before a camera, speak softly, or fall silent. Their resistance is neutralized without resort to spectacular violence. But this success of the ruling power is ephemeral. It must be generated again and again through the ever more intensified, threatening presence of suspended violence and by more frequent outbursts of spectacular violence, deployed in direct relation to the shrinking deterrent power of suspended violence. Deterrence shrinks not because less military might is involved—of that there is only more—but because the Palestinians have less and less to lose. It takes ever more awesome displays of power to achieve the same result: the submission of the Palestinians.

The presence of suspended violence is required and intensified due to the fact that the ruling apparatus in the territories lacks three main forms of domination that, in normal circumstances, enable the government to rely mainly on signs and symbols of suspended violence, reduce its visible presence, and avoid resort to spectacular violence. *First*, there is no law: the legal system in its entirety has been suspended, being replaced by a series of ever-changing ad hoc orders and regulations.[9] The arbitrary nature of the ruling power means that no rule is effective unless it is accompanied by the visible presence of suspended violence. The ruling apparatus requires the massive presence of suspended violence simply in order to announce and change the rules and use them to regulate the behavior of the occupied. The latter too need the same violent presence in order to learn about the rules and understand what is expected of them: how to go to work, to school, which way to take in order to buy bread, or how to plant a bomb.

Second, the ruling apparatus operates almost no disciplinary sites, except for prisons and detention camps whose role is not to discipline, indoctrinate, or reform, but to exclude and intimidate power's unwanted subjects. *Third*, as far as the Palestinian population goes, no ideological apparatus functions either, whether through or independently of disciplinary practices. Of course, the Israeli ruling power is deeply invested in ideological production, but the consumers of this ideology are Israeli citizens.[10] The Palestinian uprising has virtually destroyed Israel's capacity to employ ideological or disciplinary means for governing the Palestinian population. In fact, the ruling power is incapable of constructing and shaping Palestinian individuals as its own subjects. While the rule of law is suspended, and as the disciplinary and ideological apparatuses have ceased functioning, the Palestinians in the territories cannot simply become subjects of the Israeli sovereign, in clear contradistinction to the Palestinian citizens of Israel. The occupied Palestinian is not a subject, neither in the modern sense of this word nor even in its ancient Latin sense: unlike the modern subject, he is not recognized as a bearer of rights and a source of knowledge and action, but neither is he a *subjectus*, or someone who was clearly distinguished from the slave, who obeyed his master out of faith and of his own volition, and whose subjection was always part of a chain of subjection and authorization in which even the sovereign took part.[11] The Palestinian under occupation is neither a subject nor a citizen. He is a noncitizen who is subjugated by the ruling power but who is not a subject of it; he obeys out of naked fear of authority, which is sheer aggression and arbitrariness to him. His political existence is reduced to the status of an object of power, as both power's target as well as an object that stands in opposition to power, an obstacle in its way. From power's point of view, he is an addressee of symbolic action only because he is conceived, first and foremost, as an address for violent action. Resistance may appear any time he dares to speak back to power, seizing the position of the addresser.

Indeed, without the mediation of law, ideology, and discipline, the ruling power must intensify the presence of suspended violence and resort to spectacular violence, always readily accessible. Instead of disciplining or educating its subjects, power injures their bodies and damages their property. Punishment is no longer related to law but to resistance—any kind of presence conceived to be addressing power in terms other than its own. And spectacular violence is no longer restricted to punishment and the preservation of law and order; it is mainly related to the preservation of the deterrent power of suspended violence itself. Resistance is an attempt to reclaim freedom and space in the midst of power's efforts to control them, but it gives power an excuse to turn control into destruction and transform the place of resistance into a disaster zone. However, it is worth mentioning that in most of the violent events that involve destruction—of space, houses, roads, wells, other kinds of infrastructure, and everything that falls under what Amira Hass called "weapons of light construction" that have transformed the Palestinian living space—that destruction has been the outcome of a planned policy which is meant to damage or annihilate the material environment without touching human bodies directly.

When citizens are good subjects of their government, power is in fact internalized to a greater or lesser degree. Noncitizens, subjugated by an arbitrary power that suspends the law and acts with no mediation, have internalized nothing; from their point of view, power must always act out in the open and be present on the surface of the space it controls; it can be understood only as an external, visible, and threatening force, always in the midst of the interplay between disastrous outbursts of spectacular violence and the intensified presence of suspended violence. As noncitizens, the Palestinians also lack most of the legal means to negotiate with the ruling power over the way they are governed.[12] If they do not want to resist openly or obey submissively, they can only try to evade power or deceive it, using all kinds of improvisations, simulations, and dissimulations in order to avoid looking suspicious. But they are always suspicious, at least as long as they maintain their ability to speak back to power. For the ruling power, their resistance is not only a matter of their actions but of their very presence and identity.

The Israeli government dismisses the possibility that the continuous exercise of violence of all kinds calls for violent resistance and creates more violence than it is supposed to prevent. After every terrorist attack, official Israeli spokespersons are quick to declare that prevention can never be absolute, and hence there is no choice but to exercise more violence in order to prevent that unpreventable violence. Journalists, politicians, and the average citizen thoughtlessly repeat these clichés Violence is always presented as preventive. One always generates violence in order to prevent violence.[13] Violence that prevents violence (VPV) assumes the existence of an inexhaustible source of violence that must not be allowed to materialize. Every Palestinian is, by his or her very presence, both a source of suspended violence and its addressee. But, in contradistinction to the visible, obtrusive presence of suspended violence on the Israeli side, the Palestinian threat is mostly clandestine, and great efforts are required to expose it. It is therefore necessary to threaten, to restrict movement, and to control it, to intrude into places in order to monitor them and to monitor in order to intrude, to detain in order to investigate and to investigate in order to detain, to destroy cultivated land in order to uncover it and to uncover it in order to destroy it, to impose curfew, closure, and siege in order to restrict movement and to restrict movement in order to reinforce curfew and closure. Thus VPV is productive as well as destructive. It transforms space, establishes new constructions, invents new instruments and methods of control, and produces and distributes anxieties, threats, rumors, and innumerable risks. This violence has a totalizing character— without it, we are told, everyone will be forsaken; to give it free rein, anyone may be forsaken. It is constantly at work, it should not cease for a moment, it will never go on vacation, and it is here to stay. The entire Israeli-Palestinian space is dominated by its crazy logic.

Walter Benjamin proposed a useful distinction—useful for "normal" political conditions, at least—between lawmaking violence (in a revolution and a coup d'état, for example) and law-preserving violence (of a military force, when it is used as a means toward legal ends, for example).[14] The suspended violence we are describing seems to be out of joint with this distinction. It does not preserve the law or constitute a new law; it does not even blur the distinction between these two forms of violence. Benjamin deconstructs his own distinction when he argues that the police, whose power is "formless" and whose presence is "nowhere-tangible, all-pervasive, ghostly," is both lawmaking and law-preserving, and in a famous work Derrida goes further in untying his text.[15] But this inherent ambiguity of violence, which is always also constitutive when it preserves, and preserving when it constitutes, is precisely what cannot be ascribed to suspended violence. Whereas the violence of the police or the army about which Benjamin and Derrida speak is *both* constitutive and preservative, suspended violence is *neither* the former *nor* the latter.

In the Occupied Territories, suspended violence is being exercised when the law has been suspended in its entirety and no effort is made to establish an alternative system of law. Suspended violence in the territories preserves not the law but its very suspension, and it constitutes not a new law but a no-law situation, which it maintains and constantly re-creates. Note, however, that law has not been abolished altogether but merely suspended. This means that unlike the anarchy created by a civil war or in the midst of natural or man-made catastrophes, law is not completely negated; the complete negation of law is suspended as well. The intensified, ubiquitous presence of suspended violence suspends not only law but also the eruption of all-encompassing violence in the form of "total war," or the creation of a spectacular, large-scale catastrophe.

Israeli officials and most of the Israeli public represent and justify this type of violence in terms of "security" and the need to protect Israeli citizens from the Palestinian version of spectacular violence. From our point of view, the truly restraining impact of this VPV is not upon Palestinian terrorists but upon the Israeli war machine. This is a form of violence exercised by the Israeli military apparatus to restrain itself and prevent a full outburst, so far suspended, of the destructive forces accumulated and deployed throughout the territories. The fantasy of such catastrophic outbursts of violence is reproduced with almost any major clash. Military operations are often conceived and presented as miniatures of and exercises for an always larger scale operation yet to come or held in reserve. There can always be a more terrible onslaught on a Palestinian neighborhood or refugee camp than the existing one. What lasts for a few days may last many months, more Palestinians may be detained, deported, and killed, more houses blown up, more cultivated land taken or "exposed." There are always political and moral reasons to keep an operation in its present, "limited" scope, to postpone its next stage, to withdraw ahead of time, and yet to declare that "all the objectives have been achieved." And while the difference between the phantasmic loosening of violent forces and the real one is flexible, and while the threshold of the intolerable is constantly moving, as people get quickly and alarmingly accustomed to kinds of violence they only recently abhorred, the real catastrophe or large-scale disaster is always kept at a distance. Only the chronic, creeping disaster may be traced and tackled; the spectacular catastrophe should always be postponed. Israeli authority would let others—local nongovernmental organizations (NGOs) and international observers and agencies—intervene, but cooperate with them to bring basic humanitarian relief only when the danger of catastrophe seems too imminent.

Suspended violence allows the ruling apparatus to function without law, discipline, and ideology, but also without war and catastrophe. The territories are on the threshold of law as much as they are on the verge of war and catastrophe, but they are not quite there. The eruption of war in the present circumstances, when the Israeli army faces scattered groups of terrorists and a few small and poorly equipped militias, would have led, in one way or another, to massive transfer or even mass killing of civilians. Since the territories are already occupied and the enemy has neither a government nor an army, the only goal of war could be to reduce dramatically the number of noncitizens—nonsubjects subjugated to Israeli rule—and to completely destroy their existence as political beings. But the Palestinians have been neither annihilated nor assimilated, neither expelled in large numbers nor integrated. They are governed as temporary human beings who belong to the Israeli state by being excluded from it, cared for by being forsaken, new kinds of *homini sacri* in the sense Giorgio Agamben gives to this term.[16] The suspended violence of the ruling apparatus suspends a final solution. Total war or catastrophe on the one hand and the rule of law on the other are two polar potentialities that structure the Israeli regime by the suspension of their presence and the presence of their suspension.

We believe that thinking about "the wall" must begin from this understanding. The wall is a seemingly perfect architectonic-geostrategic machine of suspended violence. As a means of security, this machine is supposed to reduce the number of successful terrorist attacks (and it is already presented by Israeli authorities as quite effective in this respect).[17] It is said to reduce Palestinian spectacular violence but also to restrain, or at least reduce, the need for Israeli counterviolence. But precisely by being a useful mechanism of VPV, entirely integrated within the existing infrastructure of checkpoints, roadblocks, and bypass roads, the wall multiplies the presence of suspended violence and increases dramatically its destructive effects. It creates conditions of a chronic disaster for the Palestinian inhabitants of Palestine.

On the Verge of Catastrophe

The wall is meant to ensure the closure—practical, potential, and virtual—of the OPT and their complete separation from Israel "proper," wherever its boundaries lie, and from the Jewish settlements within the Occupied Territories. What is new about it is not closure itself but the attempt to enforce and ensure it with no exception and the presumption that total closure is possible. Under martial law, as well as under police control in times of emergency, the closure of an area is declarative much before it becomes (if it ever becomes) architectonic. The delineation of the space as closed and of closure as a quality of a certain space are concepts that may—but do not necessarily need to—rely upon material obstacles. Walls, fences, and ditches can help the erection of a closure, but they may also exist as obstacle to movement without pretending to create a system of total closure. How strong, long, or deep these constructions should be depends on both the resistance to closure and the will to enforce it. The wall is not a means to *create* closure but to ensure and sustain an already existing system of closures in the face of a growing resistance to the *geography of separation* in local and international circles, on the one hand, and a growing will to enforce *total separation without respect for any geopolitical lines* on the other hand.

This becomes clear when one considers the fact that the territories have long been sealed off, or at least capable of being closed off, from the rest of the world. The first complete closure of the Occupied Territories was declared during the war in Iraq in 1991. For more than six weeks the entire Palestinian space in the Occupied Territories was completely seperated from the Jewish space within and outside of it. For their Palestinian inhabitants, the territories became an enclosed camp. What was at first an extreme, straightforward, and not very sophisticated measure taken in an exceptional situation has long since become routine. Closure has been developed as a sophisticated, sui generis apparatus, a coordinated set of quasi-legal, architectonic, observatory, and military means to circumscribe space, isolate it, and control the location where and the degree to which it can be penetrated. This development took place mainly during the Oslo years, under the veil of the so-called peace process. The territories have become a puzzle of semi-isolated demarcated spaces whose boundaries can be redrawn at any moment according to the decision (whimsical or strategic, it does not matter) of local Israeli commanders. Each isolated space is connected to or disconnected from others by unpredictable military decrees that may turn, within minutes or hours, each such demarcated space into an isolated camp. The second intifada only accelerated and provided a pretext for the consolidation of this mechanism of domination which had already been largely in place before its outbreak; it also forced this mechanism to become more visible (we shall return to this point later).

But where precisely are "the territories"? The green line that supposedly separates Israel from the Palestinian land occupied by Israel in 1967 has long been erased; it functions only on the maps of Palestinian officials and Israeli leftists, designating the separation between Israeli and Jordanian forces declared by the 1949 armistice accord, as well as the line that one day will hopefully separate the state of Israel from a future Palestinian state. Along the green line and on both of its sides many villages and towns have been established, and together with older Israeli—both Jewish and Arab—villages and towns they form the so-called seam line, which has become a wide and long stretch of land. From the points of view of Israeli civilians, soldiers, settlers, and Palestinians alike, "the territories" begin where the "seam line" ends—except that nobody has ever drawn a map of that end. It is a very flexible line that every day can be inscribed anew in the maps and on the ground according to "the needs of the hour." Recently, the needs of the hour have meant a series of more or less local closures, more or less extensive sealing of Palestinian areas. "The territories" actually designate—and this is the most prudent, if not most accurate definition—the area that may be sealed off without warning and without any due process, except for a decree issued by certain army generals. The "closureable" area does not have to be closed in its entirety or at once. In extreme circumstances (such as the wars in Iraq or major military operations) but also on certain marked days of the year (the High Holidays, Passover, and Independence Day), closure is a means for integration of the entire area. At other times closure is partial and local, and it becomes a means of division and separation.

The authority to declare an area "a closed military zone" is not restricted to the Palestinian Territories; it is given to the military on both sides of the green line as part of the legal fact that the state of emergency declared at the time of the British

Mandate has not been abdicated by the Israeli lawgiver. Since the dismantling of the military regime imposed on Arab villages and towns between 1948 and 1966, this measure has been used several times in areas where Israeli Arabs and Bedouins live but almost never in Jewish areas. And whereas since 1966, closure has become a really exceptional situation for Israeli citizens, it has since 1991 become the rule for its Palestinian noncitizens. The Palestinian "closureable area" is now represented, organized, articulated, and coordinated through at least three incommensurable maps used by the three groups that mainly inhabit and move in that area: Palestinian residents, Jewish settlers, and Israeli soldiers.[18]

Members of the three groups cannot coexist, let alone reside permanently in the same places. They can hardly move along the same roads, and when using the same roads they do it in a very different manner. For the soldiers, the entire space is permeable, no place is inaccessible,[19] and no hideout is really out of sight, though penetration into some enclaves may be harder and more costly than into others. Closure and restrictions of movement work for both Palestinians and settlers but in a very different way: for the settlers, the sealing of their space and the restriction on their movement are means of protection; in the Palestinian case, the same measures are means of intrusion and penetration, a network for the deployment of suspended violence as well as a pretext and a solid support for its spectacular outbursts.

These three incommensurable maps represent and reproduce the constant effort to keep Palestinians and Jews apart. Living areas, working places, shopping areas, and above all the roads among them are mostly ethnically segregated, although segregation is not strict, formal, or effective in the same way in these various spaces. However, the spread of Jewish settlements and military bases throughout the West Bank and the limited economic, medical, and infrastructural facilities there create a situation in which no group can be contained within its own zone, kept moving only on the roads allocated to it, and do it without crossing others' zones. Constant friction between members of the three groups is an inevitable outcome of this situation, and it leads to further attempts at keeping the groups apart, which in turn creates further points of friction. The wall is part of the old dream to put an end to the friction and keep the separate zones as "clean" and as "pure" as possible. But, like the more local means of segregation, the wall too is means of partition that only rearranges and determines the location of friction, the moment of coming together, and the means of contaminating "sterile spaces."

Thus, space is not only ethnically and functionally segregated, its organization has become a mechanism for creating ethnic and functional segregation. At the same time, the control of movement by the Israeli army and the free movement it enjoys serve as means of integration of what is being constantly segregated. The violence used to enforce a spatial segregation or intrude into enclosed sites relates both sides of any boundary to the encompassing ruling apparatus. Hence, the deployment of suspended violence and the occasional eruption of spectacular violence integrate what has been spatially segregated, while at the same time the spacing out of power resegregates what sheer violence has integrated. But this dialectic is not symmetrical, for, after all, the space of the military encompasses both the settlers' and the Palestinian spaces and is capable of compressing them into one, changing their outlines, redrawing their boundaries, and enforcing new forms of interlacing between them.

There is, of course, another space that claims superiority: the imaginary settlers' space, the whole Land of Israel (*Eretz Israel hashlema*), that supposedly contains both the Palestinian and the military spaces. This space has a very tangible correlate: a detailed map of land allocations, of environmental and architectonic planning, of "outposts" and "enlargements" of new neighborhoods, and of new villages that respect no neighbor. This is the constantly changing space of colonization. It is often said that the army only follows the settlers' initiatives, protects them from Palestinian violence wherever they go, and forsakes the Palestinians whenever Jewish settlers go into and out of their fields and orchards. However, no matter how geopolitically important this colonized space, nor how powerful the peculiar combination between the imaginary space and its detailed representations in maps of environmental planning, the fact remains that only the military commander, not the settlers' leadership, is both authorized and capable of proclaiming and enforcing closure of the colonized space and determining exceptions to this closure. No matter how often settlers break into both military and Palestinian space (through "illegal" outposts, incursions into Palestinian villages and orchards, bypassing roadblocks, etc.) and redraw their boundaries, it is only through the presence of the military and the articulation of space in its language and maps that spatial segregation and (re)integration take place. Furthermore, in the same way that a sovereign is characterized by its authority to declare an exception, only the sovereign (in the person of the government, the defense minister, the chief of staff, or the local commander) can order "disengage-ment" or any other form of withdrawal from certain spaces. As much as exception and exclusion are means for reappropriating the excluded and reestablishing the law,[20] disengagement or withdrawal is a means for reappropriating control over the entire space and reestablishing the occupier's rule over it.

Indeed, the so-called disengagement plan is a means to regain control and reassert authority over the entire Gaza Strip. Regardless of the intentions ascribed to the plan, this has already been its effect—long before the first settler has been forced to leave his house—and will remain one of its effects if it ever materializes. The same is true for the wall. Long before the project is finished, and in some areas long before it has even started, space has been redrawn and redistributed, with new partitions of land, new restrictions on movement, and new methods to reintegrate the space that the planned or constructed wall divides. In both cases space is unilaterally redrawn and rearranged so as to regain full control over the way Palestinians move in and out of their enclaves, without hindering the penetrability of the Palestinian space that remains always open for the incursions of Israeli forces. Also in both cases, some settlers' space is threatened by the rearrangement of military space; in the Gaza Strip this space is meant to be annulled altogether, while in the West Bank more restric-tions on settlers' movements are expected in settlements that will not be encircled by the wall. These future injuries, for which a great machinery of compensation has already been set in place, are the result of the fact that despite all their colonial privi-leges, Jewish settlers in the Occupied Territories are not normal citizens: all their rights are fully protected by Israeli law except for their rights to the colonized space itself. The territories have never been fully annexed and the settlers' presence in them has never been fully "naturalized" in Israeli minds, let alone recognized by non-Israelis. Neither the settlers' free movement in the territories nor their possession of the land can be guaranteed by the Israeli legal system. From the point of view of this system, the colonized space has never been pacified and "civilized" (except for the annexed territory in the greater Jerusalem area) and is in a permanent state of emer-gency. It is a space where the law has never been fully established—or withdrawn—and therefore exception has become the rule, having a zone of its own. It is space itself (mainly, but not only, Palestinian space) that can be forsaken, abandoned, dam-aged, and destroyed without punishment.[21] At the same time, for many years the

Israeli government acted as if this space cannot be sacrificed either, not even for the sake of peace, and this is still the position of many Jewish nationalists and religious fundamentalists. The settlers' space—abandoned to unpunishable injuries and excluded from the realm of religious sacrifice—has itself become sacred, a sort of *spatium sacer*, as if space itself has taken upon itself two characteristics of a *homo sacer*,[22] mirroring the Palestinians' situation as *homini sacri*. In fact, it was the supposedly sacred nature of the settlers' space, in which colonization was led by a vanguard of messianic fundamentalists who worked to transform space as a means to transform historical time, that had forsaken the Palestinians in the first place.

Every aspect of Palestinian life—economy, labor and leisure, politics and armed resistance, culture and education—is contained within this sacred/forsaken space, constrained and constructed by the system of segregation and integration that operates within and through it. This system abides by no law except the regulations it constantly invents, inscribes, and reinscribes into the space it controls and constantly transforms. The plethora of rules and regulations used to articulate, direct, restrain, or describe after-the-fact the operations of the ruling apparatus have only this in common: they are anchored in the present temporary phase of spatialization of this apparatus, to which they give form and which they constantly transform. Nothing is more constant than the changing spatial aspect of these rules. They may derive their authority from Israeli law, they may be restrained by an occasional, limited, and partial respect for international humanitarian law, and they may reflect the changing intensity of Palestinian resistance, settlers' pressure, diplomatic maneuvers, or economic interests. But all these sources of influence are always mediated by and articulated through the spacing out of power and the triple segregation/integration of space. With no special additional effort and within a very short time the mechanism of closure and restrictions of movement can render meaningless any external input—legal, political, economic, moral, or other—into the system of domination, preventing its proper realization.

This fact accounts for the obvious but irregular differences between the situation and well-being of Palestinians in different dominated areas. The government reacts to Palestinian resistance, and sometimes to Palestinian submissiveness as well, while local commanders have a certain degree of freedom in making decisions regarding closure and movement. In some places, on some days, people can get to work, study, and even have uninterrupted social lives while on others no one can go to work for weeks, schools are closed, and people are stuck in their homes for many long days and nights. This difference is always explained as a matter of security, which means precisely that space must be resegregated or reintegrated according to the changing needs of the ruling apparatus that respects no rules but its own. Closure and restrictions on movement are means of security, they say, but security itself is always already spatially articulated and distributed: security for Jews, forsakenness for Palestinians. To ensure security means to perpetuate the spacing out of a power whose law is suspended and whose presence takes the form of a pendulum movement between suspended and spectacular violence and between violent segregation and violent reintegration of space: a sacred space, always on the verge of a disaster zone.

The more violent this spatial segregation and reintegration becomes the more apparent is its resemblance to a camp, in the sense Agamben gives to this notion.[23] This is neither a concentration camp, nor a labor or a refugee camp, but a camp it is nonetheless: an enclosed space in which law has been suspended and power works through a series of spatial segregations of already-segregated segments of the population. In the camp, the exceptional and temporary suspension of the law becomes the rule, and a state of emergency becomes the normal state of affairs. Life turns into "bare life" because, lacking the protection of any legal system and political status, it is completely invaded by mechanisms of power which make it at one and the same time an object of knowledge and an addressee of violence. In the camp, bare life becomes a medium in which knowledge and power meet, exchange, nurture, and produce each other incessantly, without the mediation of law or political discourse. The rules of power are immediatley inscribed in the inhabitants' bodies, property, and space, while any attempt by the inhabitants to reclaim their space, property, or bodies is immediately construed as resistance to power.

This camp, however, is not a place to which Palestinians have been sent or deported but a construction enforced on their place of living. For Palestinians the camp is inside their own homes, villages and towns, orchards and fields. In addition to, and through, the fragmentation of space and the complete control over all movements, the ruling power also made the very presence of Palestinians in their own living spaces a temporary matter. Both regular and unexpected restrictions of movement are temporary; identity cards and permits allowing movement in and out of the enclosed zones are also temporary and must be renewed frequently;[24] in the greater Jerusalem area thousands of people literally have lost their right to return to their place for all kinds of administrative reasons.[25] The demolition of houses has become so frequent that in certain areas the very existence of one's house seems temporary;[26] and the danger of deportation and expulsion is always hanging in the air, the suspended presence of the ultimate spatial weapon.

In most camps, people are in a state of transition, and this state is more or less temporary. The temporariness, transience, deferral, and suspension which characterize any camp create or assign a common identity to the camp dwellers, be they tourists, soldiers, detainees, refugees, or deportees. Having lost or given up their identities and roots in their places of origin, either temporarily or for good, and not having reached their destinations yet, they all undergo a similar experience: the camp suspends or erases their many differences with respect to origin and destination and becomes their common destiny. In the territories, people are thrown into a state of transition because their living spaces are in transition, and by virtue of this transition the Palestinian common destiny is severely fractured; the fragmentation of space creates many local destinies according to the specific, contingent conditions in each of the enclaves or separate cells of the large camp. Still, the inhabitants of the separate spatial cells have one important attribute in common: they are all deprived of citizenship, and this status of noncitizen is their form of belonging to the Israeli state.[27] This deprivation defines their political existence in a way that has now made it possible to turn their villages and towns into the cells of a new camp which, in its turn, makes possible their continuous expulsion from the realms of law and politics, of civility and culture. The camp is not the place where Palestinians have been gathered; it is rather the "encampment" of their birthplace that allows the continuous reduction of their existence into "bare life."

This "encampment" of the Palestinians has now become visible with the construction of the wall. The wall has concrete destructive effects on the population caught within its serpentine tentacles; apparently, it is also having quite dramatic psychological effects on both Israelis and Palestinians. The wall has even contributed to the emergence of new, nonviolent, and multinational forms of resistance to the occupation in the form of a series of demonstrations in which Palestinian villagers,

Israelis from the radical left, and volunteers from various international organizations take part in civil disobedience at the construction sites. But the wall has not introduced any new methods of domination that have not already been put to use at a more local level. The system of separation, fragmentation of space, and spatial segregation according to national identity, the attempt to "clean" more and more space of Palestinian presence, the radical reduction of the volume of Palestinian movement in space, and the detailed, rigorous control over anything that is still moving were all already in place before the erection of the wall. What the wall is adding is both a momentous destruction of the Palestinian environment along a line whose logic lies precisely in the lack of any comprehensible guiding principle, and the phantasm of total separation construed through numerous new points of friction.

In other words, it is not the wall that has created the camp, but rather the strategy and reality of encampment which has led to the construction of the wall. The transformation of the territories into a sacred space, a zone of exception at the outskirts of law produced entirely without residue through an unrestrained interplay between suspended and spectacular violence, into a dynamic of destruction and construction, fragmentation, segregation, and reintegration, is now performed most conspicuously—but by no means only—through and around the construction of the wall. It is the *construction* of the wall that has to be emphasized here, not the constructed wall: the long process of planning, the legal, military, and physical preparations, the diplomatic and political—local and international—struggles, the frequent changes in the wall's line, the dismantling of certain parts of it and their displacement, the recurrent postponements of construction of some other parts (due to lack of money, political and diplomatic pressure, court decisions, local compromises with villagers or settlers, etc.), the frequent changes in the number of open and operating gates, their status and regulations. Every moment of this process, every curve along the hundred kilometers of the wall's itinerary, every opening or closure of any of the gates, have been occasions for segregation and reintegration of space, redeployment of forces, interplay between suspended and spectacular violence. The wall may have already brought more security to many Israelis, but only at the expense of bringing havoc on many Palestinians, and only because "security" itself has remained a principle of segregation and colonization. At every turn of this long route, new ways to render space sacred have appeared and new forms of forsaking its inhabitants have been exercised. A static instrument of spatial separation has turned out be the tail of a crawling monster that devours space and re-territorializes it at the same time, without ever splitting the territory into two.

The wall is not simply a major project under construction; it is an unfinished project in which nontermination seems structural rather than accidental. Therefore, it seems safe to predict that the wall will remain unfinished "forever" (until one day some new project—of full annexation or true reconciliation—puts an end to it altogether). The wall's role is not to reduce violence but to extend and reproduce domination and reinscribe it in space. The wall is not a means for total separation of two communities in conflict but part of a mechanism of spatial segregation and reintegration through which conflict management is carried out by the ruling partner. For the purpose of segregation and reintegration, the thousands of tons of reinforced concrete are less important than the numerous gates and their changing status and regulations.[28] "The facts on the ground" are not inscribed by the concrete wall; they are inscribed by, in, and around these gates and the zones of friction around them, which, *together with the unfinished parts of the wall*, constitute the constantly changing network of permeability through which power is spaced out, the colonizing process continues, the Palestinian population is encamped, and its daily life dissected.

The wall, so argue Israeli officials and opinion makers, is merely a substitute for a political solution; it is temporary, and it can be removed in peacetime or relocated according to a future agreement between the two parties. In the meantime it represents a suspended political solution. The wall is an architectonic-geographic-military solution to a lack of political solution. In the meantime, the wall that protects "us" is the wall that forsakes "them." But the only way to bring "our" protection to perfection is to make "their" abandonment complete. Indeed, the wall embodies and helps articulate two complementary fantasies: total disengagement from the Palestinians ("We don't want to see any of them around any longer") and their total abandonment ("Let them kill each other, let them starve there, let them drink the sea of Gaza"). But it is precisely because total disengagement means total abandonment that both fantasies can never come true for a full-scale, "total" disaster is suspended as much as the political solution is postponed. While evading and postponing the latter has been the tacit policy of most Israeli governments since 1967, a policy Israel often shared with its Palestinian partner, suspension of a wholesale disaster has been a constituent element of its ruling apparatus in the territories since the outbreak of the second intifada.[29]

The reduction of Palestinian livelihood to sub-Saharan standards[30] is no doubt an effect of the geography of segregation, but it is also a means to reproduce it. Bringing the population to the verge of disaster creates submissiveness, fosters dependency among Palestinians, and mobilizes the international humanitarian community that subsidizes the Palestinian economy—and hence the occupation itself—in a proportion unparalleled by any other contemporary humanitarian crisis.[31] Despite obvious frictions and tense relationships, the mechanisms of suspended violence and humanitarian action are at work simultaneously, complementing each other and often well coordinated. The hinge that today connects the two apparatuses—military and humanitarian—is suspension. In the new Palestinian camp, everything has been suspended and is on hold: normal daily life, law and the legal system in its entirety, total war, disengagement (which is itself a form of suspension), mass dislocation of population, a full-fledged humanitarian catastrophe, a permanent political resolution of the conflict, a final solution of this or that nature. The violent apparatus of the ruling power suspends not only daily life and the law, but total war and mass dislocation as well. The humanitarian apparatus takes an active role in achieving this suspension. By their direct distribution of aid and indirect impact on public opinion and on the Israeli authorities, the humanitarians prevent unemployment from becoming malnutrition and malnutrition from becoming famine, thus suspending the disaster which a widespread famine would have created. By their very presence, as part of the so-called international community and its representatives, they also contribute, temporarily at least, to the suspension of more brutal policies of domination; they contribute to the prevention of targeted killings becoming mass murders and local house demolitions becoming the full-fledged transfer of an entire population.

In moments of severe crisis, in order to prevent further deterioration and the crossing of that imaginary threshold of "true" catastrophe (which can always be redrawn according to the assumed changing sensibility and attentiveness of a no less imaginary "international community"), the ruling apparatus is always ready to consider certain alleviations of its yoke, to open new gates, to allocate more soldiers to the checkpoints to allow faster passage, and so on. Most of the engagements between Israeli soldiers and the Palestinian residents take place in these circumstances and thus concern endless negotiations over passage within, into, and out of the territories, negotiations in which "humanitarian reasons" are one of very few things a Palestinian can bring to the exchange in order to get a permit to pass.[32] Palestinians are constantly forced to exchange presentations and representations of the basic needs of their bare lives, their suffering and losses, for permits that would allow them to maintain bare lives and mitigate some of their suffering.[33] The immense suffering and humiliation of the crossing points themselves cannot be included in this negotiation, for they are part of the conditions for negotiation. The numerous gates in the wall, together with the numerous other checkpoints on both sides of the wall, function as a network of theaters in which these (re)presentations of bare life take place, sometimes several times a day for one person.

The wall has not reduced the Palestinian existence to bare life and has not created the theater where this existence is represented; it has only given this theater a more visible, more threatening presence, creating for it a stage whose size is enormous. And it has no doubt intensified the specter of a final solution (in the figure of separation or deportation) and the sense of temporariness in light of this specter.

The rising concrete, in view everywhere, means that total separation is imminent, that the very existence of bare life is at stake, that every passage is temporary, and that everything gained at the checkpoint is ephemeral and has to be regained through another tortuous round of negotiation. But there are always openings in the wall, there is always the possibility that closed gates will be opened, and there are still wall-less areas, which means that the real disaster has not happened yet, that some lines of flight are still possible, that resistance—not only submissiveness—should be channeled and redirected according to the advance of the monster's tail. And it is precisely this continuation of resistance that reaffirms the necessity of the wall in Israeli eyes.

Notes

1. This text is an excerpt from a larger work in progress. Some parts were presented at a conference on "The Politics of Humanitarianism in the Occupied Territories" at the Van Leer Jerusalem Institute, April 20–21, 2004.

2. The demarcating line is the first closure imposed on the entire Palestinian Territories by the Shamir government during the Gulf War in 1991. Amira Hass, "Colonialism Sponsored by the Peace Process" (in Hebrew), October 2003; and page 12.

3. Jean Ziegler, special rapporteur,"Report Submitted to United Nations on the Right to Food in the Occupied Palestinian Territories" (advance, unedited version — unpublished draft), September 2003. Due to Israeli and American pressure, the report has never been officially published. This is but one example among numerous reports of this kind issued by various governments and international agencies that monitor what is arguably the most surveyed and best-documented humanitarian crisis in the world today. The first conclusion stated in the special report of the International Development Committee of the British House of Commons on "Development, Assistance and the Palestinian Occupied Territories" in May 2004 is that "rates of malnutrition in Gaza and parts of the West Bank are as bad as anywhere one would find in sub-Saharan Africa. The Palestinian economy has all but collapsed." See also the report of John Dugard, special rapporteur of the European Commission on Human Rights, submitted to the commission in September 2003. On the specific impact of the wall on the humanitarian crisis, see the United Nations' report, "The Humanitarian Impact of the West Bank Barrier on Palestinian Communities," September 2004.

4. Sometimes a legal exercise of force is distinguished from an illegal one, and only the latter is called violent. Sometimes the use of force (legal or not) that does not yield direct contact with an exposed body is not considered violent. We would consider an action violent irrespective of its legality and of the existence of an actual contact between physical forces and exposed bodies. In this context, however, we deal not with the relation between the legality and illegality of a violent act but only with the interplay between eruption of physical forces and its suspension.

5. Compare Louis Marin's excellent analysis of power and representation in the Introduction to *The Portrait of the King* (Minneapolis: Minnesota University Press, 1987).

6. We borrow Giorgio Agamben's term here. See *Homo Sacer: Sovereign Power and Bare Life* (Stanford: Stanford University Press, 1998), 18. However, as will become clear later, our debt to Agamben goes much beyond the borrowing of this phrase.

7. We are thinking, for example, of some of the newly constructed checkpoints where dozens or hundreds, sometime thousands, of people are caged in a small wired area. Waiting for hours in lines before passing through the carousel gate, they are humiliated, deprived of their rights, and robbed of their time. The close area in front of the gate is so crowded that people are constantly stepping on each other, pushed and pressed to the wire fence, almost suffocating, hardly carrying their belongings, unable to help the crying children, the elderly, and the sick. And while the deferred passage has become a torturous waiting, the passage itself is now computerized, well controlled, and, from the army's point of view, more efficient. For a thorough analysis of the checkpoint see Tal Arbel, "Measured Abandonment, a Political Technique: The Checkpoint Apparatus in the West Bank," work in progress.

8. In the checkpoints discussed in the previous note, violence is constantly exercised by caging numerous people in a tiny closed space, lining them up, leading them through a single carousel gate, and so forth, but this violence almost never becomes spectacular. Bodies are touched, pushed, detained for hours, but not penetrated or butchered, and the soldiers hardly ever shoot and very rarely use their sticks.

9. On the legal aspects of power in the Occupied Palestinian Territories see Eyal Benvenisti, *Legal Dualism: The Absorption of the Occupied Territories into Israel* (Boulder: Westview, 1990), and *The International Law of Occupation* (Princeton, NJ: Princeton University Press, 1993), ch. 5. See also Orna Ben-Naftali, Aeyal M. Gross, and Keren Michaeli, "Illegal Occupation: Framing the Occupied Palestinian Territory," *Berkeley Journal of International Law,* forthcoming.

10. Note that we are not thinking here merely about propaganda, to which consumers of the news are exposed everywhere, but about the ideological shaping of subjects through education, literature, public memory, etc.

11. Compare Etienne Balibar, "Citizen Subject," in *Who Comes after the Subject,* ed. Eduardo Cadava et al. (London and New York: Routledge, 1991), 33-60. The discussion of the ancient figure of subjectus is on pp. 40–44.

12. The partial success of some pleas against the construction of the wall at the Israeli supreme court which might have been presented here as counterexamples only demonstrate our point: the construction of the wall was halted in some places but accelerated in others; the army has never stopped putting pressure on villagers in the areas where the wall was to be constructed; demonstrations along the wall have become more fierce; and their oppression has become more violent and sometimes deadly.

13. To win means to strike the last blow, but the last blow is only the latest in an infinite series, and it creates the conditions for the next blow; hence, winning is always an embryonic moment of losing, and vice versa. The only real difference that exists is between more and less deadly and destructive violence. On this quantitative scale, the Palestinians are worse off.

14. Walter Benjamin, "Critique of Violence," in *Selected Writings, vol 1, 1913–1926* (Cambridge, MA: Harvard University Press, 1996), 236–252.

15. Ibid., 242; Jacques Derrida, "Force of Law: The Mystical Foundation of Authority," *Cardozo Law Review*, 11, no. 5-6 (1990): 921-1045.

16. Agamben, *Homo Sacer,* ch. 1.

17. The reduction in the number of both attempted and successful terrorist attacks in 2004 is a fact, and its ascription to the wall may be true but is very hard to prove. Many other factors may be involved, including the daily killings of Palestinians who are said to be combatants, and change in the political atmosphere in which less and less support of suicide bombing is expressed now. The security discourse of the wall conceives the Palestinians as walking bombs to be stopped at Israel's gate and gives no account of their position as free-thinking and -acting subjects. Without considering the Palestinians will and perseverance, how could one explain the fact that in the Gaza Strip, which is completely sealed off (by a fence, not a wall), Palestinians are constantly shooting into and shelling Israeli areas? And why this does not happen in the West Bank?

18. Other groups, e.g., Israeli Jews who are not settlers or Palestinian citizens of Israel, may have their own maps as well, but these maps are not as distinct from the major three discussed here.

19. This is the case in principle, at least, although some areas may be less permeable for a while, depending on the level of Palestinian resistance.

20. Agamben, *Homo Sacer,* part 1.

21. The Palestinian sociologist Sari Hanafi has described in detail this destructive relation of Israelis to the inhabited Palestinian space and to its environment, calling it "spacio-cide." See Sari Hanafi, "Spacio-cide, réfugiés, crisis de l'Etat-Nation. Vers un Etat palestinien Extraterritorialisé," in *Multitudes,* no. 18, 2004. See also Hanafi's essay in this volume.

22. Giorgio Agamben, who resurrects the ancient Roman figure of *homo sacer,* presents it as someone who may be killed without punishment and yet whose religious sacrifice is not permitted. See Agamben, *Homo Sacer,* part 2.

23. Agamben, *Homo Sacer,* part 3, especially chapter 7. Paraphrasing Agamben's title of this section of the book, one may say that the camp has become "the paradigm" or "the Nomos" of Israeli domination in the Occupied Territories. It is important, however, to note that, as explained on pages 12–13, this camp has no fixed external boundaries.

24. Renewal requires movement, but movement is restricted when documents are no longer valid. This vicious circle of the permission policy is well documented in Tal Arbel, "Measured Abandonment, a Political Technique: The Checkpoint Apparatus in the West Bank," work in progress.

25. More than three years before the second intifada the human rights organization B'Tselem reported "the quiet transfer" of thousands of residents (special report on the quiet transfer, April 1997). After September 2000 the pace of administrative denial of residents' rights only increased.

26. "More than 3,000 homes, hundreds of public buildings and private commercial properties, and vast areas of agricultural land have been destroyed by the Israeli army and security forces in Israel and the Occupied Territories in the past three and a half years. Tens of thousands of men, women and children have been forcibly evicted from their homes and made homeless or have lost their source of livelihood. Thousands of other houses and properties have been damaged, many beyond repair. In addition, tens of thousands of other homes are under threat of demolition, their occupants living in fear of forced eviction and homelessness," in "Israel and the Occupied Territories under the Rubble: House Demolition and Destruction of Land and Property," report by Amnesty International, May 2004.

27. It is worth noting that Israel administers a cluster of camps that comprises almost a fourth of its governed territory and encompasses about a third of the population that lives under its official direct and indirect control. There were in the past regimes that constructed and administered camps much vaster and much more terrible than this one, but the Israeli regime is perhaps the first to construct a camp so disproportionally large that it threatens to swallow the power that has erected it.

28. For a survey and classification of over fifty gates in the wall, see, for example, the United Nations report, "The Humanitarian Impact of the West Bank Barrier on Palestinian Communities" (September 1, 2004).

29. It is reasonable to assume that external political forces would intervene if and when the situation in the territories became truly catastrophic and was recognized by Western countries as a "complex humanitarian emergency." So far Israel has been very careful not to reach that point. We are interested here only with the way Israel, having brought the territories "to the verge of catastrophe," has used this threshold as a means of domination.

30. See note 2, above.

31. See Anne Le More's, "Foreign Aid Strategy," in *The Economics of Palestine: Economic Policy and Institutional Reform for a Viable Palestinian State*, ed. David Cobham and Nu'man Kanafani (London: Routledge, 2004); Adi Ophir, "The Role of the EU," paper delivered at Faculty For Israeli-Palestinian Peace (FFIPP), third conference in Brussels, July 2004. See also Mary B. Anderson, "'Do No Harm'—Reflections on the Impacts of International Assistance Provided to the Occupied Palestinian Territories," report from a visit to the Occupied Palestinian Territories from May 9–17, 2004, www.jerusalemites.org/reports.html.

32. The other thing a Palestinian can always give is collaboration with the ruling apparatus.

33. These presentations take place not only at the checkpoints, but also in about ten offices of the "civil administration," the so-called District Civil Liaison Offices, where the requests for permits are submitted. But the work of these offices is part and parcel of the entire mechanism of the restriction on movement, and they should be integrated into any geography of the wall and the entire network of checkpoints and roadblocks, gates, and passages. See the report, "The Bureaucracy of Occupation: The District Civil Liaison Offices", Physicians for Human Rights and Machsom Watch, December 2004. Tal Arbel, , "Measured Abandonment, a Political Technique: The Checkpoint Apparatus in the West Bank," work in progress.

Primitive Separations

Dean MacCannell

The wall now being built to prevent the movement of Palestinians into Israel
is called variously the "Israeli West Bank Barrier," the "West Bank Security Fence,"
the "West Bank Wall," or simply the "separation fence." Each label reflects a different
political position on, for instance, the location and route of the wall, the effectiveness
of the barrier in reducing suicide bombings, and the fate of Palestinians who are
being placed on "reservations" between the wall and the green line. After visiting the
wall I could see reason in several of these positions. But my aim here is not primarily
to recoup or defend any part of the politics surrounding it. Here I am interested in the
wall as a cultural artifact and as symptomatic of specific psychic formations.

Israeli proponents of the wall like to point out that it is modeled on the barrier the
United States has constructed along the most porous sections of its border with
Mexico. Some Israelis apparently believe that there are fewer Mexicans in the United

States now that the border is partially sealed. These are not the only walls currently under construction. Saudi Arabia is building a similar barrier along its border with Yemen. (If its first sections succeed in keeping the Yemenis out, the Saudis say they will consider walling their entire country). India is building a similar barrier on the "line of control" between Indian- and Pakistani-administered portions of Kashmir. The European Union is building several around Spanish enclaves in Morocco.

Any social division implies a relationship based in fantasy between the divided parties. Walls in the form of neighborhood fences, the walls between apartments in a high-rise building, walls with doors and windows that can be knocked upon and peeked through, movable walls . . . these are crucial supports to the thousands of small dramas that make up everyday life.

A wall of absolute separation, a barrier between peoples that is supposed to be impenetrable, is an entirely different matter. It functions rather as a mirror, reflecting the fantasy form of the other back onto its creator. It cannot but fail in its security purpose because it will inevitably eventually produce on its own side the hated stereotypical qualities of the people it is trying to keep out.

We are today beset by conflicts said to be based on religious fundamentalism. This is strange because these conflicts actually do little to foreground the fine points of theological difference. We get occasional quasi-religious rationales for this or that action: "It is against the teaching of the Koran to capture civilians in war"; and Netanyahu's infamous "Jews are condemned to live by the sword . . . in a state of constant siege until the end of time."[1] Christians suggest that they are not fighting for Christian principles per se but for "freedom" and "democracy," thereby affirming the superiority of their religion over others as better adapted to the geopolitical realities of the *modern* world. Who could believe that George W. Bush really went into Iraq to clear the ground for a Jerry Falwell ministry, or a Billy Graham "crusade"?

If we are not exactly fighting *for* religion but only *through* religion, what exactly are we fighting for? Some say it is for oil, or land, or markets. No doubt a few secular elites profit from wars of fundamentalism. But what about the believers who do the fighting? From a religious standpoint, the strangest outcome of all would be if some future Max Weber were to demonstrate that fundamentalist religious beliefs were only a beard for secular economic adventures.

Let me suggest the conflicts go deeper than religion. These are wars of social theory. While this is one of the ugliest prospects imaginable, we should consider the possibility that the battles are being fought over what is, or ought to be, the basis of the human community itself. Fundamentalists, of no matter what religion, avow that the strength of their communities requires an embrace of common values steeped in tradition and the unquestioned support of co-familiars who share the same set of beliefs. What they are affirming is their right to shield themselves and their children from contamination by ideas different from their own. The strategy they have settled on is the simplest one possible: to close the circle of sacred sameness from which all but the pure are excluded, to wall out any discordant imagery, to cleanse conscious- ness of any difference and all doubt.

Isn't this, a fundamentalist might ask, merely a return to the kinds of communities we had before life was sundered by competing religions and ideologies? Isn't it just an effort to get back to the way things were before our world became fragmented and different peoples were forced to share the same space? Isn't the fundamentalist ideal of a community unified in a faith in the "natural" human condition that prevailed before the advent of "anthropology," "secular humanism," "cultural relativism," "judicial activism," mixed marriages, gay marriages, and such?

Actually, it is not.

Before the beginning, six magical beings emerged from the great water and mingled among the Indians. One of the supernatural beings had his eyes covered and could not look at the Indians. But he wanted to look. Finally he was unable to restrain his curiosity and he peeked. When the spirit's eyes beheld a human, the man dropped dead. The spirit meant the Indians no harm, but his gaze was simply too powerful and it inflicted cer- tain death. The other five magical beings escorted him back beneath the great water and left him there. The five remaining spirits then rejoined the Indians and became a blessing to them. From these supernatural beings originated the great clans or totems of Ojibwa society: catfish, crane, loon, bear, and marten.

—Ojibwa myth, after Lévi-Strauss

It is very easy for us to misplace details of our human heritage. But anyone who carefully examines the ethnological record will easily arrive at an opposite conclusion: *at the beginning there was difference.* Not sameness. Difference.

Before undertaking the establishment of any commonalities, the Ojibwa separated themselves into five groups. They even went so far as to establish a basis for a separation more radical still between the first five clans and an empty term marking pure potential difference, a sixth clan that could not come into existence because its spirit totem was simply too powerful.

The early ethnological record is saturated with observations of a set of so-called primitive beliefs and practices surrounding the naming of descent groups or clans. Research into the organization, meaning, and function of these naming practices was once done under the heading "totemism." The word *totem* comes from the Ojibwa *ototeman* and in the Algonquin language means "he is a relative of mine."[2] Originally, in its native usage, it designated a logical category, *relation.* As ethnological observations of totemism accumulated, it came to mean much more. When a nonspecialist encounters a remnant of totemism, it is usually in the practice of naming different lineages and descent groups after animals, plants, and other features of the natural world: jaguar clan, hummingbird clan, rainbow clan, for instance. Old Hollywood westerns dependably provide this much knowledge of totemic naming. Many students of cultural anthropology can add further insight. They would know that clan members mystically identify with their totem animal and that there may be specific ritual requirements, such as a taboo on killing your totem. Those who know a little Freud could add that our primitive ancestors believed they had descended from their totemic animal. Readers of E. B. Taylor's (1899) essay on the subject may go so far as to conclude that modern religions are an outgrowth of earlier totemic beliefs.[3]

As is the case for every cultural complex "discovered" in different parts of the world, close examination reveals more variability than similarities and the "complex" tends to fall apart. As ethnographic reports continued to come in, we learned that not all social divisions into clans were named after animals, plants, or other natural phenomena. And not all of those that were so named required a special ritual attitude toward their totem. Today, the term has been discredited, by anthropologists such as Claude Lévi-Strauss, as having suggested too much cultural commonality between dispersed practices that are only superficially similar, and more integrity to the "totemic complex" than can be supported by careful study of the facts.

Before taking this second look, it is worthwhile to review more of the criticism that has been leveled at theories of totemism. Early on, hard-nosed—mainly British— social anthropologists argued that the so-called totemic complex was little more than an imaginative projection onto the ethnographic record by theory zealots trying to make names for themselves. Even back then, these overreaching theorists were French. In an article originally published in *L'Année sociologique* in 1903, Émile Durkheim and Marcel Mauss take up the question of early forms of symbolic classification that have moral and religious signification. They argue that all such systems of classification are based on the structural features of the societies that produced them. The symbolic schema the group invents to account for themselves and the natural world around them is differentiated in a way that reflects the differentiations of the group. According to Durkheim and Mauss, systems of totemic classification mirror primitive social structure.

In his introduction to the 1963 English translation of Durkheim and Mauss's essay, Rodney Needham summarizes the discomfort with their theories. He especially concerns himself with the causal arrows they drew, particularly their claim that social divisions *precede* the mental faculty for symbolic classification (e.g., that "logical hierarchy is only another aspect of social hierarchy").[4] Needham argues that the same data Durkheim and Mauss examined can be used in support of the opposite claim: that the logical powers of a superior (human) intellect produced the plans for the original divisions of the human groups in question, not vice versa.

In its drive to discredit its own theories of totemism, anthropology covered over one of its most important insights. In all the disagreements over the generality and/or the significance of the "totemic complex," there is no disagreement about one of its features. Every account of primitive social structure and symbolic systems accepts without comment that "at the beginning there was difference." Our savage ancestors, who were organized in societies as culturally homogeneous as human groups can be, embarked on a project of differentiating themselves internally at the instant of their formation into coherent collective entities. Or perhaps they engineered these primitive separations just before they came together as a condition of their original formation. Collectives can only be formed around some object or principle that belongs to no one. It is only after they are formed in this way that they can pretentiously claim the founding principles belong to everyone. Durkheim and Mauss were especially interested in Australian and American aboriginal societies, specifically the Arunta, the Zuni, and the Omaha. These three societies exhibit several of the most elementary divisions: in half, into reciprocal moieties; in quarters, corresponding to the cardinal division of space; and in multiples, by clans or lineages.

When all the controversy over totemism is swept away, the ineluctable remainder is that human societies, even the earliest and simplest ones, did not come into being or survive unless they were organized around differences of their own devising. We achieved our humanity by dividing ourselves from ourselves in order to deal with these divisions. Society can not exist except as an occasion for ongoing interaction between parties whose interests are not perfectly aligned. Erving Goffman would make this a basic principle in his kind of sociology. He wrote:

> The study of every unit of social organization must eventually lead to an analysis of the interaction of its elements. The analytical distinction between units of organization and processes of interaction is, therefore, not destined to divide up our work for us.[5]

And:

> The image that emerges of the individual is that of a juggler and a synthesizer, an accommodator and appeaser, who fulfills one function while apparently engaged in another; he stands guard at the door of the tent but lets his friends and relatives crawl in under the flap.[6]

Lévi-Strauss goes so far as to suggest that theories of totemism are themselves caught up in this differentiating and separating process. At the historical moment when ethnographic investigation was on the threshold of claiming an enormous common ground for all humanity, it was necessary to come up with a cultural complex separating "us" from "them." The "totemic illusion" (Lévi-Strauss's term) works perfectly to construct a separation of modern from primitive; a separation of peoples who understand themselves to be outside nature from those who think themselves to be part of nature (those who willingly trace their ancestry to animals, for instance); a separation of peoples who are science-based from those who are ignorant of the role of the father in conception; and so on. Lévi-Strauss summarizes, saying that totemism was invented by anthropology as a kind of prophylactic defense against its own findings, a "touchstone which allowed the savage, within culture itself, to be isolated from civilized man."[7]

The division of society (or societies) into two opposing parts is found everywhere: Republican-Democrat, Arab-Jew, white-black, etc. Can we say then that polarization is a normal or original state of society, a "primitive separation"? Certainly there is ample ethnographic evidence that our primitive ancestors were frequently divided into two opposing moieties. The Winnebago divide themselves into those who are above the earth and those who are on the earth. Lévi-Strauss turns his attention to this question in his essay "Do Dual Organizations Exist?" His argument is instructive: there can be no primal dualism because duality is already divided in itself; in other words, there are two fundamentally different types of dualism. He labels these "concentric" dualism, which establishes *hierarchies* (A over B), and "diametric" dualism, which establishes fluid *differences* (A and B).

If every duality is itself divided, a simple duality (A:B) could never have been an original basis for separation into two parts. Any primitive dualism would have been the kernel for an immediate and ever-expanding differentiation: A against itself, A over B, B against itself, B over A, and so on. Along these lines, some apparent dualities are actually more complex when they are examined closely. In a two-party system, for example, the moderate wings of both parties may have more in common with each other than they do with the radical wings of their own parties. Under these conditions, there are grounds for an enormously more nuanced political process than occurs when there are really only two opposing positions defined by political fundamentalism. So how can we account for the proliferation of simple polarizations in the world today? It can only be the result of a logical collapse, a retreat from possibility, a de-differentiation by peoples who become exhausted in the face of their full human potential.

There is no ethnological evidence to suggest that primitive schema inevitably adjust themselves in the direction of simplification. In fact, there is much to suggest that the opposite occurs. Realization of the self-generative potential of symbolic systems is in evidence throughout the primitive world. The Ojibwa, whose origin myth was retold ealier, made very flexible use of their system of social classification to expand it. The original groups (with the exception of the bear clan—perhaps they were Ojibwa fundamentalists) gave birth to additional groups. The catfish gave birth to merman, sturgeon, pike, whitefish, and sucker. The crane gave birth to the eagle, the loon to the cormorant and goose, and the marten to the moose and reindeer. When white men arrived, it was impossible to assign their half-caste offspring to any clan because, among the Ojibwa, descent is figured patrilineally. Noting that pigs and chickens also arrived with the white men, the Ojibwa assigned their mixed offspring to new pig and chicken clans. When the caribou disappeared from southern Canada, an anthropologist asked members of the caribou clan if the disappearance of their totem animal worried or upset them. "It's only a name," they answered.[8]

We have arrived ethnologically at the same destination Derrida arrived at philosophically. But there is a problem. Derrida presented his position as radically *opposed* to anthropology. He claimed that structural anthropology posits an original unity; that the first human groups were undivided, harmonious wholes. "Lévi-Strauss . . . must always conceive of the origin of new structure on the model of a catastrophe—an overturning of nature in nature, a natural interruption of the natural sequence, a brushing aside of nature," he writes.[9] Derrida argues that the anthropological idea of "structure" is based on a desire for oneness, truth, security in knowledge, clear boundaries, an evident center, the transparency of thought to itself, and of "full presence." Against this desire (can we call it fundamentalist?) Derrida mobilized poststructuralism, an indeterminacy without origin, a game which does not begin or end in which there can be no security, the free play of discourse, a field where the center is not merely lost—it was never there.

I believe Derrida has given us the best description we have of the situation faced by the earliest human thinkers. It is also a superior description of the exigencies that are encoded in primitive social organization and continue to be evident in all ethnological accounts. Rena Swentzell,[10] a Tewa architect, writes about the *nan-sipu,* a sacred hole in the ground in the dance plaza of the pueblo. It is the place where the ancestors emerged from under the earth and it is said to be the center of the universe. Every pueblo has one. There are as many "centers" of the universe as there are pueblos. Clearly it was some prototypical Derrida and not some fundamentalist who laid out the first pueblos. For Derrida to separate poststructuralism from structuralism he apparently found it necessary to repackage the insights of anthropology as if they were founded on a fundamentalist desire. I suspect his accusation has merit in some cases, but it has nothing to do with the ethnographic record. The Ojibwa said it long before Derrida raised it to the dignity of a philosophical principle: "It's only a name." Derrida needed to stage a historical rupture between structuralism and the fields he was seeking to found. In his own words, "these two interpretations of interpretation are absolutely irreconcilable." It is not "a question of *choosing* ... The category of choice seems particularly trivial ... because we must first try to conceive of the common ground and the *difference* of this irreducible difference."[11] Could there be any more elegant demonstration of the continued operation of the totemic impulse in thought today?

Before there were walls, primitive separations necessarily manifested themselves in myth, ritual, adornment, other dramaturgy, stylized interactions, and spatial arrangements. Pride of difference, ritualized conflicts, routine competition between clans, and other social divisions are marked features of the ethnographic record. In some ancient societies that made more than necessary of sexual difference, men and women developed separate languages, sometimes mutually unintelligible within the same community. There are reports from Australia that women had to sustain the fiction, under pain of death, that they could not comprehend what the men were speaking about among themselves. Of course, they *did* comprehend. The "wall" between the sexes was founded on the women's acting ability, their success at convincing the men they were ignorant of the men's affairs. This arrangement is not entirely restricted to Australian aboriginal groups. Primitive myth very often depicts the conceptual space between social categories as filled with monsters, ogres, and the like, erecting a symbolic wall of terror. It is only after there are walls—real walls, not metaphorical ones—that we get fundamentalisms.

In the Bororo village Lévi-Strauss studied, the physical layout of the houses in a circle around the men's meeting house became his model for concentric (hierarchical) duality. The rings of houses were also bisected on a north-south axis, dividing the matrilineal, exogamous clans corresponding to diametric (or reciprocal) duality. The lines were imaginary in that they were not marked by lines in the soil or by stones, but they were very real in their consequences. The arrangement of houses and common areas did not deviate from the system of social separations as spatially expressed.

Early social separations were maintained without walls, through interaction, strategic secrecy, and reciprocal knowledge. Robert Heizer[12] has reconstructed the methods California Indians used to maintain their tribal territorial boundaries. The

Indians learned to speak the languages of neighboring groups and negotiating a mutual understanding of where the lines between them should be drawn. These negotiations had to be accomplished with considerable dignity and integrity when, for example, it was necessary to determine on which side of the line (i.e., in whose territory) a game animal was standing when it was shot.

There are a number of accounts from the American frontier of whites who were taken captive by Indians. After a day or two on the trail, the Indians would make no effort physically to restrain their captives even when they were left alone while the Indians went in search of food. The Indians knew that the prisoners knew the Indians to be superior trackers who would have no difficulty hunting them down and recapturing them before they could find their way back to a white settlement. They were imprisoned by a mutual understanding more secure than iron bars.

A nine-year-old white boy taken captive by the Shawnee in 1790 near the current Ohio-Pennsylvania border reports on the Indians' approach to security. The first night, the Indians elaborately stretched and dried the scalp they had taken earlier in the day from the boy's traveling companion, watching him intently and making certain he could closely observe their operations. The account continues:

> Having finished their meal, the Indians prepared for rest; first tying the middle of a cord around my neck, and extending its ends around my wrists separately, they spread a blanket on the ground and ordered me to lie down; then, lying down on each side of me, passing the ends of the cord under their bodies, and covering themselves with the remaining blanket, soon sunk into a profound sleep.[13]

After traveling through the wilderness for over a week, the boy is finally delivered to a medicine woman who keeps him as her helper. He notes:

> The Indians use neither bolts nor locks, and when they leave for a time their cabins, either empty or with any articles in them, a log placed against its door affords ample protection to its contents, and abundant evidence of the right of possession in its owner; a right seldom, if ever, violated.[14]

Before there were walls and locked gates, apparently symbols alone sufficed for security.

Erving Goffman, in his classic *Presentation of Self in Everyday Life,* elevated the wall to the status of an analytic category basic to understanding Western society. He noted that every social division is:

> Bounded to some degree by barriers to perception ... [t]hick glass panels, such as those found in broadcasting control rooms, can isolate a region aurally but not visually, while an office bounded by beaverboard partitions is closed off in the opposite way.[15]

There are numerous ways to erect "barriers to perception" that do not involve building walls. Among the millions of other strategies that conform to Goffman's insight, we would need to include the fleeting reticence expressed by a Japanese woman who hides her laugh behind her hand. Another would be Robert Murphy's description of Tuareg warriors who wrap their heads with long indigo-blue head scarves. In ordinary dealings with tribal familiars, most of their face shows between the folds. But in dealings with strangers or enemies, the scarves imperceptibly wind tighter until only an occasional glint from their eyes appears through a narrow opening.[16]

Wall building is only the most rigid, permanent, and dramatic kind of barrier used to limn social separations. Walled communities are found widely dispersed throughout the ancient and even the primitive world. The Indians who captured the young Spencer (quoted earlier) built walls, or at least their neighbors to the east and south did. Some 370 wooden-stake-palisaded communities have been excavated in the area of the Mississippian culture complex. Most of these were built between 1100 and 1400, long before the Europeans arrived.[17] There are ruins of spectacular walls, some of them over sixty feet high, throughout the Middle East dating from the Bronze Age. The Romans built walls, as did the Irish, and of course the Greeks pretty much exhausted the logical possibilities in wall construction.

I want to set aside for the moment the most obvious reason for surrounding a district, city, or country with a wall—security and defense—and consider the ancillary *social* and *communicational* functions of walls. Any big wall can function in all three of the following ways.

1. **Staging interactions between peoples.** It has been noted that American Indian chiefs who had built reputations as great warriors became interested in avoiding war. They were afraid, even in victory, that their people would notice their lack of judgment or blind luck, and their reputations would be tarnished. So they built flimsy stake barricades around their encampments and told their people this would thwart attack, obviating the need for war parties. The barricades would have been worthless defenses against serious attack, but they served to maintain the local reputations of the warrior chiefs under conditions of collusive peace.

2. **Bearing messages.** In other words, a wall can be a "barrier to perception" but can also be used as a signboard bearing a message the wall builder or a graffiti artist wishes to communicate. Fifth-century Marwanid inscriptions on the walls of Diyarbekir near Mosul six times repeat the name of Abu Ali, an early occupier of the city. The repetition of the name carved on the exterior of the wall has been interpreted as a sign to potential enemies that Abu Ali had quelled internal resistance to his occupation and united the people of the city under his rule. In other words, "If you attack, don't assume the people will join on your side."[18]

3. **Reducing or obviating the need for symbolic exchanges between the peoples divided by it.** While this is historically and logically the most pitiful and hopeless rationale for walls, it is today the most common reason given for their construction. It is, of course, contradicted by 1 and 2 already.

No one loved to fight more than the Greeks, and no one built better walls. The first fortifications of large cities (as opposed to military posts and small villages) appeared in the Greek colonies in the late eighth, and early seventh centuries B.C., and for these, aesthetic considerations weighed as heavily as economy of construction and strength against attack.[19] What is perhaps most interesting about Greek walls to a modern observer is that they had, in addition to their gates, *posturns* or openings every thirty to one hundred meters. These posturns were not cut straight through but were made by overlapping sections of wall, leaving a gap between the overlaps. Arrows shot through the posturn would not go into the city but would rattle along the inner wall. A heavily armed man could pass through them. From the Greek standpoint they were strategically necessary for two reasons: (1) to permit the defending army to slip out at night to harass the attackers, and (2) to produce obvious points of entry for the enemy to come in single file and be killed one at a time, should anyone be brave or stupid enough to try such a thing. In short, the walls were porous as a principle of security. They were constructed not to keep the enemy out, but to invite him in on the defenders' terms.

During the Peloponnesian War the battering ram came into widespread use. City defenders quickly replaced fragile brick walls with stone. The battles consisted mainly of attackers pounding on the wall from the outside and frenzied construction by the defenders of a new wall behind the section being battered. Positioned with bows and arrows in towers standing slightly out from the walls, the defenders could counterattack anyone battering on the outer wall from the side, above, and slightly behind. The batterers, for their part, could work under a portable armored roof called a turtle. An attack became an occasion for collective work and ingenuity: demolition and construction under a hail of arrows and a rain of fiery oil. This kind of exchange could go on for days and would end only with the physical exhaustion of one or both sides. Under siege, the Greeks would disassemble their houses for materials to increase the height of their walls and to rebuild sections shaken down by battering. They would destroy what they were protecting in order to protect it. The first walls were 3.5–4.5 meters high and 1.75 meters thick.

Anticipating attackers' use of the battering ram, walls were made thicker and the number of fortified towers was increased. Attackers trying to work between two closely placed towers could not withstand the withering defense (the rain of arrows and oil from above) the towers provided. The combination of thicker walls and more towers neutralized the ram as an effective weapon.

From the fourth century forward, undermining became the preferred method of breaking walls. The problem with this approach was that the wall would often collapse on the digging army before it could pull back from its underground work.

The tower eventually superseded the wall as defending armies realized that with enough towers even an invasion breaching the walls could be stopped from above. Early in the fourth century, Philo warned that curtain walls hung between towers and bonded into them should be untied so they could fall free without compromising the integrity of the towers.

Also during the fourth century, stone-throwing artillery (the catapult) was invented. The walls then had to be built higher and thicker to block the stones coming into the city and to withstand the force of the blows. The walls could no longer be crenellated because the flying stones easily crumbled the thin crenellations. Mounting artillery in the towers gave it greater range than the same caliber machine on the ground, so defenders briefly enjoyed an advantage and were able to keep attackers away from their walls.

Attackers responded with Carthaginian siege towers, which were catapults mounted on portable towers matching the height and range of those of the defenders. Both sides increased the range and caliber of their catapults. Siege towers reaching a height of 100 cubits (about 175 feet) required a crew of 3,400 men to move and operate. Deep ditches outside the wall were dug to keep the cumbersome siege towers out of range. But the defenders faced another problem: as they increased the range and throw weight of their projectiles, the recoil from their own weapons began shaking their towers down.

Eventually the walls were redesigned to be easily breached from the outside, opening into hardened courtyards where the invading army would become compressed and could be attacked on all sides from above. Gates hanging above ground level on the outer wall were designed to slam shut behind the attackers, trapping them in the hardened-gate courts so they could be attacked on all sides from above with no avenue of escape.

What we have here is definitely not a failure to communicate. It is bloody and violent, but it is also an exquisite dance based on very high levels of mutual understanding. With every escalation in the balance of power between attackers and defenders, intelligence, counterintelligence, surprise attack, and feigned vulnerability became increasingly important strategies. The wall and especially its gaps provided crucial support for ongoing strategic interaction.

What is key to this kind of real, historic wall, as opposed to a symbolic one? It was designed to be porous. Controlled passage through the wall in both directions was, from the beginning, its most important strategic feature.

Rommel failed to secure the beach at Normandy in World War II because he set his green recruits to building "impenetrable" fortifications along the coast to repulse the Allied invasion. All they did was build a wall. They did not train to fight. There is an old military adage, "If you try to secure everything, you secure nothing." A wall that cannot be breached is something that occurs only in the imagination. Greek walls had holes

in them and strategic weaknesses purposefully built into them, the better to keep enemies out. An impenetrable barrier is something that can only appear as a pure fantasy between fundamentalisms.

The idea for an "iron wall" around Israel was first put forth in the writings and speeches of Ze'ev Jabotinsky in the 1920s.[20] Jabotinsky clearly saw the problem of establishing a Jewish state in Palestine, but he did not give up on the idea. He argued that there would never be a voluntary agreement between Jews and Arabs regarding Israel. Jabotinsky was the Zionist who most respected the Arabs, especially their resolve to prevent the establishment of Israel. He argued that, as a condition of its existence, Israel would have to have overwhelming military superiority and be prepared to defend itself against its neighbors in perpetuity. He proposed this in his influential paper, "On the Iron Wall (We and the Arabs)." There is no evidence of fundamentalism here. Not yet. Jabotinsky laid down the terms of dialogue, engagement, and survival under adverse conditions. The "Iron Wall" was a metaphor referencing the need to build a strong military and a vigilant defensive posture. It did not refer to the literal construction of an iron (or even reinforced concrete) wall.

When the metaphor became reality, it took on an opposite meaning. It suggests there is no possibility for further engagement, and no need for dialogue. Nuanced dialogue collapses into binaries; binaries collapse into fundamentalist unities. The Iron Curtain and the Cold War laid the foundation for the eventual free play of capital in the former Soviet Union and the Sovietization of the United States, which is now almost complete. The security fence is the basis for the eventual flowering of despised Arab stereotypes in Israel, which it will accomplish all the more perfectly if it succeeds in keeping all the Arabs out.

In April 2004 Juliet Flower MacCannell and I traveled to Israel to give lectures at Tel Aviv and Bar-Ilan Universities, and to visit the wall. On our arrival, we were advised not to try to visit the wall except as a part of a protest demonstration. If we went by ourselves, we were told, we would be subject to harassment and removal by the Israeli army. We ignored this advice on one occasion and were politely but firmly sent away. "It is simply too dangerous for you to be here," a tough-looking civilian contractor told us. So we went as part of a protest demonstration, with representatives of the Israeli Women's Watch for Peace, to a place north of Tel Aviv. The cement section of the wall we visited was under construction and there was an army checkpoint. It was a holiday, so not many Palestinians were attempting to pass. But we saw discarded water bottles and large piles of cigarette butts where people had waited in line in the sun on previous days.

The young soldiers at the checkpoints were heavily armed and tense. It is true that, since the wall was built, the numbers of suicide bombers able to penetrate and target Israel has declined; most of the explosions now take place at the checkpoints. The protesters, for their part, were going up to the soldiers to witness their handling of Palestinians seeking to pass into Israel. Sometimes a Palestinian lacked a document and would be sent back to get it. The protesters might remind the soldier that the same person passes the checkpoint every day with valid papers and ask that he or she be allowed to pass. Sometimes the soldier would yield, other times not.

Where the wall separates Palestinian homes from their places of work, worship, and school, the issue of being sent back is a bitter one. With checkpoints positioned five, ten, or more kilometers apart, what was once a short walk between house and fields, or house and school, can now take several hours. It involves walking down to the nearest checkpoint, waiting in line to pass, and then, assuming one is not sent back, walking on to a location that might be no more than a loud shout from one's house but is on the other side of the wall.

Palestinian bitterness is exacerbated when they must wait at the checkpoints while cars filled with Israeli settlers from the Occupied Territories go through without stopping. The settlers are allowed to pass, not even needing to touch their brakes, and sometimes speeding up as they pass to make a point of their privilege. They may get a tired salute or wave from the soldiers and cover the waiting Palestinians with a plume of hot road dust.

We saw places where schoolchildren waited for half the school day before being allowed to pass. This wait was unprotected from the dust and hot sun until the United Nations Children's Fund built shelters to provide shade.

The army watched us closely throughout our visit, but did not ask us to leave. Civilian contractors driving heavy earth-moving equipment made a game of speeding up and seeing how close they could come to us with their huge machines. They laughed uproariously if one of us flinched or jumped to safety. It became a kind of bull(dozer) fight, with the protesters as the matadors.

On the last night of our visit to Israel, Juliet and I were taken to a section of the wall in Jerusalem by Miki Kratsman, a respected photographer. He had conceived and helped to organize a joint Palestinian and Israeli protest. During our previous visits, we had repeatedly asked what other purpose the wall might serve other than its security function, if this eventually proved to be illusory or unnecessary. Miki Kratsman gave us one: it works incredibly well as an outdoor cinema screen. On our arrival at the Israeli side, we found a growing group of artists, other protesters, and reporters, and were told a similar group was forming on the other side. Two video feeds were pushed through drainage holes in the base of the wall. We put a camera against the wall on our side facing us. This camera was connected through the wall to a video projector set up to project everything we were doing on our side against the wall on the Palestinian side. The signal from their camera was sent to our projector so we could see them as they could see us. When both sets of images were projected simultaneously, the effect was a very large virtual hole in the wall. We were able to protest together, singing, dancing, and cheering as though the wall was not there. With a prodigious act of the imagination, even this most forbidding wall can be used as a device to bring people together.

There was also a very sweet interaction I observed, between a frail Palestinian woman, probably around seventy years old, and a twenty-something male Israeli soldier with a sidearm and an automatic rifle. It was at an isolated segment of the wall near Tulkarm. The soldier blocked the woman's way with his arm and tried to explain that she lacked a necessary document and could not pass. The woman begged the soldier. She urgently needed to pass even though she didn't have her documents. They were talking over each other, each in their own language, and their voices were getting louder. The woman, adamantly demanding to be heard, grabbed the soldier by the ear and pulled his head down to the level of her mouth and shouted louder directly into his ear. He was evidently in some pain and tried to pull back but she maintained her fierce grip and even turned his body in a tight circle as she continued her entreaties. What I loved about this incident was that all the while it was happening,

Dean MacCannell

this old Palestinian woman did not consider even for a second that the heavily armed Israeli soldier might resort to the use of force against her. And I also felt that the soldier, for his part, never once considered force to be an option under the circumstances. They were two human beings disagreeing under conditions of full mutual understanding that it was okay for them to disagree. The two were eventually separated by my companions from the Women's Watch for Peace, who found someone much younger to run back for the woman's papers.

I asked myself how this would have played out between a policeman and a resident of East Los Angeles. It gave me some hope that even with the wall, and even with the failed fundamentalisms the wall signifies, the people, left to their own wit and wisdom, are still capable of working things out.

Dean MacCannell

Notes

1. Avi Shlaim, *The Iron Wall: Israel and the Arab World* (New York: Norton, 2001), 574.

2. Claude Lévi-Strauss, *Totemism* (Boston: Beacon Press, 1962), 18.

3. E. B. Taylor, "Remarks on Totemism with Especial Reference to some Modern Theories Concerning It," *Journal of the Royal Anthropological Institute*, V. XXVIII, 38–48.

4. Émile Durkheim and Marcel Mauss, *Primitive Classification* (Chicago: University of Chicago, 1963).

5. Erving Goffman, *Encounters: Two Studies in the Sociology of Interaction* (Indianapolis: Bobbs-Merrill, 1961), 7.

6. Ibid., 139.

7. Lévi-Strauss, *Totemism*, 2.

8. Ibid., 20–21.

9. Jacques Derrida, "Structure, Sign, and Play in the Discourse of the Human Sciences," in *The Languages of Criticism and the Sciences of Man*, ed. Richard Macksey and E. Donato (Baltimore: Johns Hopkins, 1970), 263.

10. Rina Swentzell, "An Understated Sacredness," *MASS: Journal of Architecture and Planning*, University of New Mexico, fall, 1985.

11. Derrida, "Structure, Sign, and Play in the Discourse of the Human Sciences," 265.

12. Robert F. Heizer, *Languages, Territories and Names of California Indian Tribes* (Berkeley: University of California Press, 1966).

13. O. M. Spencer, *Indian Captivity: A True Narrative of the Capture of the Rev. O. M. Spencer by the Indians in the Neighborhood of Cincinnati Written by Himself* (New York: J. Collard, 1835), 44–45.

14. Ibid., 66.

15. Erving Goffman, *The Presentation of Self in Everyday Life* (New York: Anchor Doubleday, 1959), 106.

16. Robert F. Murphy, "Social Distance and the Veil," *American Anthropology*, vol. 66 (1964), 1257–1274.

17. George R. Milner, "Palisaded Settlements in Pre-historic Eastern North America," in *City Walls: The Urban Enceinte in Global Perspective*, ed. James D. Tracy (Cambridge: Cambridge University Press, 2000), 46–70.

18. Sheila S. Blair, "Decoration of City Walls in the Medieval Islamic world: The Epigraphic Message," in *City Walls: The Urban Enceinte in Global Perspective*, 488–529.

19. For this and the descriptions that follow I am indebted to a marvelously detailed account. See F. E. Winter, *Greek Fortifications* (Toronto: University of Toronto, 1971).

20. Shlaim, *The Iron Wall: Israel and the Arab World*, 11 ff.

Why This Wall?
Stephanie Koury

Dafna Kaplan

I wish every Palestinian could have been present in the court to hear other
countries talk about Palestinian rights. It was the most empowering feeling in
the world. At the same time, it made me realize how far is the divide between
the internationally sanctioned peace process and the quest for achieving
Palestinian basic rights.

—A Palestinian observer during the International Court of Justice hearings of February 2004

The use of walls or barriers by governments and militaries is not a new phen-
omenon. Throughout history, walls have been constructed to delineate boundaries, for
defensive purposes, to consolidate territorial conquests, and even occasionally in the
name of peace. Consider the Berlin Wall, for instance, or the twenty-seven barriers
built by the British in Northern Ireland in an attempt to control the "troubles" there, or
the "berm," which runs along almost the entire length of the western Sahara and will

secure for Morocco around 80 percent of that territory's resources.[1] So why is so much focus concentrated on Israel's construction of the wall in the Occupied Palestinian Territories (OPT)?

One reason may be the sheer scale and material nature of the wall. In some places, particularly in Palestinian-populated areas, Israel has erected eight-to-nine-meter-high concrete panels protruding from the earth on hilltops or in flat lands next to Palestinian homes or farmland. In other places, it is composed of coils of barbed wire with two ditches, a trace path, and patrol roads, all forming a 50–100-meter-deep barrier that separates Palestinians from their families, their land, their schools and places of work.

The wall is one continuous line, with a planned route of some 652 km, 200 km of which are completed to date. It has limited crossing points and restricted operating hours, and so is ill-suited for the movement of people, goods, and motorized vehicles to and from adjoining areas. Over 95 percent of the wall built to date intrudes into the West Bank; less than 1 percent is planned for construction on Israeli territory.

Another reason for the intense focus on the wall may be the political strategy behind it. Israel has created a new administrative regime by declaring the areas between the green line and the wall to be "closed" and establishing a permit system for access to and fro.[2] Palestinian residents and nonresidents of the area must now obtain a written permit (sometimes valid for only one month and occasionally declined outright) to remain in their homes, access their land and places of work, or simply visit friends or family. In contrast, Israeli citizens or those eligible for citizenship are exempt from the permit regime and may remain in or move freely to and from the closed zone to access and remain in their settlement.[3]

To Palestinians, the wall is the conclusion to a complex but carefully planned demographic-based policy that Israel has implemented in the Occupied Palestinian Territories since 1967 in order to permanently retain parts of the West Bank. This policy, undertaken in the name of security, has involved (1) the systematic confiscation of Palestinian land through military orders and other "legal" mechanisms; (2) an induced transfer of Israeli civilians into the OPT by government subsidies and incentives to settle there; and (3) a gradual blurring of differences between Israeli citizens residing in Israel and those in the OPT through the extension of Israeli law to those settlers and their areas of settlement.[4] Facilitating these demographic changes is the network of roads that Israel is constructing, which, when complete, will extend some 450 km and link these settlement areas with each other and with the state of Israel.[5]

The route of the wall entrenches the Israeli settler presence within the OPT. It weaves extensively into the West Bank, protruding seven to eight kilometers in places, as in East Jerusalem, and in other areas twenty-two kilometers into the northern West Bank, in order to accommodate Israeli settlements and their bypass roads to the "Israeli" side of the wall. The wall has also captured large areas of Palestinian farmland and as yet undeveloped commercial areas to reserve space for Israeli settlement expansion in the OPT. In recent months, Israel has begun construction or advertised plans for at least five new settlements situated to the west of the wall in the OPT.[6]

The macro effect of the policy of wall construction is the same as that caused by Israeli construction of settlements: the displacement of Palestinians from their land, accompanied by the gradual destruction of community ties and diminishing opportunities for sustained economic livelihood. The wall represents the continuation of the "Nakba," or the displacement of approximately 700,000 Palestinians from their land, their homes, and their way of life when the state of Israel came into being in 1948—except that in this case many additional Palestinians will be displaced because access to their land and places of employment will be increasingly denied, along with other resources critical for future demographic growth and economic development.

The Palestinian town of Qalqilyah, for example, with a population of approximately 43,000, has been encircled by the wall in order to facilitate the expansion of the Zufin and Alfei Menashe settlements and ensure that settlers can travel on bypass roads in the area. According to a UN report by the special rapporteur on the right to food, approximately 6,000 Palestinians have left the Qalqilyah area to date.[7]

Israel's wall, combined with its settlements and settler-only bypass roads, is projected to divide the Palestinian West Bank into a series of enclaves on 52 percent of the West Bank, with "transportation contiguity" of roads but without significant territorial expanse or adequate access to natural resources such as water. In short, the wall is viewed as rendering permanent the Israeli efforts to date to secure their hold on Palestinian territory and prevent the establishment of a viable Palestinian state.

Going to Court: Israel's Biggest Fear[8]

The quest for achieving the enforcement of respect for Palestinians' human rights in an international forum is not new. In the early 1980s, three prominent Palestinian lawyers attempted (unsuccessfully) to get the UN Committee on the Inalienable Rights of the Palestinian People to garner support for a request for an advisory opinion from the International Court of Justice (ICJ) on Israel's confiscation of Palestinian land to build the network of settler bypass roads known as Plan 50. The UN General Assembly passed Resolution ES-9/1 in 1982 calling on member states to suspend economic cooperation with Israel. Trying a different tack, Belgian and Lebanese lawyers tried (again unsuccessfully) in the late 1990s to secure the prosecution of current Israeli prime minister Ariel Sharon for his role in the murder of Palestinians in the Sabra and Shatila refugee camps in Beirut.

In the case of the ICJ and the matter of the wall, however, Israel had several things to fear. First, although an advisory opinion by the ICJ itself is not binding, the international law on which the opinion is based would be binding. Thus, Israel would be obligated to comply with the legal findings of the court. Perhaps even more threatening, Israel feared that a question on the wall put to the ICJ would risk exposing and discrediting the complex legal framework it has constructed over the last thirty-six years in relation to the Occupied Palestinian Territories and their Palestinian inhabitants.

Territory is considered occupied when it is placed under the authority of a hostile army, as occurred in 1967 when Israel took control of the West Bank and Gaza Strip. The occupation extends only to that territory where the occupying power exercises effective control or retains the ability to do so.[9] Early on in its occupation, however, Israel took a strategic decision not to relinquish, in any future agreements with neighboring Arab states, parts of the territory it had occupied in 1967:[10] it therefore became important for Israel to undermine any applicable legal framework that would prohibit it from taking measures aimed at permanently securing Israel's hold on the territory and to construct its own legal framework to support this objective, including denying the status of the territory as occupied. Thus, almost from the outset of the 1967 occupation, Israel maintained that the West Bank and Gaza Strip were not occupied territories but rather that they were "liberated" or "disputed."[11] Despite international consensus to the contrary,[12] including determinations by Israel's own High Court, the Israeli government has maintained this position of "disputed" territory to date.

Dafna Kaplan

There was also a fear that an ICJ opinion might venture beyond the immediate matter of the wall and address the issue of the legality (or otherwise) of settlements. Israel has since 1967 exercised a policy of establishing civilian settlements within the OPT in direct contravention of Article 49(6) of the Fourth Geneva Convention. Since Israel maintains that the territories are not occupied, however, it claims that the Fourth Geneva Convention is not de jure applicable to the West Bank and Gaza Strip. Israel instead relies on Article 2 of the convention to argue that, because the West Bank and Gaza did not belong to a "high contracting party" at the point of Israel's occupation, the convention is not formally applicable to that territory.[13] Israel has said, however, that it will apply those provisions of the convention that *it* deemed to be humanitarian, excluding from its obligations, for example, the prohibition on the establishment of settlements in the Occupied Territories or other measures that result in the transfer or deportation of the Palestinian population.

For its part, the Israeli High Court has avoided determining whether the convention is de jure applicable and maintains that, because the convention was not ratified by the Knesset into domestic legislation, it is not enforceable in domestic courts.[14] While the court has selectively relied on some of the convention's provisions, it has steadfastly avoided specific examination of whether the establishment of civilian settlements in the OPT is or is not compatible with Article 49(6).[15]

Events Leading Up to the ICJ Opinion

On October 9, 2003, in light of Israel's ongoing construction of the wall, Syria, in its capacity as chair of the Arab Group, requested an immediate meeting of the United Nations Security Council to consider the "grave and ongoing Israeli violations of international law, including international humanitarian law. . . ." The United States, as a permanent member of the Security Council, vetoed a proposed draft resolution on October 14 and subsequently, on October 20, the General Assembly reconvened in an emergency special session under the Uniting for Peace Resolution 377(A). Uniting for Peace enables the General Assembly to immediately consider an issue which appears to be a threat to peace, a breach of peace, or an act of aggression, with a view to making appropriate recommendations to members for collective measures, when the Security Council is unable to act due to the negative vote of a permanent member.

On October 27, 2003, the General Assembly adopted Resolution ES (Emergency Session)-10/13, demanding that Israel stop and reverse construction of the wall in the OPT, and requesting that the United Nations secretary-general report back in one month on Israel's compliance. In the meantime, the Security Council adopted resolution 1515 by which it endorsed the U.S. "Roadmap." The secretary-generals report of November 24 found that Israel was not in compliance, and the tenth Emergency Special Session was reconvened; Resolution ES-10/14 was adopted on December 8 by a vote of 90–8 (with 74 abstentions), requesting the "advisory opinion" by the ICJ.

The General Assembly sought advice, in the context of the applicable international law, including the Fourth Geneva Convention and Security Council resolutions, on the legal consequences for Israel, for United Nations bodies, and for member states in light of Israel's continued construction of the wall. For its part, the government of Israel (GOI) had argued in official documents provided to the UN that the construction of the wall is necessary to protect "Israeli populated centers from terrorist infiltrations and attacks"[16]; and also that the establishment of a "security zone" is essential for delaying infiltrations into Israel.[17]

As momentum was building in the United Nations, Palestinians, as well as Israelis, were bringing cases in the Israeli High Court on certain aspects of the wall or parts of it. In one case, two Israeli organizations were challenging the closures of the gates built into the wall and the permit system established in the closed area. In another, Palestinians from eight villages in northwest Jerusalem were contesting a 40-kilometer stretch of the wall that would result in the seizure of approximately 4,000 dunums (approximately 1,000 acres) of their land and the separation of villagers from a vast swath of their agricultural land, schools, and health services.[18] The Israeli High Court was due to rule on this latter case on June 30, nine days before the ICJ issued its opinion.

It was clear that the scope of the decisions raised in the two forums would vary to a great extent. First, the Israeli High Court was concerned only with alleged harm caused by a short section of the wall, whereas the ICJ opinion was to provide legal guidance to the General Assembly of the United Nations regarding the legal consequences of Israel's action of construction of a wall *anywhere* within the OPT. Moreover, by the very nature of the question put to the ICJ, answers were sought regarding not only Israel's obligations but also those of third states and international organizations in the face of continued Israeli violation of international law.

Many third states, including several European countries, were opposed to the ICJ hearing for fear that an advisory opinion would obligate them to act against Israel's transgressions. Acting unilaterally would, in their eyes, run counter to their policy of promoting a resumption of political dialogue between the two sides and risk jeopar-dizing the possibility of a European seat at the negotiating table in the future. It would also upset their political posture to date of treating the parties as two governments with equal power, rather than in the legal framework of "occupied" and "occupier."

In light of what was at risk, Israel and several third states tried through written submissions to convince the ICJ, on jurisdictional grounds or for reasons of propriety, to exercise its discretion to decline from giving an advisory opinion. One argument put forth was that the General Assembly had acted *ultra vires* in reconvening the Emergency Special Session and adopting the resolution because the Security Council was seized of the matter at the time. The ICJ found, however, that the tenth Emergency Special Session was duly convened in accordance with the conditions of the Uniting for Peace Resolution 377 (A) because the Security Council had failed to act due to a veto by the United States of the draft resolution in October condemning the wall. In making this finding, the court noted that it was a redundant veto by the

United States in 1977 of a draft resolution pertaining to Israel's construction of the Har Homa settlement in the OPT that triggered the convening of the tenth Emergency Special Session in 1997. The court also noted that the Security Council Resolution adopted on November 19 endorsing the roadmap was not sufficient to show that the Security Council was seized of the matter of the wall because neither the resolution itself nor the text of the "Roadmap" mentions the wall. (With this finding, the court indirectly brought about the result the United States had been trying to avoid through its October veto: the censure of Israeli actions in the OPT and the infusion of international law standards into the Israeli-Palestinian peace process.)

Others argued that an opinion by the court could impede progress on securing the sort of political, negotiated solution to the conflict suggested by the "Roadmap" and the Quartet-sponsored peace plan, or that the subject matter was essentially a bilateral dispute between two parties, one of whom, Israel, had not given its consent to ICJ jurisdiction. The court found that these factors also did not constitute a compelling reason to decline to give an opinion. On the first point, the court said that states expressed differing views on the potential impact of an ICJ opinion on securing a negotiated agreement. On the second, the court affirmed that the subject matter could not be regarded as only a bilateral dispute. Rather, "given the power and responsibilities of the UN in questions relating to international peace and security . . . the construction of the wall must be deemed to be directly of concern to the UN," and, further, "Palestine remains a permanent responsibility of the UN until the question is resolved in all aspects in a satisfactory manner in accordance with international legitimacy."[19]

What Did the Courts Decide?

Not surprisingly, the Advisory Opinion by the International Court of Justice affirmed the status of the West Bank, including East Jerusalem, as occupied territory, noting that events subsequent to the start of the occupation—such as Israel's unilateral annexation of East Jerusalem or the Oslo Accords—that provided the PA with certain limited powers did not alter the status of the territory. Moreover, the exercise of effective Israeli control over the OPT—the construction of some 750 barriers to movement around Palestinian villages, towns, and roads throughout the West Bank, for instance—has only increased since the start of the intifada, further entrenching the occupation.[20]

The ICJ also definitively discredited the GOI's long-standing position on the applicability of the Fourth Geneva Convention, noting that the fact that Jordan was not the recognized sovereign of the OPT when Israel conquered the West Bank in 1967 is irrelevant, and that, consequently, armed conflict between two high contracting parties—the basis for the applicability of the convention, as we have noted—could be said to have occurred.

The ICJ also rejected Israel's reasoning that, since in their view human rights treaties are intended for the protection of civilians from their own government and in times of peace, human rights conventions were not applicable to the OPT. Instead, it affirmed the finding of the UN Human Rights Committee that human rights instruments such as the International Covenant on Civil and Political Rights, the International Covenant on Economic, Social and Cultural Rights, and the Convention on the Rights of the Child are applicable to the OPT, noting that the instruments apply where a state exercises its jurisdiction on foreign territory.

As for the Israeli High Court, it again avoided determining the de jure applicability of the convention[21] or certain human rights instruments in its June 30 decision. As it had done in previous cases, it used a general formula: "The parties agree that the humanitarian rules of the Fourth Geneva Convention apply to the issue under review."[22] In doing so, its point of departure for legal analysis varied significantly from that of the ICJ and, as I will show in the following paragraphs, led to quite different findings on the matter of the wall.

First, in examining the legality of the route of the wall, the Israeli High Court did not distinguish between Israeli citizens living lawfully within Israel and settlers residing unlawfully in the Occupied Palestinian Territories at the permission of the Israeli government. In contrast, the relationship between Israeli settlements and the wall factored extensively in the ICJ opinion. In affirming that the settlements had been established in breach of international law, and that the route of the wall should consequently be considered in the context of that and other prior illegal measures, the ICJ found that the route chosen . . . gives expression *in loco* to the illegal measures taken by Israel with regard to Jerusalem and the settlements . . . ," referring explicitly to Israel's unilateral annexation of Jerusalem in June 1967. Some 80 percent (325,000) of Israel's settlers would be situated between the wall and the green line.[23] Given this context, the ICJ was not convinced that the specific route Israel had chosen for the wall was necessary to attain the security objectives the government claimed. Nor was it convinced, given the way in which the settlements had been previously described as temporary, that the Israeli government's claims about the temporary nature of the wall could be relied upon. On this matter, the ICJ noted that the wall creates a "fait accompli on the ground that could well become permanent ... and would be tantamount to *de facto* annexation," contrary to the prohibition on the acquisition of territory by force.

The ICJ also considered the impact of the route of the wall in the context of the larger political situation: the right of Palestinians to the exercise of self-determination, for which a "sacred trust" is enshrined in the UN Charter and in General Assembly Resolution 2625 (XXV) of 1971. It first established that it considers that Israel recognized this right by reference to terms such as "legitimate rights" used in the Oslo Accords.[24] The court went on to find that Israel is in breach of its obligation not to take measures that impede the exercise of self-determination due to the risk of de facto annexation of the OPT and further demographic changes posed by the wall.

In sharp contrast, the Israeli High Court's findings started from the point that the wall is intended to realize a security objective.[25] Its failure to recognize Israel's settler policy as an unlawful attempt to change the demographic composition of the occupied territory dictated that the court "must examine the route on its security merits alone, without regard for the location of the green line."[26] It also enabled the Israeli court to assert a legal standard relating to belligerent occupation—that the military command must balance between the needs of the army on one hand and the needs of local inhabitants on the other, without additional systems of considerations.[27] Because the court does not recognize the unlawful presence of Israeli settlers within the OPT, however, consideration of the settlers' needs were included in the judgment about the exercise of this balance. Rather than ensuring their security by evacuation, as international law would dictate, these settlers become part of the "security needs" for which the military is responsible.[28] Thus, the court was able to rely on testimony from Israeli commanders that the route of the wall is well chosen to achieve its security objective regardlessof the fact that it follows the location of Israeli settlements throughout the West Bank.

By extension, the Israeli High Court gave no serious consideration to the wall as a political tool for furthering Israel's policy of de facto annexation of territory by settling its citizens in the OPT. It disregarded the petitioners' argument that the fence was moti-vated by political considerations because it was built not on the green line but within the OPT. It also relied on government statements about the temporary nature of the wall, just as it had previously relied on statements that Israeli settlements are temporary.

In determining the legality of the specific segments of the wall under its review, the Israeli court did not attempt to examine whether particular human rights conven-tions were applicable. Rather, it limited itself to the principle of proportionality. The principle of proportionality provides that the harm or damage caused by any measure taken by the occupying army must be in proportion to the threats posed or the perceived military advantages to be gained by the measure.[29] Accordingly, a disproportionate measure is one in which the magnitude of harm the measure causes cannot be justi-fied by the importance of the military advantage gained or the benefits of security gained. Consequently, the Israeli court confined itself to determining whether the route of the wall chosen was within the "zone of reasonableness" to achieve its secu-rity objective, and, if it was, whether the gain sought by the route was proportionate to the harm that it would inflict upon the Palestinian population.

The court found that approximately thirty kilometers of the forty sections under review violated the principle of proportionality. It noted that the wall would separate large numbers of Palestinians from their land[30] and that the licensing regime (the permit system) would not substantially decrease or prevent injury to the farmers. Access to land would be dependent upon gates which were often closed and spread far apart, and security checks would cause hours of waiting.[31] The court also found that the wall "strikes across the fabric of life of the entire population" as it passes right next to Palestinian homes or surrounds villages almost entirely, and that it directly affects the links between local inhabitants and urban centers such as Bir Naballah and Ramallah.

The ICJ's Final Verdict

A core tenet of Israel's legal framework for the OPT has been its characterization of the conflict as an ongoing dispute or "armed conflict short of war." This interpretation has enabled it both to maintain in force its state-of-emergency regulations since 1948 and to justify its use of excessive force and weaponry within the OPT. It further enabled the Israeli government, in its November 2003 submissions to the UN, to rely on Article 23(g) of the Hague provisions relating to armed hostilities rather than on those applicable to situations of occupation.

The ICJ, however, noted that, since military operations leading to the occupation had ended, the applicable provisions in both the Hague and the Fourth Geneva Conventions are indeed those relating to occupied territory. It consequently affirmed Israel's obligation to ensure the protection and well-being of the civilian population under occupation, implicitly confining its use of force to measures appropriate to policing rather than those appropriate to armed conflict.

By a vote of 14–1, the ICJ found that Israel "gravely infringed a number of rights of Palestinians residing in the OPT by the construction of the wall and its regime. These include rights relating to prohibitions on the creation of demographic changes within occupied territory, the confiscation of private property, the freedom of movement, the right to choose one's residence, the freedom of passage of relief consignments, and the rights to work, health, education, and an adequate standard of living."

The ICJ recognized that Israel had a right and even a duty to ensure the safety of its citizens. But it underscored that the measures Israel takes in effecting this duty must be in conformity with applicable international law. The court went on to examine possible Israeli defenses to preclude the wrongfulness of actions. It recognized that rights protected under human rights instruments are qualified by the requirements of national security or public order, and that "military exigencies" may be invoked in occupied territory after the close of military operations, but it was not convinced that the infringements of Palestinian rights could be justified by either of these qualifications. The court was convinced, for example, "that the destruction of private property carried out [in contravention of] the prohibition in Article 53 of the Geneva Convention was not rendered absolutely necessary by military operations."[32]

The ICJ also rejected the relevance of Article 51 of the UN Charter, which provides for an inherent right of self-defense in the case of armed attack by another state. The court, taking a formalistic approach, maintained that, because Israel had never alleged that Palestinian actions were attacks by a foreign state, Article 51 was not relevant. (Two judges, Higgins and Kooijmans, agreed with the conclusion but disagreed, in a nod to the evolving nature of the law of self-defense in light of international terrorism, with the court's reasoning that the attack had to emanate from another state.) Moreover, the court was not convinced that Israel had met the requirements for the customary defense of "state of necessity" to preclude the wrongfulness of its actions. To do so, Israel would have had to show that the route chosen by the construction of the wall was "the only way for the state to safeguard an essential interest against a grave and imminent peril."[33]

Legal Obligations: What Next?

In light of the ICJ findings, Israel is obliged to stop construction of the wall, remove existing sections of it built within the OPT, and repeal all related legislative and regulatory acts. It is also required to undertake restitution by returning property that has been confiscated and paying reparations for any damage caused.

There are legal obligations too for third states and the UN. The ICJ reaffirmed an earlier finding that the right of self-determination constitutes obligations *erga omnes*, obligations that by their very nature are the concern of all states and which all states have a legal interest in protecting.[34] It stated too that, because many rules of international humanitarian law are "so fundamental to the respect of the human person" or are "elementary considerations of humanity," they also incorporate obligations that are essentially *erga omnes*. By a vote of 13–2, the court found that third states are under an obligation not to recognize the illegal situation resulting from the construction of the wall in the OPT, nor are they to render any aid or assistance in maintaining the situation created by such construction. They are also under an obligation to ensure Israel's respect for the Fourth Geneva Convention. As for the UN, the court called on the General Assembly and the Security Council to consider what further action is required to bring an end to the illegal situation resulting from the construction of the wall and its regime in the OPT.

Following the ICJ opinion, the General Assembly reconvened in emergency session and passed resolution ES-10/15 on July 20, 2004, by a vote of 150–6, with ten abstentions. Among other things, this resolution demanded that Israel comply with its obligations as outlined in the opinion and called upon all member states to fulfill their obligations as mentioned in the advisory opinion. It also requested the UN secretary-general to establish a register of damage in connection with Israel's obligations to make reparations for the harm caused by the construction of the wall and its regime. The court also invited Switzerland, in its capacity as the depository of the Geneva Convention, to conduct consultations regarding the resumption of the Conference of

High Contracting Parties to the Fourth Geneva Convention, the last meeting of which was held in December 2001. One possible outcome of the conference is the establishment of working groups of states to consider measures available to ensure Israel's compliance with international humanitarian law. All twenty-five member states of the European Union supported the UN resolution, while the United States and Australia were among the few who voted against it. For its part, the United States has said it supports the Israeli High Court decision.

At a technical level, third states are now reexamining their donor-sponsored projects in the OPT to ensure that they are not financing projects that support the wall and its regime, and efforts are being made to provide guidelines for donors to ensure their compliance. The projects' aims are often not clear-cut: supplying equipment for use at cargo terminals built at the wall but within the OPT, for instance, might appear to facilitate the much-needed movement of Palestinian goods (indeed, this is the basis on which donations would be made), but its ultimate purpose would be to contribute to Israeli plans for establishing permanent border crossings and terminals at particular junctures in the wall. Consequently, any donation by a third state would violate its legal obligations. Similiarly, aid granted for the construction of Palestinian-use roads which lead away from the closed zone would also be illegal, because those roads will facilitate Israel's efforts to create such unsustainable conditions within the zone that large numbers of Palestinians will leave.

The Non-Aligned Movement, at its Ministerial Conference on August 17–19, 2004, adopted a declaration which called upon member states to undertake certain measures—among other things, to impose sanctions against companies and entities involved in the construction of the wall and other illegal activities in the OPT, including East Jerusalem, to decline entry to settlers, and to prevent any products of Israeli settlements from entering their markets. It also called on the UN Security Council to fulfill its responsibilities by adopting a clear resolution and undertaking necessary measures in this regard, and on the secretary-general of the UN both to expedite the work regarding the register of damages and to ensure that the positions and documents of the Secretariat were fully consistent with the advisory opinion.

Church actors are also taking measures to bring about an end to the Israeli violations of international law. In July 2004, in a vote of 431–62, the General Assembly of the Presbyterian Church USA adopted a resolution instructing its Mission

Responsibility Through Investment Committee to initiate a process of phased selective divestment in multinational corporations operating in Israel and to make appropriate recommendations to the General Assembly Council for action. Anglican Church leaders in the United States are also to recommend divestment at their 2005 meeting of the Anglican Council in Wales.

The challenge will be for third states, particularly the Quartet members, to make the difference. Israel will not act otherwise. Will the Quartet members continue to make security reform by the Palestinian Authority a condition of taking concrete measures against the wall and Israeli settlements? Or will they finally, as the ICJ opinion gave them the opportunity to do, insert a human rights and humanitarian law framework into the peace process, a framework which differentiates these obligations from the issues to be negotiated in a final status agreement?

And within Israel? Immediately following the decision Israeli prime minister Ariel Sharon announced that Israel rejected the ruling of the ICJ in the Hague, stating that it was "one-sided" and "politically motivated." Israeli justice minister Yosef Lapid said that Israel would honor its own court's ruling. Israel appears to continue to negotiate with the United States alone any potential changes to the route in light of the Israeli High Court case.

In spite of this, however, the findings of the ICJ, and the fear of potential sanctions, have opened the door to some critical examination of the legal framework Israel has constructed since 1967 to govern its relations with the OPT and the Palestinian population residing there. In fact, in late August 2004, Israeli attorney general Menahem Mazuz, heading a team of legal jurists, recommended to the government that it thoroughly examine the possibility of recognizing the de jure applicability of the Fourth Geneva Convention to the OPT. Other Israeli government officials have not joined the call, however, recognizing that such a position would mean an end to a "legally" sanctioned Israeli settlement policy within the OPT. The legal findings of the ICJ vindicate those Israeli jurists who for years maintained that Fourth Geneva Convention is de jure applicable to the OPT but who were criticized as "anti-Israeli" for their position. It will now be more difficult for the Israeli High Court to avoid making the politically difficult, but legally correct, findings of law in future cases argued on the basis of the findings of the ICJ, particularly in relation to the Geneva Convention and Israeli settlements. And the Israeli government can no longer maintain its legal construct with any semblance of credibility or legitimacy. In the meantime, however, Israel continues construction of the wall down the length of the West Bank.

Notes

1. Berlin history, from *The Columbia Electronic Encylopedia*, 6th ed., copyright 2004, Columbia University Press, www.info-please.com/ce6/world/A0856909.html (accessed August 8, 2004). See also www.wsahara.net/morberm.html and www.forcedmigration.org/guides/fmo035/fmo035-2.htm.

2. Israel Defense Forces Order Concerning Security Directives (Judea and Samaria), no. 378, 1970 Declaration Concerning Closing of Area Number s/2/03 (seam area) (Judea and Samaria), effective, October 2, 2003.

3. Ibid.

4. "Land Grab: Israel's Settlement Policy in the West Bank," *B'tselem, the Israeli Information Center for Human Rights in the Occupied Territories*, May 2002, 50–52, see www.btselem.org/Download/200205/Land_Grab_Eng.pdf.

5. Meron Benvenisti, *The West Bank and Gaza Atlas (West Bank Data Base Project)*, (Boulder: Westview Press, 1988), 35.

6. These settlements include Kidmat Zion, Nov Zahaf in East Jerusalem; Givat Y'air near Bethlehem, and around Nof HaSharon, Givat Tal Qalqilyah.

7. Report by the special rapporteur, Jean Ziegler, Addendum, Mission to the Occupied Palestinian Territories, The Right to Food, E/CN.4/2004/10 Add.2, October 31, 2003, paragraph 51.

8. The primary legal frameworks applicable to the Israel-Palestine situation are international humanitarian law and human rights law. International humanitarian law is the body of law intended to minimize the effects of armed conflict or occupation by providing provisions for the protection of persons no longer or not taking part in conflict and by restricting the means and methods of warfare. Most relevant to the Occupied Palestinian Territories is the Fourth Geneva Convention of August 12, 1949: Relative to the Protection of Civilians in time of Armed Conflict. Also applicable are the regulations annexed to the Hague Convention (IV): Respecting the Laws and Customs of War on Land, 1907. See "What is International Humanitarian Law," International Committeé for the Red Cross, Advisory Service, July 2004.

    Human rights law is the body of law that seeks to protect individuals at all times, whether in peace or armed conflict, and it serves to further individual development through, for example, the right to education or employment. Particularly relevant in light of Israel's construction of the wall in the OPT are the International Covenant on Civil and Political Rights, the International Covenant on Economic, Social and Cultural Rights, and the Convention on the Right of the Child. These instruments, along with the international humanitarian law (IHL), include prohibitions on, among others, creating demographic changes to occupied territory, destruction and requisition of property, restrictions on the freedom of movement, impediments to the exercise of the right to education, health, and work and to an adequate standard of living.

9. Article 42 of the regulations annexed to the Hague Convention (IV): Respecting the Laws and Customs of War on Land, 1907.

10. Geoffrey Aronson, *Israel, Palestinians and the Intifada: Creating Facts on the West Bank* (London: Kegan Paul International, 1990), 14–15.

11. Annex 1, Summary Legal Position of the Government of Israel, Report of Secretary-General to the UN General Assembly. Israel's military proclamation in June 1967 implicitly recognized the application of the Geneva Convention but, as we have noted, the government changed its position within weeks of the proclamation and began labeling the territory "liberated" and not occupied. See David Kretzmer, *The Occupation of Justice: The Supreme Court of Israel and the Occupied Territories* (New York: State University of New York Press, 2002), 32–33.

12. See UN Security Council Resolutions 242 (1967), 298 (1971), 478 (1990).

13.   Israel makes a highly formalistic argument: "the Convention shall also apply to all cases of partial or total occupation of the *territory of a High Contracting Party*, even if the said occupation meets with no armed resistance" (italics added). In 1967, both Jordan and Egypt were occupying powers of the West Bank and Gaza, respectively. Jordan's formal annexation of the West Bank was not recognized internationally.

14.   Kretzmer, *The Occupation of Justice: The Supreme Court of Israel and the Occupied Territories*, 45 and 31–42.

15.   Ibid., 43–44.

16.   Statement by Ambassador Dan Gillerman, permanent representative of Israel to the United Nations Security Council, on the situation in the Middle East, including the Palestinian Question, October 14, 2003, 9.

17.   Israeli High Court of Justice, HCJ 2056/04, "Beit Sourik Village Council v. the Government of Israel," paragraph 29.

18.   Ibid., paragraph 9.

19.   International Court of Justice, "Legal Consequences of the Construction of a Wall in the Occupied Palestinian Territory, Advisory Opinion," July 9, 2004, paragraph 51.

20.   United Nations Office for the Coordination of Humanitarian Affairs (OCHA), www.ochaonline.un.org.

21.   Israeli High Court of Justice, HCJ 2056/04, "Beit Sourik Village Council v. the Government of Israel," paragraph 23.

22.   Ibid.; Kretzmer, *The Occupation of Justice: The Supreme Court of Israel and the Occupied Territories*, 41.

23.   International Court of Justice, "Legal Consequences of the Construction of a Wall in the Occupied Palestinian Territory, Advisory Opinion," July 9, 2004, paragraph 122.

24.   Israeli High Court of Justice, HCJ 2056/04, "Beit Sourik Village Council v. the Government of Israel," paragraph 46.

25.   Ibid., paragraph 44.

26.   Ibid., paragraph 30.

27.   Ibid., paragraph 27.

28.   In previous cases, the court explicitly considered settlers to be part of the "local inhabitants" in order to justify allowing construction of settler byroads. See "Tabeeb v. Minister of Defense," 1981, and "Ja'amait Ascan v. IDF Commander in Judea and Samaria Minister of Defense," 1980.

29.   International Court of Justice, "Report Legality of the Threat or Use of Nuclear Weapons, Advisory Opinion," July 8, 1996, paragraph 30, from *How Does the Law Protect in War* (International Committee of the Red Cross, 1999), commentary to article 53 of the Fourth Geneva Convention, 302.

30.   Ibid., paragraph 76, 82.

31.   Ibid.

32.   International Court of Justice, "Legal Consequences of the Construction of a Wall in the Occupied Palestinian Territory, Advisory Opinion," July 9, 2004, paragraph 135.

33.   International Court of Justice, "Legal Consequences of the Construction of a Wall in the Occupied Palestinian Territory, Advisory Opinion," July 9, 2004, paragraph 140. Citing Article 25 of the International Law Commission's Articles on Responsibility of States for Internationally Wrongful Acts.

34.   International Court of Justice, "Legal Consequences of the Construction of a Wall in the Occupied Palestinian Territory, Advisory Opinion," July 9, 2004, paragraph 157.

Wall Notes
Tom Kay

Tom Kay

Since the summer of 2002, the Israelis have been announcing proposed routes for the wall. For various reasons, these often change—in most cases making the situation worse, while in a few, making the situation for the Palestinians seem better than the original proposal. To my mind there is an absolute and insidious intention to reduce protest by announcing a doomsday position—total disaster—and then redrawing the map to make it doomsday minus 1 percent. Still impossible, but "proof" that the Israelis are "listening."

Having read through my notes and examined the maps again, it is clear that, in many places, the wall has been sited specifically to cut off villages from their best farmland: in many areas I visited, there were no settlements to be "protected." Given the Israeli track record, my guess is that as soon as the wall is completed, new settlements will be started along the wall on West Bank land: Facts on the Ground.

Tuesday, March 4, 2003

Wadi Natuf in the Western Aquifers West of Ramallah

I accompanied C., a hydrogeologist working for SUSMAC, a water research NGO, on a field trip to his study area, Wadi Natuf in the Western Aquifer—a basin of valleys with mini-mountain humps in the middle west of Ramallah to the green line, an oval area perhaps ten by twenty kilometers. Both Israeli settlements and Palestinian villages are dotted over the hills. The Israelis always build on the crests with fortress-like walls rising out of the mountain below. Then they build miles of wire and search-lit fences, taking swaths of land for future expansion. SUSMAC is carrying out a study of the underground aquifers, surface springs, and wells up to 600 meters deep in this area.

To get from one village to another, we often had to drive on crazily rutted steep dirt tracks the settlers and soldiers controlling virtually every road. So the trip was a series of trial moves, driving until we came to a roadblock and had to back off. In some cases, villages two kilometers apart were separated in such a way that the tracks to be covered were five to twenty kilometers long. In many cases, "track" was an exaggeration.

C. is well known in many of the villages and we could never drive more than a few minutes without a conversation out of the window. In one village, we visited the pumping installation of a well which served a number of villages. The pump guy was away, but the young mayor brought us coffee while C. read the pump dials. The wall will pass the village. But Jamil, the mayor, says that the latest proposal here puts the pumping station on the Israeli (west) side of the wall. Without the well, will these villages survive?

At one point, we drove steeply down a track for ten minutes to find, at the bottom of the wadi, a river running across it. A bulldozer, in water a meter deep, was building an earth bridge, shovelling out the wadi bed onto a series of oil drums, which allowed the water to pass. For most of the year the wadi is completely dry, but the snows have now built the flow to a point where nothing can drive across. It is the only access to a village. The ad hoc civil engineering was the subject of great interest for a large number of villagers. Women sat by the flow upstream, with kids swimming in the freezing water. The men jumped around the rubble as it was being shifted, generally as interested onlookers but occasionally positioning the battered oil drums. There was a festive

Wadi Natuf:
Left: Getting home to the village, avoiding the soldiers.

Right: Detour around the roadblock to a village.

Tom Kay (2)

atmosphere ... and come to think of it, it was the Muslim New Year's Day. Eventually we turned around and found another route of perhaps ten kilometers, rather than the 500 meters to the village. Of course, there was a perfectly sound, if potholed, tarmac road to the village off the main road. But this was blocked with an earth barrier, as was every Palestinian village off that road. In the end, the trip took eight hours, covering ground which, without the settlements, might have taken two. (Some of the villages were Ain Arik, Deir Ibzia, Kuf'r Na'ame, Ras Kharkar, Kharbata, Deir Qaddis, Ne'alin, Qibbiya, Shuq'ba, Shib'tin, Jammala, Deir Nizam, Kobar, Beitillu. Some of the Israeli settlements commanding the high ground were Nili, Na'ale, Dolev, Talmoun, Halamish, and Ateret.)

Tuesday, February 11, 2003
Izbat Salmon, South of Qalqilyah

The Eid Al Adha starts today. Four days of visiting family and eating. In meaning, different—but in feeling, similar—to Christmas. Inevitably, the Israelis have imposed strict closure to Palestinians of all checkpoints throughout the territories. With Israeli number plates and foreign passports, we can travel. We have been invited by the M's (K.'s family) to their home village of Izbat Salman, a few kilometers south of Qalqilyah.

Near Luba Sharqiya, H. stops to pick up an old man. We repack so that he can sit in the front. Afterward, it clicked that this was not a bright thing to do. It is illegal to pick up a Palestinian in an Israeli plated car. The old man is trying to get to family in Nablus. H. is, at times, embarrassed; the old man keeps picking up her hand from the steering wheel and kissing it. We drop him some distance in front of Huwara junction, the checkpoint before Nablus, and watch him hobble toward the soldiers. Don't know if he got through. Backtracked onto Route 60 southwest of Nablus and then west onto Route 55. One village after another, cut off from this road. Occasionally, there was a tunnel under the road, connecting donkey tracks between the villages. I have seen in other areas that these tunnels are very easy to block on a whim or as punishment.

Izbet Salmon: Excavation for wall at the edge of the village.

Tom Kay

Out of the mountains into gentle hills with villages and settlements above and below us. Stretches of this road are through villages. Very confusing. In the village the Palestinians can drive, but no Palestinian plates on the road either side of the village. Passing military vehicles every few minutes. As we move west, it begins to look more and more like Israel, with residential and industrial settlements.

Just before Azun, there are three roads off to the south, leading to three completely separate settlements a kilometer apart: Ma'ale Shomron, Ginot Shomron, and Karnei Shomron. After Oslo, no new settlements were to be built. Only natural growth. All over the West Bank, new settlements have been built, but by using the same name as the original settlement. . . . Who are they fooling?

Within sight of Qalqilyah on the green line, we stop at a petrol station, looking out over the Israeli coastal plain to Kfar Saba and Herzelia beyond. We are still in Palestine, but the petrol pumps and the little shop serve Israelis, who act like slave masters. We are close to the green line and there is little doubt that this neck of the woods will be annexed. On the other side of the road sits a tank and a couple of jeeps on an outcrop ten meters above the road. Looks like a very permanent installation. We park at the back of the forecourt, near a group of young Israelis unloading from the back of a car. Weapons slung across their backs, they look like a hunting party out for a day's fun. We start a scramble down an embankment through a rubbish dump onto a dirt track. Very quickly this becomes a melted milk chocolate slurry through deep-plowed fields.

We are due to be picked up by one of the M. brothers. But today no car can negotiate this steep track in the mud. After a twenty-minute slither and slide, we come to the bottom. One or two cars are stuck there. K.'s brothers reach us and we start up the dirt track to Hable. At Hable, a village road appears and we drive south through two or three villages to Izbat Salman. Our welcome is delicious. All four brothers, their wives, and about fifteen children and grandchildren. Plus the old M. couple. Today, the first day of the Eid, sons visit parents. The sons have all reached "home." This is by no means guaranteed. Some of the journeys, a few kilometers, can take as long as going from London to New York. During the next three days, the sons will visit their sisters, if they can. We all sit on the roof terrace. Presents are distributed. Most of the family had eaten before we came. The meal, including wonderful stewed lamb, is set up just for us.

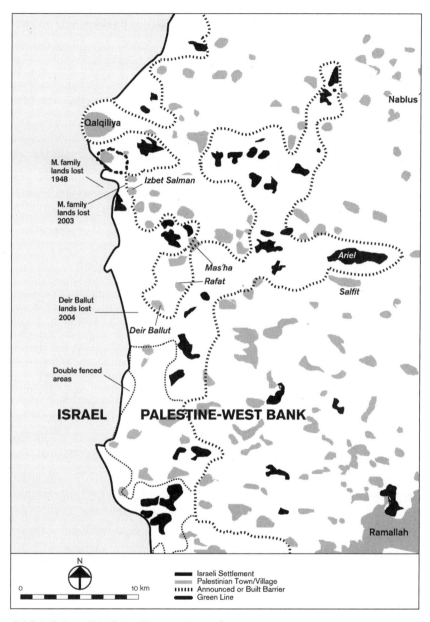

Deir Ballut Enclave and Izbet Salmon Village.

Israeli Settlement
Palestinian Town/Village
Announced or Built Barrier
Green Line

0   10 km

N

ISRAEL   PALESTINE-WEST BANK

Qalqiliya

M. family
lands lost
1948

Izbet Salman

M. family
lands lost
2003

Deir Ballut
lands lost
2004

Mas'ha
Rafat

Deir Ballut

Double fenced
areas

Nablus

Ariel

Salfit

Ramallah

In 1948 the family had land on both sides of the green line. After the war the family moved from a village, just on the Israeli side, to Izbat Salman in then-Jordan, because the larger part of their land was to the east of the new border. They lost a little less than half to the Israelis. Now the Israelis are building a wall, effectively moving the border eastward, and much of the rest of their olives and greenhouses will be lost west of the wall.

Two of the young men of the family take us to see the newly lost lands and the bulldozed strip showing the line of the new wall, just outside the village. We are dropped at the bottom of the track. Clambering upward toward the petrol station, it is inevitable (and funny) that A. should fall flat into the chocolate pudding mix. Other villagers are returning on this track . . . in their Sunday best, white shoes and all. Retraced the road back to Route 60 and Huwara checkpoint five kilometers from Nablus.

Saturday, February 28, 2004
Al Mutilla, twelve kilometers East of Jenin

Al Mutilla is a tiny hill village east of Jenin close to the northern green line. The inhabitants are part of an extended family, perhaps fifty people over four generations. Today we went there to talk to the two brothers, both in their late fifties, the working heads of the village, and to their aging parents. On this northern section of the green line, the wall is being built generally following the line, with some incursions. I assume that these are either to take the high ground or simply because the opportunity exists to take land. As always, the land occupied by the wall, its road, no-man's-land, and fences, are on West Bank land.

However, at this village the wall will leave the green line to start its southward journey, separating the Palestinian Jordan Valley from the remainder of the West Bank. Much of the Jordan Valley, some kilometers to the east, has in effect already been stolen by the army and the Israeli settlements. Here, the Israeli settlers farm with total and profligate dependence on irrigation, further reducing the already scarce Palestinian water supply and contributing to the drying up of the Jordan River. Here also, the army declares huge tracts as firing and bombing ranges, effectively dispossessing Palestinians of their grazing lands.

The wall will formalize the situation. The map shows only about ten kilometers of the wall, but the southerly direction it is taking, if continued, is tantamount to annexing about a third of the West Bank. The brothers took us onto the hills on the eastern edge of the village. From here we watched the heavy machinery on the green line. A narrow track has been cleared by the bulldozers from the green line to the village olive groves. Here the contractors have lopped the olive branches in a swath about sixty meters wide, leaving the trunks and roots to be pulled out by the machines. The groves are to the east of the village and most of village lands will soon be on the other side of the wall.

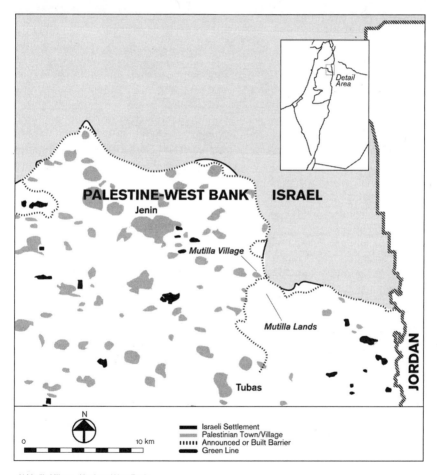

Al Mutilla Village—Northern West Bank.

Tom Kay

Mutilla: First Day of tree lopping by hand, before bulldozers start.

Sunday, May 23, 2004
Deir Ballut-Rafat-As Sawiya-Mas'ha Enclave

We went north, just south of Qalqilyah to three villages that will be surrounded by the wall, forming an enclave about five kilometers by two kilometers. The western edge of the enclave is from two to four kilometers inside the West Bank; the land outside the wall is the farmland of the predominantly agricultural village of Deir Ballut (pop. 3,000). We sat with the mayor, who showed us his maps. This village will lose approximately 85 percent of its land. The "Annexation Wall" has been marked out with red paint on stones on the edge of the village, with markers in the olive groved hills beyond.

At the north end of the enclave at Mas'ha, they have built a short section of wall with a bright yellow swing barrier, lines of razor wire, and a concrete tower gun emplacement. The wall is in the back gardens of the houses and stands more than twice their height. The early stages of the wall building reminds me very much of the dog who goes from tree to tree releasing a short burst, marking out his domain. Short sections of the wall are established, the dots to be joined up later.

Above: The red paint marking the wall is just to the left of the people. Whichever way the wall runs, the olive grove across the photo will be lost by the village. The Israelis will no doubt move the bedouin encampment on the righthand side.

Left: House near wall.

Once the wall is completed, a Deir Ballut farmer will have to travel five kilometers north to Mas'ha, go through the gate, which is opened twice a day (unless it is not opened), and then five kilometers south to within half a kilometer of the village. There will be no road for the second half of the journey. How long before the Israeli settlers take over the land with the excuse that it not being properly cultivated?

Tom Kay

Saturday, June 5, 2004
Ar'ram, 80,000 Palestinians between Jerusalem and Qalandiyah

To a demonstration in Ar'ram. Here the wall will be built down the middle of the road from Ar'ram to Qalandiyah. A thousand Palestinians and fifty photographers. The march ended in front of Israeli troops, with Palestinians trying to stop the shabab (young lads) from throwing stones. To the extent that the army did not open fire the stones not coming within 100 meters of the soldiers, one might say that the restrainers were successful.

Wednesday, June 9, 2004
Ar'ram

Army in strength on road between Ar'ram and Qalandiyah, about two kilometers. They have started the excavations for the wall down the middle of the road. Questioned by border police for taking photos, I replied that the wall had certain significance concerning urban planning.

Women in Black.

Prayers at the excavation of the wall.

Protest fire.

Opposite left: A youth is restrained.

Tom Kay (4)

Stepped foundations for wall.

A person living in Ar'ram (part of annexed West Bank territory) wanting to get into Jerusalem a few minutes to the south will have to travel north . . . go out through the Qalandiyah checkpoint, then queue to come back through the checkpoint. By taxi-foot-taxi, it will add a minimum of an hour, unless as often happens, the Israel Defense Forces (IDF) closes the checkpoint for the day. By car, it could easily add two to three hours for the five-minute journey. A very clever way to get rid of about 80,000 Palestinians, many with Jerusalem IDs. So the people of Ar'ram will be isolated, stuck in a hole between Qalandiyah and Jerusalem. The wall is sometimes positioned to steal more West Bank land and include illegal Israeli settlements. At other times, as here, it is designed to dump Palestinians into ever-shrinking parcels of land.

It reminds me of *The Death Ship* by B. Traven . . . written in the 1930s about displaced people or refugees in Europe being forever dumped across borders in the middle of the night. The hero, a sailor who had lost his papers, ships out in desperation aboard a cargo boat, which he knows will be scuttled for the insurance.

Of course, he drowns. The depression was hard for the shipping companies, but they had the scuttle option. The Israelis have the enclave option. A slower death, but a death all the same.

Every day I think I have heard the worst . . . every day I am more disgusted and have to adjust. Crying wolf? The first wolf was certainly there. But each day that wolf gets bigger or meaner.

Friday, June 11, 2004
Ar'ram

Just south of Qalandiyah, they have taken two days to lay the stepped foundation for approximately 200 meters of wall down the middle of the road toward Ar'ram. It will stretch to Jerusalem and underline the annexation . . . as if that were necessary. They have already off-loaded huge precast slabs, ready to lift into position. In another context, I would admire their efficiency. I gather they are pretty good in the science lab. They must be world leaders in super-heavyweight precast technology. Each section of wall is about 1.5 meters long, 20 centimeters thick, and 8 meters high with a precast concrete double-sided toe about 1.5 meters wide. Each precast has a perfectly formed 20 centimeter diameter hole near the top . . . presumably for lifting. Elegant punctuation when the wall is standing.

At Ar'ram crossroad the imam from the main mosque was conducting the Friday midday prayers in the middle of the wall excavation. I think the twenty or so movie cameras kept the IDF from interfering. The soldiers stood 300 meters away in both directions.

Friday, July 2, 2004
Ar'ram

Passing through Qalandiyah, I notice that the Israelis have added a ten-meter-tall cylindrical precast concrete watchtower-cum–gun post at the end of the wall that follows the northern edge of the disused Atarot airport, now a fast-growing industrial estate. The slots for the soldiers are above the top of the wall. Already in the last couple of days, it has been rather ineffectually attacked with a Molotov cocktail and is blackened at its base, now guarded by soldiers.

A hunger strike against the wall started today at Ar'ram. A tent has been erected for the strikers and another to accommodate visitors.

Tom Kay

Qalandiya Gun Tower after a Molotov

Wednesday, July 7, 2004
Ar'ram

Accompanied A. who was interviewing Nahed's family in Ar'ram. All have Jerusalem IDs. Fifteen years ago, they moved out of Jerusalem and built a house in Ar'ram. Her father, a lawyer, and brothers work in annexed East Jerusalem and in Israel. Her mother's life is still solidly connected to people in Jerusalem.

They are considering a move back into Jerusalem. Not a real option. The problem is that the house has dropped 75 percent in value since the announcement of the wall, while property in Jerusalem is and was always much more expensive than in Ar'ram.

Saturday, July 10, 2004

Ar'ram

The hunger strike finished yesterday. An Israeli minister has been quoted as saying words to the effect that it doesn't concern him if they all die.

Today at Ar'ram, Palestinian and Israeli women came together to demonstrate against the wall. Some Palestinians held placards written in Hebrew, some Israelis held placards written in Arabic.

The Israelis have cast the foundations for two-thirds of the two-kilometer stretch and have off-loaded next to the road the last of the 1,500 precast units. Following an application to the High Court in Jerusalem, there is a stay of execution of this section of the wall. Nobody expects the stay to last.

Postscript: The stay of execution was lifted during the summer of 2004 and this section of the wall has been completed.

Keeping a One-Week Diary, or, Pastrami Sandwich with Concrete Wrapping

Suad Amiry

Dafna Kaplan

What a bore it must be for me to write (and for others to read) a one-week diary of my daily routine driving back and forth between my home next to the Surda checkpoint (one of the four Israeli checkpoints totally isolating Ramallah) and my work in Riwaq, a distance of three kilometers.

I rarely use third gear on my car.

Why not bore others, as a punishment, for not lifting a hand about our siege.

That in mind, I started.

Sunday, October 26, 2003

"Nura ... do you want nunu?"

She runs toward the door.

With half-open eyes, I drag myself to open the door; she runs out to the garden. As I am preparing my two huge mugs of tea with milk, I hear a gunshot from the Surda checkpoint less than a kilometer away. I carry my two mugs and go back to bed. Nura had also made it back to her bed, next to ours; neither my husband Salim nor Nura ... get cups of tea.

Salim, with closed eyes, is listening to the news.

I was standing against the Rafat wall, which prevents me and other colleagues at Riwaq from reaching our conservation projects outside Ramallah.

"*No*, this stupid wall has nothing to do with Israel's security. Look at it. It does not separate Israel from Palestine, it separates Palestinians from Palestine. This wall, like the majority of the 320 checkpoints, has *nothing* to do with Israel's security! If Israel wants a security separation wall, it must build the wall and the checkpoints on the 1967 borders, not inside our land. This is the biggest land and water *grab* in the history of Israel. While claiming to separate themselves from us, they have taken up to 55 percent of our land. Do you call this security?"

I find myself screaming my head off at Bob Simon, who is interviewing me for *60 Minutes*, a CBS program that is profiling the impact of the wall on our lives. I think Bob Simon regretted choosing a middle-aged menopausal woman to talk about *separation*.

That afternoon I had an even longer siesta. It was so long, I woke up Monday morning.

Monday, October 27

"Nura … nunu?"

Runs toward the door, half-open eyes, opens the door, runs to the garden; two huge mugs of tea with milk. I hear an Israeli helicopter roaming in the sky of Ramallah; carry my two mugs to bed, back to her bed, Salim listening to the news:

"The American administration is critical of Israel's construction of the security wall inside the Palestinian Territories, hence preventing Palestinians from reaching their farms."

Has my interview with Bob Simon (which has not been transmitted yet) already influenced the American administration?

Tuesday, October 28

I was trying hard to hide my anxiety and fear while accompanying Leila Shahid on her trip to the town of Qalqilyah some fifty kilometers north of Ramallah. She wanted to see the worst-case scenario of the "separation wall."

It was not the three types of permits I needed to "legally" accompany Leila on her trip, nor the impossibility of getting such permits from the Israeli army on such short notice, but rather the mental and psychological barriers, checkpoints, and separation walls I have personally built in and around myself, and my life, in besieged Ramallah. I must admit I was in a state of complete denial about the harsh realities of the wall.

Denial seems to me an effective way of dealing with the unbearable encounters of life under occupation.

To drive "illegally" through Israel seems to be the only way to make it to Qalqilyah.

Also, the only way to challenge Sharon's "security wall"!

It was my *age* that got us through the Qalandiyah checkpoint, Leila's *elegance* that got us through the second checkpoint into Israel, and the soldiers' total *confusion* with Leila's passport and my Jordanian passport that got us through the *only* entry and exit point for the 45,000 residents of Qalqilyah. We later learned that we were lucky to get through, as the gate had been closed by the Israeli army for the last twelve consecutive days.

"Back up, *erghjaa la wargha*," the soldiers kept yelling at us and all others trying to get into town.

"Back where?" Leila and I inquired.

"Don't listen to him, he is stupid, all he wants is to give orders, and his orders are even more stupid," says an elderly woman standing just behind us.

We only take orders from older women, so we just continued our conversation.

"Are you from Qalqilyah?" asks Leila of the three young women standing next to her.

"Yes, we're from Qalqilyah, but we teach in the girls' school in the neighboring village of Jayyous."

"*Azab* [it's a hassle]," says her friend. "Going and coming, we have to cross this checkpoint and another checkpoint in Jayyous. We have to take four Fords [taxis], walk up and down mounds of rubble in order to reach our students. *Umsh eisheh*—it's not a life."

"And most of the times the checkpoint is closed," says a third teacher to Leila.

Leila was tentatively listening to the three teachers. I was watching the long queue of women on the other side of the checkpoint. The only aspect of Arab traditions the Israeli soldiers seem to reenforce (overrespect), while humiliating every man and woman, is gender separation.

As two Israeli female soldiers were body-searching each one of these women, my eyes were moving from one face to the other. I felt myself absorbing the feelings expressed on the faces of these women the second they were touched by the soldiers: anger, frustration, weariness, pity, helplessness, humiliation, defiance, disgust, and resentment.

I was enraged.

"Look, there is a male soldier searching the poor women; unbelievable," says Leila.

"No, Loulou, these are women soldiers."

"Really?"

I guess once you are a soldier all sex differences disappear.

"Come forward," calls the same "stupid" soldier to us.

The three teachers went first, Leila second, and I followed.

Leila and I were met by Abu Ma'zoz from the Municipality of Qalqilyah. Abu Ma'zoz realized that Leila and I had come to see the "separation wall," so immediately after greeting us he says: "You see, we are like a Coca-Cola bottle with only one cap." Why Coca-Cola? I wondered if this was a good ad for Coca-Cola.

Abu Ma'zoz started familiarizing us with the surroundings. He was pointing east:

"You see the Jewish settlement over there? That's Egal Alef and next to it Egal Beit. The one straight ahead is Sufin. It is Sufin's settlers that stole our *jarraffeh* [caterpillar], but we managed to get it back."

I wanted to stop Abu Ma'zoz and ask him how one can steal a caterpillar? But then I felt embarrassed to see all the stolen land in front of my eyes and inquire only about the *jarraffeh*.

I stopped myself from asking and continued listening to Abu Ma'zoz:

"See that huge settlement over there, to the south, that is Alfeh Manasheh."

We drove along the Nablus road, Qalqilyah's main shopping street. Having very few people in the street compelled me to inquire if the town was under curfew.

"No, it is Ramadan and since the checkpoint has been closed for twelve consecutive days people stopped venturing in or out of Qalqilyah," says Abu Ma'zoz.

Leila and I were driven alongside the high wall which totally surrounds Qalqilyah. We learned that 45 percent of the town's land and nineteen water wells are now out of reach, i.e., on the "other side" of the wall. To get to their agricultural fields, villagers have to pass through the one entry/exit to their town. Even though it was the end of October, villagers have not been permitted to pick their olive trees yet.

Against the eight-meter-high brutal concrete wall stood the seventy-year-old farmer Abu Mohammad. He was wearing the biggest square eyeglasses ever. "I am replacing the olive, palm, and fig trees which were uprooted by the Israelis to build this wall," Abu Mohammad points toward the wall and bends back and continues digging. At that very moment I wondered if Abu Mohammad would ever live long enough to see these slow-growing trees blossom. I wished I had the same-size eyeglasses (but dark ones) to hide my tears from Abu Mohammad's wrinkled face. As Leila and I walked away from the wall I heard Abu Mohammad say, "This is the third time I start all over again."

The running tears across my face did not allow me to go back and listen to what more he wanted to say.

Wednesday, October 29

"Yes, we'd love to visit the zoo," both Leila and I answered enthusiastically.

Even though Leila and I knew that Qalqilyah was a pioneering open town in many aspects (the Arab mayor of Qalqilyah and the Meretz mayor of the neighboring Israeli town of Kfar Saba have twined the two towns; the progressive Israelis in Kfar Saba made a petition to Sharon's government asking it to take Jewish land for the construction of the wall), still—a zoo in Qalqilyah! That is real pioneering work.

Our tour in the zoo started at the delightful baby giraffe shipped all the way from South Africa. I wondered if this was a present from the African National Congress to the Palestinian people. Unlike the rest of the animals in the Qalqilyah zoo, the baby giraffe seems to be totally ambivalent about the political situation, perhaps because she could see behind the separation wall.

Next to the giraffe, on a concrete platform in the middle of a tiny barbed-wire cage, sat the proud elderly lioness. We were discreetly informed that she had recently lost her beloved husband. The minute I got close to the lioness and before I even could utter words of condolence, she looked me straight in the eyes and said:

"Now you know what it means to be living in a cage, isolated and cut away from your natural habitat."

"I know, I am really sorry, we owe you an apology."

"It's okay, it is the Israelis that owe us both many apologies," adds the lioness. We hug one another and cry.

Having nothing else to tell the lioness, I walk away toward the monkeys' cage.

At first, the almost thirty stock-still monkeys looked depressed like the lioness and the rest of us living under occupation. Not having seen any visitors in months, though, they soon got excited and started showing off: some were hanging from their hands, others were hanging from their tails, a few were swinging from their legs, and some were bouncing between the four walls of their cage.

It was so touching I cried.

Behind us Said appeared, carrying two huge buckets of persimmons. He opened the cage door and started throwing in the delicious big-size persimmons. Soon the cage floor had a fluffy orange carpet.

"As the farmers of Qalqilyah are unable to sell their fruits and vegetables in the markets beyond the wall and the checkpoint, we feed it to the monkeys," says Said.

As Said was explaining, each monkey had five to six persimmons in its lap while pushing another two or three into its mouth.

I like monkey spirit.

I took one persimmon and joined in, as we drove away from the zoo.

Thursday, October 30

With a severe pain in my stomach I took Nura out for a nunu. With no mugs of tea, I spent most of Thursday sick in bed.

Friday, October 31

It was the severe pain in my stomach that woke me up early on my weekend day. I don't know why I started my day by recalling what Ariel Sharon had said in 1973, when asked by Winston S. Churchill III, grandson of the British prime minister, how Israel would deal with the Palestinians:

"We'll make a pastrami sandwich of them, we'll insert a strip of Jewish settlements in between the Palestinians, and then another strip of Jewish settlements right across the West Bank so that in twenty-five years, neither the United Nations, nor the United States, nobody, will be able to tear it apart."

It may have taken Sharon an extra five years to make the concrete wrapping around the pastrami sandwich.

I could not quite tell whether it was the image of the high concrete wall, or the image of Abu Mohammad planting olive trees against the wall, or the deadly sad look of the lioness in the zoo, or the Palestinian being beaten up in the military cage at the Qalandiyah checkpoint, or the quietly running tears on Leila's face as we were driving back that caused the severe stomachache for the whole day of Friday. I, with a worried mind and weary body, kept moving between my bed and my computer to share with you my last week's diary.

Of course, the roaming Israeli planes in the sky of Ramallah for hours at end did not help either the writing of my diaries or my nervous stomach.

An earlier version of this article appeared in Le Nouvel Observateur, *October 22–31, 2003.*

The Great Wall of Capital

Mike Davis

Mlki Kratsman

When delirious crowds tore down the Berlin Wall in 1989, many hallucinated that a millennium of borderless freedom was at hand. The people themselves had abolished a dark age of electrified death-fences, frontiers strewn with antipersonnel mines, and cities guillotined by walls. Globalization was supposed to inaugurate an era of unprecedented physical and virtual-electronic mobility: free trade and personal freedom were supposed to grow together.

Instead, the global triumph of neoliberal capitalism has stimulated the greatest wave of wall building and border fortification in history. The physical reality looks more like the late-Roman or Sung empires than the Victorian Liberal golden age of Cobden and Gladstone. A dozen different countries are currently building their own versions of the Berlin Wall or the Iron Curtain. Ariel Sharon's wall, of course, is the most tragically ironic, since it is built in the name of a people who have suffered more than any other in history from restrictive borders and barriers to free movement. But the Likud's construction of prison walls around Palestinian shtetls has many eager imitators.

Saudi Arabia, for instance, has torn up its international treaty with Yemen to build a massive concrete "isolating wall" along their border with the putative aim of stopping "terrorists," illegal immigrants, and qat smugglers. India, poorer than Saudia Arabia, has built a thick, ten-foot-high mud wall across Kashmir, part of a half-finshed scheme to fence or wall its entire 1,800-kilometer border with Pakistan. India has also fenced its border with Bangladesh to keep out immigrants. (It is frightening, of course, to think of hordes of people so poor that they risk life and limb to reach the promised land of Calcutta's infamous slums).

Exotic Bhutan, on the other hand, is walling its border against India to keep out infiltrators from the obscure National Democratic Front of Boroland. Botswana is building an electrified eight-foot-high fence along its border with Zimbabwe that reminds many Africans of the infamous high-voltage "death fences" built by the former apartheid government in South Africa. Botswana claims the fence is to control livestock, but Zimbabweans insist it is really meant to exclude them. In Central America, meanwhile, Costa Rica (home to an estimated 500,000 illegal Nicaraguan immigrants) has walled its border crossing at Penas Blancas in explicit emulation of the U.S.-Mexico frontier.

Such examples could easily be multiplied. But the internal borders of the Third World are dwarfed by the Great Wall of Capital that now brutally separates a few dozen rich countries from the earth's poor majority. This is not just a figurative addition of national borders but, increasingly, a single interlocking system of fortification, surveillance, armed patrol, and incarceration. It girds half the earth, cordons off at least 12,000 kilometers of terrestrial borderline, and is far more deadly to desperate trespassers than the old Iron Curtain. Unlike China's Great Wall, the free market's new wall is only partially visible from space. Although it includes traditional ramparts (the Mexican border of the United States) and barbed-wire-fenced minefields (between Greece and Turkey), much of globalized border enforcement today takes place at sea or in the air. Moreover, borders are now digital as well as geographical, virtual as well as architectural.

In historical terms, the current walling of the West is analogous to the Roman Empire's transition in the second century from the relatively open borders—protected by mobile legions and client states—of the Julio-Claudian era to the massive linear walls, *limes,* and *fossatum* of the post-Flavian emperors. Just as the late-Roman frontier consisted of distinctive systems of fortifications (Hadrian's Wall, the *Limes*

Porolissensis, the *Fossatum Africae*, and so on), so the Great Wall of Capital consists of three continental regimes of exclusion and border enforcement: the U.S.-Mexican *frontera*, Fortress Europe, and what might be called the Howard Line (analogous to the zoological Wallace Line) separating white Australia from Asia. Since the fall of the World Trade Center, these mega-borders have become the ramparts of empire in several literal and paradoxical senses. What follows is a brief tour.

Gatekeeper

The militarization of *La Linea*, from Brownsville to San Diego, has gone hand in hand with the passage and implementation of the North American Free Trade Agreement (NAFTA). The almost exponential increase in the flow of capital and goods across the border has been accompanied by a doubling of the border patrol and the walling of major urban crossing points. Starting with "Operation Hold the Line" in the El Paso border sector in 1992, followed by "Operation Gatekeeper" the next year in San Diego, the border patrol, with support from the Pentagon, has gone to war against illegal immigration. The most dramatic symbol of the new policy is the triple wall currently being completed between San Diego and Tijuana at earth's busiest intersection of First World affluence and Third World poverty Three layers of fifteen-foot-high steel walls—sunk deep into the ground to prevent tunneling—are augmented by state-of-the-art sensors and video surveillance, backed up by a huge contingent of border patrol officers in 4x4s and helicopters. (Maquiladora managers and binational professionals, on the other hand, use electronic IDs to zip back and forth across the border in special SENTRI—Secure Electronic Network for Travelers Rapid Inspection—lanes.)

This brutal monumentalization of Operation Gatekeeper—the walls will cut like a meat cleaver across the ironically named "Border Friendship Park"—is, to say the least, a hyperbolic assertion of nation-state sovereignty. Yet the triple wall speaks more about the appearance of border control than its actual achievement. Just thirty miles east of San Diego, in the Campo sector, one can easily walk, even drive, through fifty-foot gaps in a discontinuous, single-layer steel fence. The fortified border simply peters out into a mere gesture of control: the old status quo of *La Frontera*. Why?

Despite official assertions that the border is simply too long and wild to fully fence or wall, there is undoubtedly a more hypocritical calculation at work. Unlike the European Community's tight new borders or Australia's fanatical attempts to quarantine itself, the modern U.S.-Mexico border has always functioned, like any good dam, to regulate but not prevent the flow of surplus labor northward. In contrast to the EU's tough employer sanctions and "thick" border enforcement, the policing of labor migration in the western United States is a game mostly played at the "line" itself or at secondary border checkpoints an hour's drive inland in California and Texas.

Workplace surveillance of undocumented labor, meanwhile, has always been fine-tuned to the business cycle and employer demand for cheap labor. During the recession and high unemployment of the early 1990s, for example, the U.S. Immigration and Naturalization Service (INS) conducted massive raids on Latino worksites in the Midwest and on the West Coast. Some 14,000 enforcement actions were taken against employers of illegal immigrants during 1991. In the booming economy of the late 1990s, however, the INS downgraded workplace immigration enforcement in order to accommodate a soaring demand for minimum-wage labor. It issued a mere 150 employer sanctions in 2001. The number of undocumented immigrants, according to Urban Institute estimates, increased from 3.5 million to 9.3 million in the same period, despite Operation Gatekeeper. Thus the "terror machine" of the border, as one writer has called it, has been cynically calibrated to criminalize labor migrants but never wholly to discourage their entry into an American economy capitalized on their labor.

Seen in this light, San Diego's triple wall and similar medieval fortifications in Arizona and Texas are political stage sets. They have "less to do with actual deterrence," writes border expert Peter Andreas, "and more to do with managing the image of the border." Operation Gatekeeper, for instance, was undertaken by the Clinton administration at the instigation of Democratic senator Dianne Feinstein in order to wrest the border issue away from California Republicans. The militarization of the border was designed to send the message that Democrats were not "soft" on illegal immigration. Feinstein, indeed, has made frequent use of the new steel wall as a backdrop for press conferences. The tripling of the wall under the George W. Bush administration, meanwhile, was an up-the-ante move by conservative San Diego congressman Duncan Hunter—powerful chair of the House Armed Services Committee—to show he was even tougher on the border than Feinstein.

Immigrants, of course, have paid for these political theatrics with their lives. Intensified border enforcement at urban crossings has rerouted *mojado* itineraries, forcing them to cross into furnace-hot deserts or freezing mountains. The American Friends Service Committee, which monitors the carnage along the U.S.-Mexico border, estimates that at least 3,000, and perhaps as many as 5,000, have died in the last decade. They have suffocated in boxcars outside Laredo, drowned in irrigation canals near El Centro, died of thirst and sunstroke in Organ Cactus National Monument, and frozen to death in the Laguna Mountains east of San Diego. Others have perished in brush fires and in highway chases with the border patrol and, so it is alleged by human rights activists, been murdered by vigilantes in Arizona.

This largely unreported and invisible slaughter is the current price of balancing an electoral image of border control with a surreptitious common market in cheap labor. It obviously conflicts with the vision of an omniscient and impregnable Homeland Security state as adumbrated by the Bush administration after 9/11. One solution, long favored by Washington think tanks, would combine vastly expanded border enforcement with some kind of legal *gastarbeiter* status for Mexican immigrants. In 2004, the White House floated a variant of this idea on the eve of the Summit of the Americas in an obvious attempt to attract Latino swing voters. To some commentators, it seemed a humane alternative, especially compared to the draconian refugee policies of the EU and Australia.

In fact, as immigrant rights and labor groups quickly pointed out, it is an initiative that combines sublime cynicism with ruthless political calculation. The Bush proposal, which resembles the infamous Bracero program of the early 1950s, would legalize a subcaste of low-wage labor without providing a mechanism for the estimated five to seven million undocumented workers already in the United States to achieve permanent residence or citizenship. A "guest" working class without votes or permanent domicile, of course, is a Republican utopia. The Bush plan, if adopted, would provide Wal-Mart and McDonald's with a stable, almost infinite supply of indentured labor. As Karl Rove undoubtedly calculates, it also would sow wonderful disarray and conflict among labor unions and liberal Latinos.

The offer of temporary legality, in addition, would be irresistible bait to draw undocumented workers into the open where the Department of Homeland Security could identify, tag, and monitor them. Those who remained ineligible and undocumented would face new sanctions and intensified enforcement. Already House Republicans are lobbying hard for legislation that would train as many as one million local police and sheriff's officers as immigration police. Indeed, Congress has already authorized pilot programs in Alabama and Florida. As always, the principal targets would be individual immigrants rather than their exploitative employers.

Regardless of specific policy choices, the Justice Department, the Pentagon, and the Department of Homeland Security are fostering a technological revolution in border surveillance. The National Security Entry-Exit Registration System, launched by Attorney General John Ashcroft in June 2002, uses biometrics to identify and track foreign visitors. New digital scanning systems at airports, harbors, and land borders will use the same biometrics to monitor and gather data on foreign individuals. Meanwhile, the San Diego–Tijuana region has become the laboratory for the Justice Department–sponsored Border Research and Technology Center (headquartered in a downtown San Diego skyscraper), which is constantly working to improve the border patrol's high-tech intrusion detection systems—the networks of hidden seismic, magnetic, and infrared sensors as well as video surveillance cameras that are now uplinked to satellites to allow remote viewing from a central command post.

The Pentagon, after a long absence, became reinvolved in border enforcement in 1989 with the establishment of Joint Task Force 6 at Fort Bliss, Texas. JTF6 (which officially "synchronizes and integrates Department of Defense resources") was originally limited to missions against major narco-trafficantes smuggling large quantities of cocaine across the southern border. Now, as the cartels supposedly have "expanded their operations to include or become intertwined with criminal syndicates engaged in human trafficking," the task force mission is being enlarged by Congress to include surveillance and interdiction of illegal immigration. The Pentagon relishes this enlarged role because "there's no better place in America to get the kind of training that will prepare a unit for deployment to Afghanistan or Iraq." The border patrol, in return, is now reinforced by Marine Super Cobra helicopter gunships, Air Force AWACS radar surveillance, and, if need be, specialized teams of Army Rangers and Navy Seals.

In a series of steps, with very little congressional oversight or debate, immigration enforcement has merged with the War on Drugs and, now, the War on Terror to create what can only be described as a permanent state of low-intensity warfare along the U.S.-Mexican border. A similar process is under way in the European Community, where the conflation of immigration and terrorism has also produced walled and deadly borders.

Fortress Europe

In July 2001, a Spanish newspaper published a photograph of beachgoers at Tarifa near Gibraltar happily sunning themselves in blithe disregard of the body of a drowned Moroccan immigrant a few yards away. The photographer labeled the image, "The Indifference of the West." Indeed, 600 to 1,000 bodies per year now have washed ashore since the European Union in the early 1990s began a common effort to seal borders against political refugees and Third World immigrants. Like the dead *mojados* in the Arizona desert, they are sacrificial victims to asylum and immigration policies that bear little relationship to either economic reality or human rights.

"Fortress Europe," to be precise, was mandated by the 1985 Schengen Treaty and its 1990 application convention. As with the political theater enacted at the U.S.-Mexico border, the Schengen-driven restructuring of Europe's frontiers is designed, first and above all, to allay voter fears of a Third World inundation. The vision of dark-skinned and usually Muslim hordes invading Europe—first popularized in Jean Raspail's lurid 1972 novel, *The Camp of the Saint*—now galvanizes the European far Right in the same way that anti-Semitism did during the era of Dreyfus. Schengen was designed by the mainstream parties to stem voter defection to the anti-immigrant movements led by populist demagogues like Jean-Marie Le Pen, Jörg Haider, Umberto Bossi, and the late Pim Fortuyn. It is aimed as much at the threat of the barbarians from within as those from without.

To this end, the EU intergovernmental groups responsible for the management of borders, asylum, and immigration have been given sweeping enforcement powers largely unconstrained by the oversight of the European Parliament or the European Court of Justice. Indeed, critical parts of the Schengen implementation agreement remain top secret. Fortress Europe, meanwhile, consists of three evolving elements: a panoptic brain, a common system of immigrant and border enforcement in depth, and an emergent buffer zone of client states.

The brain is the Schengen Information System (SIS), which went online in 1995. An unprecedented pooling of police and immigration intelligence, the Strasbourg-based SIS contains information on eight million "undesirables" forbidden entry into the EU. It is being upgraded through the addition of biometric data and increased adoption of national and, eventually, EU identification cards. An offshoot with the sinister acronym of PROSECUR will allow SIS data to be utilized instantly across the EU by the newly authorized European Border Guards Corps. A "white list" of visitors from preferred countries like the United States, Israel, and Switzerland will eventually be speeded through immigration by ABG (Automated and Biometrics-Supported Border Controls) systems, while the Third World visitors (or groups like the European Roma) will be subject to the extraordinary surveillance of movement that the United States is now demanding of its allies.

Border enforcement in the EU under Schengen begins with uniform restrictions on legal entry by nationals from high-emigration countries. Thus Spain, in alignment with the 1990 agreement, has been required to refuse visas to most African and Moroccan visitors. Tough new laws punish those who harbor or employ illegal immigrants, while high-tech inspection systems (like retinal scans at Heathrow and Frankfurt Airports or CO_2 detectors in German ports) provide a level of surveillance considerably more advanced than in North America. Border control has been upgraded through the so-called Electronic Curtain in the East and joint task-force operations in the Mediterranean.

The major weak points in Fortress Europe are perceived to be Spain and Italy. Former Spanish prime minister Felipe Gonzales once gave other EU leaders a photo of Morocco taken from southern Spain. "This is our Rio Grande," he told them, pointing to the Strait of Gibraltar "It's not far and the living standards are four, five, ten times lower on the other side." Thanks to EU financing, the Spanish government has now fortified its North African enclaves of Ceuta and Melilla with formidable double razor-wire fences, watch towers, and state-of-the-art sensors, while the surveillance system for the strait supposedly provides rapid detection of the armada of overloaded rubber boats attempting to smuggle poor Moroccans and other Africans into Spain. This maritime equivalent of Operation Gatekeeper, however, has only diverted part of the migrant stream into the even more dangerous 100-kilometer journey between Morocco and the Canary Islands.

Italy, with one of the most rapidly aging workforces in the world, has been the destination of seaborne immigrants from both North Africa and Albania. The journeys are even more perilous than attempts to cross the Strait of Gibraltar. In June 2003 alone, for example, nearly 300 immigrants drowned in shipwrecks trying to reach the Italian island of Lampedusa, off Tunisia. Although Italy proportionally has one of the smallest immigrant populations in Europe, the anti-Mediterranean Northern League and neo-Fascist National Alliance, as powerful political partners of Prime Minister Berlusconi, have dictated a policy of national hysteria ("an assault on the Italian coast by criminal gangs"), culminating in dramatic naval chases and deportations on arrival without opportunity for asylum application. In July 2004, Italy created an international scandal by refusing for three weeks to allow a German rescue boat to land thirty-seven shipwrecked Africans. Although Vatican pressure finally forced Berlusconi to let the Africans come ashore, he had the rescue crew arrested for "abetting illegal immigration."

The EU solution to the carnage in the Mediterranean (at least 4,000 deaths since 1993) is simply to transfer border enforcement to the countries of North and sub-Saharan Africa. The Schengen system has hardened the Eastern marches of the EU by forcing ex-Comecon countries to police the flow of migrants and potential asylum-seekers. Now the EU is debating a British and German proposal, supported by Italy, for a new system of immigration buffer zones in Eastern Europe, Africa, and elsewhere. Some commentators believe that the recent mass deportations in Italy have been a deliberate attempt to foment a crisis that will force reluctant EU countries like France to accept this remote-control strategy of border policing.

"Friendly Neighborhood" is the official euphemism for a proposed migrant cordon sanitaire that would include Russia, Ukraine, Moldova, Belarus, Albania, Morocco, Tunisia, Libya, and possibly Syria and Israel. "These countries," says human rights watchdog Statewatch, "will be expected to institute 'reform' (free market capitalism) and to implement key parts of the EU's *acquis communautaire* [Schengen]—especially on 'enhanced cooperation of justice and security issues' including illegal migration, judicial and police cooperation, and 'threats to security.'" In the idealized model championed by Britain, Germany, and Italy, migrants would be intercepted and detained long before they set to sea in their desperate journeys to the EU. The impact on human rights and civil liberties in the buffer states, of course, would be huge, and some critics have compared the proposed detention camps to the infamous U.S. facility at Guantánamo Bay.

Tony Blair has proposed the further step of establishing so-called protection zones in key conflict areas of Africa and Asia where potential refugees could be quarantined in the deadly squalor of refugee camps for years on end. Countries would be induced to provide such zones (Tanzania and Kenya have been mentioned) by a combination of carrots (aid and trade) and sticks (no aid or trade): a policy trajectory whose logical conclusion would be to link access to OECD markets to governments' willingness to control emigration.

The Howard Line

Right-wing prime minister John Howard of Australia has become the idol of American and European opponents of open immigration. Reversing the more liberal asylum policies of the previous generation, Howard (prodded by the rise of the xenophobic National Party on his right) has declared war on wretched Kurdish, Afghan, and Timorese refugees trying to reach Australia by sea. He has sent the Australian navy to intercept ships in international waters, interned refugees and their children in notorious desert detention camps, and, more recently, deported asylum-seekers to equally grim camps on the tiny island republic of Nauru. His government has also made lurid equations between Muslim refugees and the terrorist threat to the antipodes. The opposition Labor Party, intimidated by popular support for Howard in the tabloid press and on radio, has partially acceded to this resurrection of "White Australia" exclusionism.

Howard's most famous victory over the invading Third World was the battle of the Tampa. On August 24, 2001, the Palapa, an overloaded wooden fishing boat carrying 460 Afghan asylum-seekers, foundered about 100 miles north of the Australian territory of Christmas Island. Australian maritime authorities, who intercepted the distress signal, asked the Singapore-bound freighter MS Tampa to go to the aid of the Palapa. The Tampa dutifully rescued the Afghans, some of whom were seriously ill, and turned back to drop them off at Christmas Island. The Howard government, however, refused the Tampa's Norwegian skipper permission to enter Australia's territorial waters and ordered him to take the refugees to Indonesia. Captain Arne Rinnan responded that the Tampa, designed for a crew of twenty-seven, lacked lifesaving gear and sanitary accommodations for the hundreds of hungry and sick refugees. When, after a several-day standoff, the Tampa and its desperate human cargo attempted to enter Australian waters, Canberra dispatched thirty-five armed SAS commandoes who boarded the ship and ordered Rinnan to return to the open sea. He courageously refused and was threatened with prosecution as a "people smuggler." The refugees were then transferred to an Australian naval vessel which took them to a detention camp on remote Nauru.

In another incident, Howard's government was advised by Indonesia that a boatload of refugees were headed toward Australia directly through the path of a cyclone. Canberra did nothing to intercept or save the doomed ship, leading one immigrant-rights activist to observe that "the death penalty has been declared a useful and acceptable means of deterring undocumented immigrants."

More recently, refugees and their children have participated in a wave of hunger strikes, riots, and mass escapes from desert hellhole detention camps like the infamous Woomera in South Australia. The United Nations has been particularly critical of the Howard government's long-term detention of minors and small children. At the beginning of 2004, Australia held at least 183 children in Woomera and Nauru detention camps, some of them for as long as five years. As one teenage detainee told human rights officials: "We have now been living in Australian detention for three years. These places I have only imagined in my nightmares. We have been imprisoned in a frightening desert camp in South Australia called Baxter. My family is separated from each other. My mother and I are in Woomera housing and my father and brother are in Baxter detention, they are surrounded by razor wire."

Despite its international notoriety, however, Howard's brutal treatment of refugees (the overwhelming majority of whom are fleeing genuine persecution or real threat of death) has been hugely popular among voters. Radio shock jocks make bad jokes about barbequeing the refugee hordes and throwing them into the ocean for the sharks. The militarization of refugee interdiction, moreover, has been blended in almost seamless continuity with Australia's own version of the War on Terror, which now includes "preemptive strikes" against terrorists in neighboring countries. Howard has aggressively staked out an Australian cordon sanitaire or informal empire that includes Papua New Guinea, the Solomon Islands, and other statelets like Nauru. The wretched of the earth have been warned: Stay Away from Australia.

Walling Off the Future

A walled world has many ironies. The rich countries building these great walls, of course, were in the nineteenth century either lands of mass emigration or settler colonies found by those emigrants. The free global movement of labor, as well as capital, was a principal article of faith to Victorian Liberalism. Neo-liberal globalization, in this decisive regard, is an altogether different animal. It enthrones the borderless sovereignty of capital upon the physical fortification of inequality and the criminalization of labor migration. In the name of the War on Terror, moreover, it unleashes forces with ominous totalitarian potential.

For example, if border enforcement has now moved far offshore, it has also come into everyone's front yard. Residents in the U.S. Southwest have long endured the long traffic jams at "second border" checkpoints far from the official linea. Now stop-and-search operations, pioneered in Germany, are becoming common in the interior of the EU. Even notional boundaries between border enforcement and domestic policing, or between immigration policy and the War on Terror, are rapidly disappearing. "No-border" activists in Europe have long warned that the Orwellian data systems used to track down and deport non-EU aliens will inevitably be turned against local antiglobalization movements as well. They are probably correct.

In obscene haste, U.S. and EU legislators are giving gatekeepers like the Department of Homeland Security and the various Schengen commissions and ministries huge, shadowy, even secret powers. Far from being a temporary aberration (as some wishful liberals initially believed), the USA Patriot Act is probably only a starting point for a radical redefinition of citizenship and the rights of dissent. Likewise, Australia's brutal antiasylum policies have opened the doorway for Italy's own summary deportations and naval interdictions. The rest of Europe may soon follow, and the "buffer states" (and their buffers) will not be far behind.

The trends are cruelly unidirectional. Walls will beget walls. Empires will beget barbarians and Wars on Terror, terrorists. In the meantime, the human toll of the new world order will grow inexorably. The utopian hope of 1989 has become the daily carnage in the Arizona desert and on the beaches of the Mediterranean.

The Long Economic Shadow of the Wall

Anita Vitullo

Anita Vitullo

A vibrant economy requires freedom of movement and control of assets and resources. It is difficult, and for many Palestinians pointless, to differentiate the impact that the wall has had on the Palestinian population and economy already battered from the cumulative effect of Israel's movement restriction policy. But in fact the wall is already causing economic disturbances far deeper than the immediate destructive force of the structure itself that could force long-term changes in social and economic behaviors. The economic distortions are so enormous that the local coordinating group for UN agencies has cautioned that a barter economy could emerge in some areas.[1] There is already increasing reliance on the informal economy, as Palestinians engage in an economy of survival.

The wall is creating disenfranchisement and pauperization of small agricultural village economies, forced migration and depopulation on both sides of the wall, limited access to labor markets, and the final severance of Jerusalem from the West

Bank—economic disasters on the scale of the impact of the 1967 war. Also of concern are the impending second-stage effects of a downward spiraling economy, such as the collapse of the public sector and private formal sector, and the impact of decreased expenditure on environmental and preventative health and on education.

When the wall is completed in 2005, it will put negative synergistic changes into motion that are likely to have lasting import for the Palestinian nation. The wall will affect Palestinian national and household economies in terms of economic assets such as land, water and energy resources, as well as employment, agriculture, commercial activity, infrastructure and property, development, and services. This article notes the immediate as well as the longer-term irreversible losses to the economy, and some possible implications they may have for demography, the future of Jerusalem, and the viability of a future Palestinian state.

A Cobweb of Restrictions

Israel has manipulated the flow of people, goods, and services through the West Bank and Gaza according to Israeli needs and interests since the beginning of its occupation. The Gaza Strip has been tightly monitored by an electrified fence and buffer area along its perimeter and military-controlled access routes. However, most of the long West Bank border had remained open, allowing the migration of up to 120,000 illegal workers daily into Israel as day laborers—and an equal number of workers with permits—that benefited both the Palestinian and Israeli economies. But Israel was unprepared for the Palestinians' political use of labor strikes during the first intifada. The first Gulf war presented Israel with an opportunity to regain economic control by holding the population immobile through region-wide curfews. Israeli agriculture and construction industries, which were particularly dependent on cheap Palestinian labor, suffered slowdowns and losses, but quickly up to 200,000 foreign workers were imported on a temporary basis from Southeast Asia and eastern Europe to replace Palestinians, until immigrants from the former Soviet Union and Ethiopia began to arrive in large numbers and ensured a Jewish labor force.

In 1993 Israel inaugurated systematic movement restrictions in the Palestinian Occupied Territories with the closure of Gaza and Jerusalem to nonresidents. Control mechanisms increased gradually and almost imperceptibly over the post–Oslo Accords period, not only along the invisible borders with Israel but also within the territories. A double road system was constructed to connect settlements, and Palestinian roads were blocked. After the start of the second intifada in late 2000, restrictions were institutionalized through hundreds of checkpoints and roadblocks (more than 750 blockages of roads were noted in a mid-2004 UN review[2]) that have paralyzed normal life.[3] In the West Bank, commercial border cargoes can be accommodated at only eight "back-to-back" terminals, delaying goods and increasing costs.[4]

The restrictions have found their ultimate shape in the form of the 622-kilometer concrete and wire barrier wall that ended any discussion about a return to the pre-intifada status quo. Israel's advantageous positioning of the wall has pushed the post–1967 war border lines farther eastward in its favor, following its vision of maxi-mum settlement expansion (and minimum Palestinian development) and abandoning the Armistice border, or green line, despite the fact that adhering to the green line would have reduced the meandering length of the wall by half as well as muffled at least some international criticism. The blocking of Palestinian workers is clearly at least part of Israel's wall strategy. The Gaza Disengagement Plan specifically men-tions Israel's desire to reduce the number of Palestinian workers entering Israel and eventually to stop them altogether, as a way of "encouraging Palestinian economic independence." While the World Bank has cautioned against a sudden halt in work-ers as counterproductive, Israel now permits only 10 percent of previous levels of the workforce to enter for jobs.[5]

A Stressed Economy Before the Wall

The macroeconomic indicators[6] for the 2000–2002 period show a clearly failing Palestinian economy. GDP was $4.1 billion in 1999 and 2000 and dropped to $2.8 bil-lion in 2002, creating one of the sharpest rates of decline in real per capita GDP (40 percent) of any country in modern history; per capita GDP was calculated at $879, down from $1,493 in 1999. Unemployment grew to 31 percent of the workforce (41 percent, including discouraged workers) in 2002 and poverty grew to 51 percent of the population.

For the same period, declines of 25 percent (122,000 jobs) were reported in pri-vate sector employment, 66 percent in private investment, 35 percent in exports, 40 percent in imports, 52 percent in manufacturing value, and 47 percent in manufactur-ing productivity per worker. The movement restrictions were chiefly to blame for a fall in construction employment and an increase in agriculture, a fall in private sector employment and increases in commerce (small trade), and for increased importance of the public sector, although with no increase in the number of jobs—all trends that have continued.

The primary factor destabilizing the economy is the system of closure. In 2003 the economy stabilized its downward trend somewhat and both unemployment and poverty rates fell by 4–5 percent. However, new jobs were poor in quality and pay, exports actually decreased, and per capita GDP grew by only 1 percent. The rate of deep poverty (expenditure of less than $1.5 per day) is now estimated at 17 percent, calculated from the percentage of the population that exists entirely on outside aid.[7] The World Bank suggests that without donor assistance, which was $898 million in 2003, absolute poverty levels would be almost 40 percent higher; donor assistance accounts for 97 percent of welfare services and basically supports the PA, which employs 22 percent of the workforce.

An earlier World Bank analysis summarized: "If donor disbursements were doubled to US $2 billion in 2003 and 2004, poverty would fall by only 7 percent. In contrast, if internal closures were lifted and exports facilitated, Palestinian GDP would surge by 21 percent in 2003 and poverty would fall by 15 percent by the end of 2004."[8] In late 2004, the World Bank reiterated: "Any sustained Palestinian economic recovery will ultimately require the dismantling of the closure system." Under a status quo scenario, and particularly with the wall in place as an impermeable barrier to trade and labor flows, by 2006 GDP would drop by almost 12 percent from 2003 levels, while real GDI would decline by 22 percent, unemployment would increase to 35 percent due to large numbers of new workers, and the poverty rate would rise to 56 percent. The limp economy weighs heavily on the young and is an effective push factor for emigration in the absence of other economic alternatives. Up to 70 percent of workers who entered the labor force during the intifada are unemployed.[9]

Estimating Losses
The impact of the wall is felt the most acutely in the economies of those living in its path. But the shadow it casts is a long one. The aggregate loss to the national and household economies includes the confiscation of land and mass destruction of trees, crops, and property; the loss of water resources; destruction of greenhouses

and businesses; future losses for the private sector; diminishing of agricultural output; and trade reductions due to the shrinking of the area where economic activity takes place. Agriculture, which has traditionally expanded to accommodate unemployed workers during economic downturns, is also the sector most harmed by the wall and therefore limited in its ability to provide economic relief for affected households.

In addition the population must deal with the increased costs for basic goods such as water, food, consumer goods, and services and transactions. Donors also find their resources diverted by "wall mitigation" projects—for example, duplicating services that had been available but, with severed networks, were put out of reach.

Some losses are incalculable, such as the loss and degradation of landscape, flora, and fauna; loss of cultural heritage and traditional village structures; loss of social ties and social solidarity; missed investment opportunities; and thwarted future development and population growth. If the wall remains, and alternative strategies for income generation fail to meet needs, the population along the wall will likely flee deeper into the West Bank or will emigrate for survival.

Israeli Gains

Of course, while the "cost" to Israel, and to its benefactors and donors, of the construction of the wall itself weighs lightly against the losses incurred by Palestinians, the drain on the Israeli treasury for construction alone is immense: $3.4 billion, as the head of the Knesset Economics Committee has calculated (and every deviation from the green line increases the length—and cost).[10] The enormous government expenditure is already forcing cuts into services and welfare programs for Israel's burgeoning poor.[11]

But some Israelis regard the wall as Israel's "largest national project," and indeed more than 500 bulldozers and earthmovers have been activated for the effort. It has been an expensive project but lucrative for private Israeli building and materials contractors, especially for those who have close relations with the Likud government, cultivated since Sharon's earlier days as minister of housing and infrastructure and settlement czar; they are making huge profits. Some of the takings filter down to smaller contractors, as well as to the entrepreneurial crop of security businesses that have sprung up. Israeli contractors sometimes even hire Palestinian workers, especially where the wall abuts crowded Jerusalem areas, since the eight-meter prefab concrete slabs still require some hard labor on the ground.[12]

Israel controls all entries, exits, and aerial space (as well as electromagnetic space) in the Palestinian territories. With fewer gaps and tighter controls on movement and goods, Israel can also more easily impose the economic rules it wrote into the post-Oslo agreements with the Palestine Liberation Organization (PLO), by which they gave themselves one-sided trade advantages with the Palestinian territories. Dumping of expired, substandard, or banned Israeli or foreign products into the captive economy of the West Bank and Gaza Strip is common; the West Bank is also used as a convenient disposal area for toxic wastes. At the Barkan industrial zone in the northern West Bank, there are eighty Israeli companies engaged in high-polluting industries such as plastics, chemical processing, and aluminum that are illegal in Israel, and that expel one million cubic meters of potentially toxic wastewater into the ground and water sources of surrounding Palestinian villages.[13] An Israeli gas factory located in Tulkarm is being left behind in the city rather than moved to Israel because it does not meet Israeli environmental standards. On the other hand, the wall has been routed to include Rachel's tomb, a site promoted for Israeli Jewish pilgrimage, despite its location within a Muslim cemetery and at the very entrance to the city of Bethlehem.

As a by-product of "land clearing" for the wall, an illegal olive tree-selling industry has grown up with the cooperation of entrepreneurial Israeli bulldozer drivers, construction companies, and, one can assume, official sanction.[14] In late July 2004, evidence of this could be found north of Jenin, where an empty plot had been turned into a "tree pound," filled with crowded rows of ancient olive trees, looking oddly naked, their limbs amputated, and stacked forlornly for "relocation." Three days later, the several thousand trees were gone from the plot; some of the thick old trees are probably among those found transplanted along new Israeli highways and in Israeli settlements.

There are also reports of apparently organized theft of public and private resources such as archaeological artifacts, factory production, vehicles, cargoes, and agricultural production—particularly the daylight theft by settlers of olive harvests, especially in West Bank areas that have been closed off to Palestinians.[15]

Land Ownership and Access

Based on the latest routing of the wall (the southern half and eastern wall is still under construction as of this writing), 631,000 dunums, a significant swath of land, will be cut out of the West Bank. This represents 25 percent of the best West Bank land that remains with Palestinians (almost 80 percent of its most fertile land).[16] This theft represents the home and livelihood for 93,200 Palestinian residents in 63 towns and villages, and represents about 11.5 percent of total land area.[17] The wall also draws into Israel 56 Israeli settlements and 140,200 settlers, accounting for 62 percent of the settler population in the West Bank. When the wall severing Jerusalem from Ramallah is completed, 400,000 Palestinians will be cut off from other West Bank towns on the other side of the wall. And with the completion of the eastern wall in the Jordan Valley area, a total of 500,000 Palestinians will be living between the wall and the green line, most with an uncertain status as their subsistence becomes more at risk.

The wall runs along the 1967 green line for only 15 percent of its length, and then only to separate Palestinian cities and large towns from Israel. The wall extends twenty-two kilometers into the West Bank in order to annex the Israeli settlement city of Ariel. A system of trenches and mounds referred to as a "depth barrier" has begun to be carved on the eastern side of these communities to obstruct the possibility of growth of Palestinian towns and refugee camps, as well as to limit movement. There are also "security zones" being constructed around all settlements as wide as 400 meters and equipped with electric fences and cameras, swallowing more land.

Caught between the green line and the wall, 46 Palestinian villages (population 16,300) on 477,200 dunums will be closed areas without access to the rest of the West Bank except with permits and when gates are opened; 17 isolated Palestinian population enclaves on 38,500 dunums will be completely enclosed by the wall and military checkpoints; and two bottlenecked partial enclaves of 16,000 dunums (population 15,400) will have only one access point. The wall completely encircles the town of Qalqilyah, save for a single gate and narrow road. Some villages, such as Tira and Beit-Sira west of Ramallah, will be marooned between the wall and an Israeli superhighway that requires a permit for them to access. Three villages that were physically split by the 1948 borders[18] will be joined again by being on the western side of the wall, but residents from the West Bank side will not be able legally to enter the Israeli side.

Land ownership and access is extremely important to local economies in the West Bank: one-third of the West Bank farms its own land and the land holdings of the vast majority of farmers are under 10 dunums. The first 145-kilometer section of the wall in the initial phase of construction resulted in the confiscation or closure of 124 square kilometers of prime West Bank agricultural land.[19] While the market value of West Bank land varies according to its registration, location, soil quality, and proximity to water resources, a rough estimate could be made, based on a JD 5,000/dunum average, of a monetary loss of $800 million for this initial land grab, not including annual income loss from agricultural production. The amounts Israel offered in compensation to landholders were 10 percent of the actual value of their plots; in any event, Palestinians have historically refused to participate in the forced sale of their property, considering it tantamount to legitimizing confiscation.

Some of the agricultural land west of the wall belongs to villages that are east of the wall, and so more villages are being affected than those behind the wall. According to Gush Shalom, 73,000 farmers in 67 villages have lost their agricultural lands and livelihoods in the first 145-kilometer stage of the wall construction. Continued access for farmers, as well as for students, teachers, and businesspeople, depends on being issued an Israeli "green" permit—for one gate only—and is unpredictable.

Owners of *miri* land—common land near villages—are concerned that if the land is left uncultivated for a three-year period, even if it is due to lack of access, it may revert to the "state" under Ottoman laws. Israel has used this pretext for land confiscation in the past, which is another reason why farmers are anxious to maintain their lands.

In the north, requisition orders are for three years and in effect until the end of 2005; however, they may be legally extended indefinitely. Some farmers have appealed the requisition orders—either individually or collectively through a municipality or local council—but typically hearings have not resulted in a reversal.[20] Faced with the publicity of court appeals, the government has redrawn the route in several areas to reduce pressure.

Of the forty-three main crossing points and "agricultural crossings" on the UN-monitored list of gates, nine were military crossings only and fifteen were closed to Palestinians.[21] In Jenin, two main gates were closed in August 2004 and a new one opened that is now the only entrance or exit for people in the entire district.[22]

Requisition orders are still being issued for the southern half of the West Bank, as the final route of the wall in this area is being drawn against fierce local opposition. Construction has also begun on the northern section of an *eastern* wall that is planned to run through the Jordan Valley, annexing fertile land and springs to a string of Israeli settlements and excluding Palestinian villages, which have been highly productive in fruits and vegetables but will be unsustainable without water and markets.

Agriculture

The northern districts of Jenin, Tulkarm, and Qalqilyah are exceptionally fertile and accounted for $220 million in agricultural income in 2000 from rain-fed and irrigated land, about 45 percent of total West Bank production. The per-square-kilometer output was $430,000, the most productive rate in the entire region due to a combination of good soil quality, rainfall, climate, and intensive farming methods. Irrigated lands total only about 5 percent of cultivated land, but their production in tons exceeds that of rain-fed land in these districts. The northern governorates have a disproportionately large share of the West Bank's agricultural and water resources, accounting for 37 percent of agricultural land, 45 percent of production value, and 80 percent of wells. Employment in these two activities is also disproportionately high, with the northern governorates accounting for 42 percent of West Bank agricultural workers and 53 percent of water-sector employment.[23] Unfortunately, the natural resources have also made the districts a favored site for the establishment of Israeli settlements that continuously expand onto the villages' agricultural lands.

Agriculture has been a natural fallback for workers who had been employed in Israel or elsewhere in the West Bank but lost jobs or access. In Jayyous village, 400 out of 550 families are now totally dependent on agriculture, up from 250 before the intifada. In Qalqilyah town, 22 percent of the city's pre-intifada economy was based on agricultural produce; this number has risen to 45 percent, with 2,000 agricultural workers supporting approximately 15,000 residents.

The theft of some of the West Bank's best land and major water resources, therefore, will have grave consequences for agricultural productivity and food security in the future. The Ministry of Agriculture estimates annual loss in agricultural production at $28 million for lands isolated beyond the wall. The cost of supplying goods to these areas may exceed sales revenues due to higher costs of transport, market disruptions, and increased costs of inputs. Lost pastureland will result in overgrazing and damage to remaining land and force reduction of animal herds.

The care with which farmers time their planting, harvesting, and marketing work, by season, weather, and crop appearance, is easily undone by requiring permits to enter and leave their lands. The two weeks of olive harvesting during the biannual "good" crop is particularly labor intensive and crucial for family economies. About 23,000 tons of olive oil are produced annually and generates about $17 million.[24]

While donkeys are still exempt, special vehicle permits are required for agricultural equipment such as small tractors. Farmers have reported that routine denial of permits and the long delays or closures of gates have caused cultivated trees and crops to perish and produce to go unharvested. In 2003, farmers in the north found the gates were never opened at harvest time to allow them access to their orchards, thus ruining their olive crop, which is the main source of household income for the entire year.

Agricultural land has been spoiled also by settler vandalism in areas near the wall, to discourage farmers from remaining. In one area south of Nablus, settlers cut down 6,000 olive trees and set fire to 400 dunums of orchards. There are regular reports of settlers shooting and beating olive harvesters. An estimated 330,000 olive trees were uprooted from Palestinian orchards by the Israeli military from 2001 to 2004.

A closer look at the first-phase land grab in the northern districts shows that it includes common agricultural land as well as land that has been allocated for village development, land privately owned by village households, and pastureland. Of the land taken for the wall from households, 95 percent was prime agricultural land. Most of the confiscated land was utilized and fully productive, as can be seen in the following breakdown:[25]

124,323 dunums confiscated for wall construction in phase 1, including:
8,008—citrus trees
62,623—olive trees
18,522—cropland
9,800—pasture land
21,002—privately owned land

Regional Poverty

The loss of land and agricultural activities and the associated increased costs for goods and services affect the villages along the wall trajectory most seriously. Their unemployment rates and associated pauperization are expected to rise dramatically and to increase over time, making them more and more dependent on outside intervention. Neighboring villages and towns that depend on agricultural trade and business markets in the region as a whole, in addition to social relationships with their neighbors, will also be adversely affected. For the fertile northern region of the West

Bank, estrangement from lands and sudden dependence on food aid will be exceptionally difficult.

In certain localities bordering the wall in the northwestern areas of the West Bank, the wall's effect on community and household economy has been noticeable and stark, if not quantifiable. The wall and the policy of forced estrangement of people from land that supports it has left these residents literally without fields to cultivate, water to drink, trees to harvest, or income-generating jobs. Seventy percent of Qalqilyah city residents are unemployed, with no prospect of being employed in the foreseeable future. More than 600 of the town's 1,800 business have closed. Residents cannot pay municipality bills for electricity, and the Israeli provider is threatening to cut the power over a debt of NIS 5 million.[26] More than 10 percent of residents thus far found the situation so bleak that they have migrated from the area in search of employment.

UNRWA[27] carried out field visits in 2003 to examine the effects of the barrier on the livelihoods of local residents, with special emphasis on registered refugees. Most of the northern green line towns and villages accommodate refugee families. Certain villages in particular—Atil, Baqa esh-Sharqiya, Barta'a esh-Sharqiya, Taibeh, Rumana, and Zububa—contain significant, even majority, refugee populations. Qalqilyah includes 4,000 refugee families, a newly refurbished UNRWA hospital, and other facilities, and will be completely surrounded by the wall except for a single access point. In May 2005 a young woman from a Qalqilyah area village was reported to have died in childbirth after being delayed for hours by checkpoints to the hospital.

In the area of Tulkarm, where 3,700 refugee families live, the wall barrier on its western side and a "depth barrier" to the east seals in most of the town's immediate hinterland, including the refugee camps of Tulkarm (15,600 registered refugees) and Nur Shams (8,000 refugees); economic opportunities are already extremely limited and living standards minimal. In the northwest Jenin district, another "depth barrier" will isolate the enclave of Rumana. Khirbet Taibe and Anin villages all have large numbers of refugee families and include an UNRWA school.

The Palestinian Central Bureau of Statistics (PCBS) surveyed households in localities through which the wall passes and found that in 52.7 percent of households, income was not sufficient to meet household needs, compared to 15.1 percent before the wall was constructed.[28] There have been several notable attempts to understand the changes wrought by their isolation through narrative summaries based on interviews.[29] It has been a period of accommodation for residents on both sides of the wall as they try to secure their survival by seeking creative solutions, from finding new markets and sources of goods to relocating businesses or migrating out of the area, for part or all of the family.

In the latest round of household economy studies in the second quarter of 2004,[30] PCBS reported that 61.9 percent of West Bank households lost more than half of their income in the previous six months, 9 percent more than in the previous round and the highest rate since the intifada began. Households that reported needing assistance to manage were 71.7 percent, while only 18.2 percent actually receive assistance, mostly in the form of food supplies worth an average of $35 per family per month. Food was a top priority for households (42.6 percent), followed by jobs (14.3 percent). When identifying priorities for the community, jobs were ranked first

Dafna Kaplan

(39.7 percent). The only question specific to the wall concerned obstacles to health care; 9 percent blamed the wall as the chief obstacle. The fact that figures for Gaza households continued to show more serious economic problems on almost every level than the West Bank in spite of the substantial impact of the wall indicates that the economic crisis is a national rather than regional crisis and affects both regions.

Food and Water

In the West Bank, where water lies in deep underground aquifers, the water-land interrelationship means that it is vital to keep access to the land above the aquifers. However, the land closed off by the wall contains 65 percent of the water sources of West Bank Palestinians. According to Palestinian sources, twenty-six water wells, generating four million cubic meters of water per year, have already been confiscated and diverted to Israeli use,[31] and fourteen more are threatened by the construction of new sections of the wall. In addition, an estimated 35,000 meters of water infrastructure—pipes, sewage lines, and irrigation networks—have been destroyed by bulldozers. Farmers are concerned that their wells that had been used for irrigation of now closed land may be seized by Israel on the pretext of "under-use," jeopardizing their ability to irrigate their remaining land east of the wall.

Qalqilyah's nineteen wells represent approximately 30 percent of the city's water supply. In the district of Qalqilyah, only 34 of its 75 wells remain accessible, while 200 cisterns and rainwater reservoirs are inaccessible beyond the wall. According to the Palestinian Agricultural Relief Committee, only five of the fifty-two Palestinian communities now isolated on the west side of the wall are connected to the Israeli national water network. A number of the villages concerned are losing their only source of water. Palestinian village households now must supplement their winter rain catchment wells by buying water in summer, some of it from Israel collected from West Bank aquifers. Ten cubic meters of water cost $23 four years ago, but because transport through access routes is often closed, the cost of trucked water has risen to $41 since the start of the intifada and continues to rise.[32]

Villages east of the wall have suffered from the arbitrary reduction in water supply: the Jenin village of Silet al-Daher had its water reduced by the Israeli water company from 11,300 cubic meters per month to 3,000, forcing people to buy more expensive tankered water to meet their household needs.

Production and distribution of agricultural produce has been severely affected, but it is loss of income that has affected household food security the most. The UN World Food Program estimates that 40 percent of the population is food insecure and another 25 percent is at risk; the situation is more serious in the area near the wall, where 55 percent of Jenin's population is at risk.[33] Land leveling particularly jeopardizes food security. In some villages near the wall that once were food producers, two-thirds are on food assistance (for example, the village of Zayta). The UN rapporteur on the right to food reported to the UN Commission on Human Rights that the wall had caused an "invisible tragedy," citing UN figures that 65 percent of Palestinian households ate only once a day and 68 percent depended on international assistance to some extent.[34]

Donor Mitigation Costs

Development under occupation is difficult, due to Israeli military orders restricting projects, resources, and personnel. Development under the conditions of the intifada has been more difficult since it must compete with constant destruction and crippling restrictions on movement, including the erection of the wall. Donor asset building projects worth $200 million were destroyed by the end of 2002, giving donors pause for thought when considering where to direct future assistance.

Instead of disbursing aid for sustainable development, donor assistance is increasingly being diverted to emergency humanitarian relief to alleviate the extreme poverty brought on by movement restrictions. A Ministry of Planning report (May 2004) calculates that $22.6 million has been spent on completed or ongoing wall mitigation projects and $7 million more is committed to additional projects. A further $15.2 million is required to fund future planned projects. Sixty percent of projects are implemented by Palestinian National Authority ministries and agencies and the rest by Palestinian NGOs, international NGOs, and multilaterals.[35] This does not include many NGO projects that are not coordinated with the PNA or not reported. The projects include basic cash relief, emergency employment generation, water and food aid, and other projects with a minimal developmental dimension. The PNA also undertook some short-term employment generation schemes, mostly in infrastructure, construction to offset labor loss.

By October 2004, the UN Office of the Coordinator of Humanitarian Affairs (OCHA) reported only 45 percent of humanitarian funding requirements had been met for the year; the shortfall jeopardized humanitarian relief for new needs in the most high-risk areas, especially the population in and around the wall. The UN is extending its Consolidated Humanitarian Appeal Process another year in view of the ongoing crisis, which it describes as: (1) growing impoverishment and vulnerability; (2) fragmentation of the economy and of society; (3) emerging pockets of acute crisis; and (4) increased need for protection of civilians.[36]

The Jerusalem "Envelope"

The impact of the wall may be most demoralizing in the Jerusalem area, where the solid concrete barrier threatens to permanently isolate 120,000 people in the northern, western, and eastern suburbs from the rest of the city. More than half of this number are registered Jerusalem residents forced to live in outlying areas as a result of the lack of licensed housing in the Arab part of the city; they will have only a single gated entrance to the city and may lose their Jerusalem residency altogether. The enclosure of the city disrupts the high level of social and economic integration of area villages with the city and their dependence on the city for services, reflective of Jerusalem's traditional role as a center for transportation, trade, education, culture, and religion in Palestine. The physical disruption of normal networks and traffic patterns also "deadens" the once vibrant commercial areas on both sides of the wall.

For residents in East Jerusalem, the wall also deprives Jerusalemites of sustaining contact with other areas of the West Bank, including extended families; it shrivels local businesses and forces the redirection of their economic activities toward Israel. It will, no doubt, dramatically raise the cost of living in East Jerusalem to near Israeli levels. The wall's construction has been accompanied by pressure on all sides: a suffocating presence of police, massive settlement housing and highway construction, tax harassment, arbitrary checkpoint delays, settler takeovers of property in the Old City, and other provocations.

For thirty-seven years of occupation, East Jerusalem residents had been able to maintain their connections and identity with fellow West Bank Palestinians and had rejected en masse the Israeli attempts to force integration into Israel. In response to almost every new Israeli regulation that attempted to limit the number of Palestinian residents in the city, Palestinians had found a creative, if temporary, solution. The wall, however, poses what may be an insurmountable logistical challenge to this struggle. And without the available support of Palestinians from outside the city, resistance to Israeli plans for relocating residents, destroying houses, closing institutions, and escalating pressure on the population is liable to be weak. An estimated 15,000 persons have chosen to move back to the city to protect their residency rights, despite the costs and crowded conditions.

The latest Israeli vision for Jerusalem was revealed in September 2004 by Israeli prime minister Sharon during the final stage of wall construction around the city. The government unveiled a plan to evacuate 15,000 Old City residents, about half of the Arab population of the historic city, to outlying areas of the city on the pretext that the Old City was overcrowded. The announcement was quickly attacked by Palestinian political leaders and human rights activists as ethnic cleansing. In May 2005 a new plan was revealed that the government had decided to remove 100 Palestinian families from Silwan neighborhood, just below the southern edge of the Old City, and destroy their homes to create a tourist area near a Jewish archaeological site.

Already, West Bank residents, who as shopkeepers and consumers formed the backbone of the wholesale and retail business in Jerusalem, are gone from the streets, shops, and businesses. Residents expect that many shops could be confiscated by Israel as "absentee property," as was done with Palestinian property in West Jerusalem after the 1948 war. The commercial area outside of the Old City is active only on weekends when Palestinians from the Galilee and east European migrant laborers visit for religious worship and shopping, while new Palestinian businesses linked directly to Israeli businesses have moved into the northern suburbs, with Israeli encouragement, and appear to be flourishing. From the banning of bayd baladi, the local West Bank egg production, and other West Bank agricultural produce from Jerusalem markets, to prohibiting West Bank employees from taking jobs in East Jerusalem hotels, restaurants, and tourist agencies, the economy of East Jerusalem is slowly but inexorably being severed from the West Bank as part of Israel's policy of annexation and "Judaization." Encircled by the wall, with access to the rest of the West Bank now only through "border terminals," Palestinians in the Jerusalem area are predictably the most pessimistic about the future.

Village Economies and Employment

Confiscations can disenfranchise whole villages. UNRWA, Negotiations Support Unit, and OCHA, as well as the Stop the Wall campaign and numerous human rights and journalistic reports, have all documented case studies about the changes in daily life for village residents living in the shadow of the wall.

Before the intifada, the economic integration of northern green line towns and villages with Arab communities in Israel across the green line had brought limited prosperity to the northern area. This was virtually stopped by the ban on workers migrating to Israel and the ban on Israeli citizens over the past four years from entering "A" areas, which are under the Palestinian Authority. The wall will add to the acute unemployment and poverty levels. An UNRWA report describes the isolation of Baqa al-Sharqiya, separated from its other half, Baqa al-Gharbiya, by the green line and separated from many of its residents by the wall; the owners of 250 of its 420 businesses live outside the town, east of the wall.

The village of Nazlat al-Issa may disappear altogether due to the wall. Caught in the area between the green line and the wall, the once prosperous village has been a target of large-scale demolitions by Israel: its entire commercial market of more than 200 shops has been destroyed. Sixteen dunums were confiscated in the heart of the central market for "defense of Israeli settlements,"[37] and the wall was built on the site, splitting families, separating children from schools. Five houses were also demolished, while another seventy-five shops, twenty small factories, twenty homes, and one primary school have demolition orders. With the wall in place, village residents fear that requisition orders will be made to clear large areas on either side of the wall as a next step. The area between Nazlat Issa and Baqa Sharqiya, one of most fertile in the entire West Bank, is now a closed military area with many of its 7,500 residents trapped between two walls.

Two Qalqilyah district villages surveyed by UNRWA reveal the multiplicity of problems for villagers severed from their environment:

Izbat Jal'ud, Qalqilyah: The inhabitants of Jal'ud (also known as Sheikh Ahmed) are refugees from the village of Zakur (a village destroyed in 1948), whose remains lie just across the green line. Some six families, about 36 persons, are registered refugees, out of a total population of 100. The barrier will cut off 250–300 dunums in the village as a whole, despite the owners possessing Ottoman and British title deeds. In addition, there is a demolition order for three homes and a mosque erected without a permit: no building permit has been issued in the village since 1978.

Abdallah Said Jal'ud, an UNRWA-registered refugee, will lose approximately 125 dunums in Jal'ud and possibly more land in Hable and Izbat Salman once the course of the barrier there is clear. Various fruits and vegetables, an apple farm and a water reservoir are affected.

Ras Atiya, Qalqilyah: In Ras Atiya (pop. 1,400) villagers worked in Israel prior to the intifada, but are now heavily dependent on local agriculture. Some 1,400 dunums are being lost to the barrier itself and 9,000 dunums will be isolated, 75 percent of the villagers' lands, affecting some 220 families. The barrier will pass within 10 meters to the north and east of the local school, a coeducational institution of 450 students, constructed through Swiss funding. Requests to move the barrier to a more reasonable 100-meter distance were refused on "security grounds." Teaching has been disrupted because of explosives used in blasting rocks, and the dynamiting caused cracks to appear in the outer barrier. Sixty pupils and twenty out of twenty-five teachers are from outside Ras Atiya and the barrier, which will cut the road to Dab'a and isolate nearby Khirbet Tira, will make access difficult for all concerned.

In **Zayta,** most of its 3,000 residents depend on agriculture for their livelihood, exporting 80 percent to the West Bank. Now two-thirds of residents are on food aid. Of the 875 dunums of land west of the wall, 443 dunums have been confiscated for "border correction," meaning land loss to 500 residents, in addition to closed land. Six thousand Zayta olive trees were uprooted.

Azzun Atma yielded the highest amount of produce per dunum in all of the West Bank prior to September 2000: ten trucks of produce left daily, nine to the West Bank and one to Israel. Now there is no access to markets.

In **Jayyous**, 480 out of 550 (87 percent) of families have lost their sole means of livelihood. The wall separates Jayyous farmers from their 120 greenhouses, 15,000 olive trees, and 50,000 citrus trees. The area annually produces 17 million kilos of vegetables and fruits. All seven of the village's water wells are behind the wall. The village now gets two hours of water every three days. Irrigated crops at one time provided 90 percent of the town's total economic revenue.

These small villages also generate income and business in their market cities. Jayyous villagers sold their fruits and vegetables in the Nablus city market and paid fees to the Nablus municipality; the city will now lose $150,000, and truck drivers, loaders, and other related workers will also experience losses.[39]

To make use of the human capital of landless unemployed workers, discussions have taken place concerning the creation of industrial estates near Taybeh-Far'un and a German-funded estate near Jalameh, but the idea has never been a popular one with Palestinians due to questions over Israeli ownership of businesses and the possible negative impact such projects may have on Palestinian wage scales, work conditions, and on local businesses. The purpose and location of the industrial parks will also be an issue if they are placed on land confiscated for construction of the wall, not to mention their political and environmental impact.

Private Sector

The impact of the wall on private-sector business has not been quantified as yet. The effect will be clearer in the medium term since the future of businesses behind the wall will depend on the predictability of access. Most definitely, income will be substantially less and transaction costs more. The private sector is still dealing with the destruction due to Israeli military activities during the intifada: there were $110 million in losses reported for the northern West Bank districts. Private-sector losses during the wall construction have been minimal, other than the Nazlat al-Issa central market. In the enclaved areas, twenty-seven out of 750 businesses were destroyed, with a loss of eighty jobs. At least eleven houses have been destroyed and sixty-three require repairs,[40] but many more have had their property devalued by their proximity to the wall.

With investment waning due to the loss of confidence, the strongest trend in the private sector is toward the informal economy, which offers low-risk and low-capital alternative employment and is exceptionally mobile. Donor enthusiasm for micro credit is also supporting entry into the informal economy, especially for women.

Final Scenario

Some of the predicted aftershocks of the wall have begun to occur: (1) development, expansion, and confluence of settlements in the area between the green line and the wall; (2) the thinning of population and migration of residents in search of livelihoods, housing, services, and social relations; (3) the pressure on Palestinians who acquired Israeli IDs through marriage and Israeli ID holders who are married to West Bank residents (as many as 10,000 in the northern area) to relocate; (4) the destruction of land and property and uprooting of trees in the 50–180 meter "buffer" area on both sides of the wall in Palestinian-populated communities such as Tulkarm and Qalqilyah and a number of villages; and (5) greater restrictions on water use in the rest of the West Bank in line with Israel's confiscation of 65 percent of Palestinian water sources.

Without international intervention, there is likely to be an eventual evacuation or transfer process of the population out of the annexed area west of the wall and the enclaved areas. Israel is likely to confiscate the numerous properties in Jerusalem owned by West Bank residents under the pretext of the Absentee Property Law, a scheme it has been threatening since the first intifada, and to create additional measures to implement the total separation of the Jerusalem economy from the rest of the West Bank. Meanwhile, settlements will be thickened and new ones established; already three are being constructed in Arab neighborhoods in Jerusalem. As this is being written, the destructive path of the wall has wound south to the Hebron district just at olive harvest time. The wall penetrates the village of Beit Awa, near homes and schools and atop the cemetery. Hundreds of olive trees have been uprooted and hundreds more isolated from farmers. Villagers who tried to defend their land were shot at, beaten, and gassed.[41]

The scenario is very similar to Sharon's $200 million, five-year plan that was begun in 2004 in the Naqab desert area. The aim of the Naqab plan is to force the remaining 70,000 Bedouin from their lands and forty-five "unrecognized" villages and confine them into seven urban reservation towns. The tactics and the goal are the same: deprivation of basic services, including water; land leveling (as well as destroying crops with herbicides and seizing herds); house demolitions and no-construction orders in order to clear the land for new immigrant Jewish settlers. The end result will be to guarantee the future demographic balance of the area in favor of Israeli Jews at the expense of the basic rights of the Palestinian people.

Notes

1. "The Impact of Israel's Separation Barrier on Affected West Bank Communities," Humanitarian and Emergency Policy Group (HEPG) and Local Aid Coordination Committee (LACC), annex 1, May 4, 2003.

2. "Mid-Year Review," *UN OCHA*, Consolidated Appeals Process (CAP), June 15, 2004. This is an increase from March 2004 when 695 roadblocks were noted: fifty-seven checkpoints, ninety-six roadblocks, 420 earth mounds, seventeen walls, thirty-eight gates, and sixty-seven trenches, in addition to "flying checkpoints" (OCHA, March 2004).

3. United Nations Conference on Trade and Development (UNCTAD) reported in 2002 that Israeli policy was largely responsible for the collapse of manufacturing, construction, and much of the public sector and precipitous drop in incomes, a situation that they deemed at the time may be irreversible.

4. "Disengagement, the Palestinian Economy and the Settlements," *World Bank*, June 23, 2004, fn. 35, p. 36.

5. Ibid., p. 1.

6. Economic figures cited here are from the World Bank unless stated otherwise. See Ibid..

7. Ibid., p. 34.

8. "27 Months of Intifada," *World Bank*, 2003, ch.4.

9. Ibid., p. 1–3.

10. "Preliminary Analysis of the Humanitarian Implications of Latest Barrier Projections," OCHA, July 2004. Estimates vary: according to Gush Shalom, the cost is at least $1.5 billion (700 kilometers @ $2 million per kilometer) while Oxfam calculates $4.7 million per kilometer. The Central Bank of Israel put the cost of Israel's intifada-related expenditure, including the wall construction, at $8 billion after three and a half years.

11. The Israeli National Insurance made a 30 percent cut in subsistence allowances for the 34 percent of households living below the poverty line, and a 15 percent cut in child support benefits in 2002, cited in "Protecting Civilians: A Cornerstone of Middle East Peace," Oxfam Briefing Paper, May 2004.

12. A few notorious Palestinian cement suppliers have also benefited financially.

13. Lucy Mair and Robyn Long, "Backs to the Wall," *Dollars & Sense: The Magazine of Economic Justice*, November 2003.

14. Stop the Wall Campaign.

15. A Ministry of Agriculture official estimated that settlers had picked olives from an area of over 300 dunums in Yanoun and Deir al-Hatab in 2003. Cited in "Danger: Olive Harvest, Settlers on the Prowl," *Palestine Report*, by Atef Saad, October 14, 2004.

16. Leaflet, Gush Shalom, no date.

17. "Preliminary Analysis of the Humanitarian Implications of Latest Barrier Projections," OCHA, July 2004, made from a map analysis. Other sources put it at 764,000 dunums or 13.5 percent of West Bank land (CAP report, 2004).

18. Baka Gharbiya and Baka Sharqiya, Barta'a and Taybe.

19. "The Annexation and Expansion Wall: Impacts and Mitigation Measures," Palestinian Ministry of Planning, May 2004.

20. "Impact of the First Phase of the Barrier on the Qalqilya, Tulkarm and Jenin districts," UNRWA.

21. "The Impact of Israel's Separation Barrier on Affected West Bank Communities," HEPG, March 2004.

22. Tura gate was closed on August 16 and Barta'a gate on August 20; the gate at Zibda is the only access point for Jenin residents living on the other side of the wall.

23. "The Impact of the First Phase of the Barrier on the Qalqilya, Tulkarm and Jenin districts," UNRWA.

24. Cited in "Danger: Olive Harvest, Settlers on the Prowl," Atef Saad.

25. "The Annexation and Expansion Wall: Impacts and Mitigation Measures."

26. "Bad Fences Make Bad Neighbors," Fact Sheets, *Negotiating Support Unit—PLO.*

27. "Impact of the First Phase of the Barrier on the Qalqilya, Tulkarm and Jenin districts," UNRWA.

28. PCBS, October 2003.

29. Notably, the Negotiating Support Unit, OCHA and UNRWA.

30. "Impact of the Israeli Measures on the Economic Conditions of Palestinian Households," 9th Round, April–June 2004, August 2004.

31. Leaflet, Gush Shalom, no date.

32. CAP, 2004, and Oxfam.

33. Ibid., p. 35.

34. "International Meeting on Impact of Construction of Wall in Occupied Palestinian Territory Continues," UN Information Service, April 15, 2004.

35. "The Annexation and Expansion Wall: Impacts and Mitigation Measures."

36. Report at meeting of Association of International Development Agencies (AIDA), October 6, 2004.

37. "The Separation Barrier: Position Paper." *B'tselem*, September, 2002, www.btselem.org/Download/ 200209_Separation _Barrier_Eng.rtf.

38. "Bad Fences Make Bad Neighbors."

39. Report #1, The Apartheid Wall Campaign, *Palestinian Agricultural Relief Committees* PENGON, November 2002.

40. "The Annexation and Expansion Wall: Impacts and Mitigation Measures."

41. "Devastation in Beit Awa," Stop the Wall, PENGON/Anti-Apartheid Wall Campaign, September 23, 2004.

Border/Skin

Lindsay Bremner

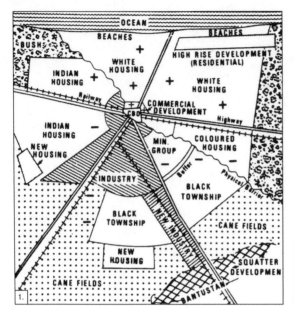

Fig 1. Graphic model of the apartheid city. (Reprinted from *Geoforum* 17, J. J. McCarthy, "Problems of Planning for Urbanization and Development in South Africa: The Case of Natal's Coastal Margins," 276–288, copyright 1986, with permission from Elsevier.)

You can be a citizen or you can be stateless, but it is difficult to imagine *being* a border.
—**Andre Green, 1990**[1]

Apartheid, the official government policy of racial segregation that existed in South Africa between 1948 and 1994, conjures up, in the global popular imaginary, visceral images of walls, fences, palisades, and barbed wire keeping black and white South Africans apart. South Africans of different race groups are assumed to have lived lives as separate as those on either side of the Berlin Wall, which, with apartheid, becomes the critical reference point for making sense of current attempts to divide Israeli and Palestinian territory in Israel and the West Bank.

Yet the wall is not a familiar trope through which apartheid was lived or its experience recalled. Any attempts it made to draw boundaries were fluctuating, porous, and ill defined. Its most concerted attempts to do so—the establishment of

"Bantustans" (or "homelands," as they were otherwise known) as self-governing or independent black labor reserves for white industry or "townships" and as temporary accommodation for those working in urban areas—produced nothing more than vague and constantly morphing blobs on land surveyors' maps and an incessant migration of people moving between the fragments of their lives.

Instead it was the countless instruments of control and humiliation (racially discriminatory laws, administration boards, commissions of inquiry, town planning schemes, health regulations, pass books, spot fines, location permits, police raids, removal vans, bulldozers) and sites of regulation and surveillance (registration offices, health clinics, post offices, recruitment bureaus, hostels, servants rooms, police cells, courtrooms, park benches, beer halls) that delineated South African society during the apartheid years and produced its characteristic landscapes.

As instruments of this utopian project of racial segregation, planners and architects contrived to construct the city as an object of administrative, control-based planning and as a technological instrument to house the Bantu. For this project, they drew on models, images, and procedures of modernity generated in the metropolitan center, in particular those of the nineteenth-century English reformers Robert Owen and Ebenezer Howard. The introverted "neighborhood unit" or "urban village" in which housing units face inward toward communal facilities embedded at their geographic centers, with internal movement orientated toward these to "stimulate social cohesion and a sense of community,"[2] provided the model for early urban slum clearance programs. The wartime government transformed this planned neighborhood approach into a distinctly South African discourse, addressing issues of urbanization and segregation. Coherent residential communities separated by green belts with carefully planned employment sites and transport between them was presented as technological solutions to the problems of cities.[3]

These themes came together in apartheid's primary spatial planning instrument, the Group Areas Act of 1950. Under this legislation, each race group was consolidated into its own residential area, which was to be able to expand in case of future development. Each consolidated area was to be self-governed and as functionally independent of other areas as possible. Each area was separated from others, preferably by natural barriers (ridges or rivers) or, if not, by highways, railways, or a buffer zone of open space. Each racial group had access to a work zone, where interaction

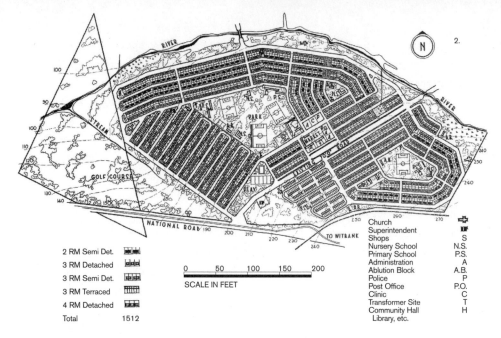

2.

2 RM Semi Det.		Church	S
3 RM Detached		Superintendent	
3 RM Semi Det.		Shops	S
3 RM Terraced		Nursery School	N.S.
4 RM Detached		Primary School	P.S.
Total	1512	Administration	A

SCALE IN FEET

0   50   100   150   200

TO WITBANK

Church   S
Superintendent
Shops   S
Nursery School   N.S.
Primary School   P.S.
Administration   A
Ablution Block   A.B.
Police   P
Post Office   P.O.
Clinic   C
Transformer Site   T
Community Hall   H
   Library, etc.

between them was permissible. However, in moving to and from work, no race group was permitted to cross the residential area of another. A centralized production and exchange facility (a central business district) accommodated white-administered civic, commercial, and financial functions (see Fig. 1 and Fig. 2).

Within this centralized, racialized, and technocratic vision of population control through urban design, architectural activity focused on the problem of housing.[4] Under a National Housing Commission, set up in 1948 by the newly elected apartheid government to address the estimated shortfall of 154,000 housing units in black urban areas at the time, a program of research was set up at the National Building Research Institute (NBRI) to assess minimum space standards, optimum neighborhood densities, performance standards of materials, and methods of construction, and to conduct a minute analysis of cost requirements to establish "valid housing for the urban Bantu."[5] Leading architects were prominent in formulating its methodology, including Dr. D. M. Calderwood, whose doctoral thesis, "Native Housing in South Africa,"[6] resulted in his becoming the head of the architectural division of the NBRI, and Norman Hanson, a leading proponent of the modern movement in South Africa in the 1930s, who was a member of the National Housing Commission from 1948 to 1963.

Calderwood framed his approach to native housing as a "technical one," aiming to "reduce the costs of housing and services."[7] J. E. Jennings, the first director of the NBRI, spoke of housing as "a problem of whole engineering,"[8] the end product of "objective technical research."[9] By 1951, plan types for native housing had been developed as modernist norms for bulk production, procurement, and supply side discounts. The single-storied types, in particular the celebrated NE 51/6 (four-roomed) and 51/9 (three-roomed), reduced the cost of building by almost three-quarters (see Fig. 3). Housing had met the technical imperative of accommodating the greatest number of people for the least possible means. "Throughout South Africa," proclaimed the South African Information Service in 1963, "areas were laid out amid clean surroundings, planned from the start like modern towns in any Western Country,"[10] Architects' drawings, "resonant with the nostalgic anti-urbanism of the Garden City movement ... delicate freehand drawings of houses surrounded by gardens ... bucolic bungalows ... isolated in the countryside like part of a Robert Owen

Opposite: Fig. 2. Final layout of Witbank's new Native Township. (Reprinted from D. M. Calderwood, *Native Housing in South Africa*, unpublished Ph.D. thesis; Johannesburg: University of the Witwatersrand, 1953, 123.)

Right: Fig 3. Plan and elevation of the NE 51/9 three-roomed house. (Reprinted from D. M. Calderwood, *Native Housing in South Africa*, unpublished Ph.D. thesis; Johannesburg: University of the Witwatersrand, 1953, 31.)

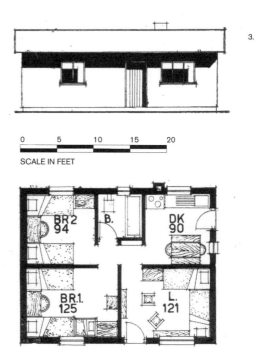

3.

| 0 | 5 | 10 | 15 | 20 |

SCALE IN FEET

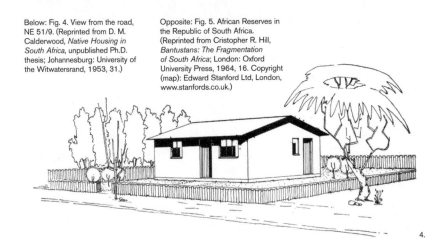

4.

ideal village,"[11] concealed the true meaning of apartheid's intentions (see Fig. 4). For it was here and in its parallel landscape, the Bantustan, that the category of "native" would be constructed, simultaneously, as dehistoricized, primitive, tribal savage and as modern, docile, urban subject.[12]

Bantustans were modern tribalized spaces, apartheid versions of colonial "native reserves" (see Fig. 5). Their location, size, and fragmented geographies were products of the processes of the South African frontier during the nineteenth century.[13] Conflict between Boer settlers, indigenous peoples, and the British government resulted in a policy of defining areas for exclusive ownership by indigenous people, first by imperial intervention and later by the South African government. It was thus a frontier geography that was consolidated in legislation in the twentieth century, beginning with the Land Act of 1913 and the Development Trust and Land Act of 1936, and later in the legislation that established Bantustans proper, the Bantu Self-Governing Act of 1959.[14]

Bantustans were either "self-governing territories" (Lebowa, Gazankulu, QwaQwa, Kwa Ndebele, KwaZulu, and KaNgawne) or "independent states" (Transkei, Boputhuthatswana, Venda, and Ciskei), the latter only distinguished from the former by having local armies, diplomats, casinos,[15] and farcical border posts. They were intended as instruments to retribalize the Bantu by defining and consolidating ethnic and tribal identities as Bantustan nationalities, where black South Africans would live according to tribal custom and practice while providing labor reserves for white industry.

Images of Bantustan life constructed it as outside of history, an idealized tribal past mapped onto the present.[16] Black citizens were supposed to identify with this paradise lost, thereby filtering and regulating their access to the modern world.

In reality, Bantustans were fragmented and discontinuous territories, located in unproductive and marginal parts of the country. Boputhuthatswana, for instance, was made up of nineteen tracts of land, most of which had no access to roads, rail, telephone, or electricity, and KwaZulu comprised seventy enclaves scattered widely over the province of Natal (see Fig. 6).[17] Despite the fact that Boputhuthatswana straddled mineral-bearing rock formations containing platinum, chrome, vanadium, iron ore, limestone, granite, and manganese, it received no direct benefit from this. Mineral rights were vested in local tribal groups, and their exploration and development was regulated by the white-directed Bantu Mining Corporation.[18] Homeland governments had no control over mineral leasing or exploitation, nor over their territorial waters.[19]

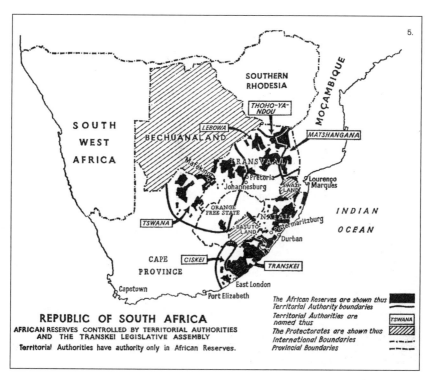

5.

REPUBLIC OF SOUTH AFRICA
AFRICAN RESERVES CONTROLLED BY TERRITORIAL AUTHORITIES AND THE TRANSKEI LEGISLATIVE ASSEMBLY
Territorial Authorities have authority only in African Reserves.

The African Reserves are shown thus
Territorial Authority boundaries
Territorial Authorities are named thus — TSWANA
The Protectorates are shown thus
International Boundaries
Provincial Boundaries

They were bleak, poor, corrupt, and repressive, governed by leaders appointed by the apartheid state and maintained by the violence of forced removals, relocations, and administrative neglect.[20] Their landscapes were sliced, Haussmann-style, by state security highways for the deployment of South African troops should anti–South African political activity emerge there, brutal insertions of modernity into "non-European space." Outside these enclaves, yet inside South Africa, a status of temporary modernity was assigned to black bodies insofar as they supplied labor for white industry. Between these two worlds—the tribal Bantustan and the urban township—bodies, goods, stories, and identities incessantly flowed and shifted, in a ceaseless migratory flux.

But Bantustans were physical, geographic territories only insofar as they were political ideas, and they were thus constantly shifting according to the vagaries of political expediency (see Fig. 7). The South African state's "ability to fiddle with the fences of the national states"[21] knew no bounds. It did this through powers it granted itself in a dizzying host of continuously evolving acts, schedules, revisions, bills, and proclamations. For instance, when powers granted to the state by the National States Constitution Act of 1971 were found by the courts to be insufficient to effect the incorporation of the township of Botshabelo (outside the city of Bloemfontein) into the self-governing homeland of QwaQwa, the Alteration of Boundaries of Self-Governing Territories bill was introduced. This would have validated the invalid proclamation and made future land shifts at the discretion of the South African State president after consultation with his own cabinet.[22] (Fortunately the bill lapsed before it could be effected.)

The whole epistemology of apartheid, like that of much of the colonial enterprise in Africa, was based on a simple equation that, between the native principle and the animal principle, there was hardly a difference.[23] To assert him/herself as human, the white man relegated the native to the status of animality, of the not-yet human. This is illustrated in a passage from Baden Powell, in South Africa during the Anglo Boer War (1898–1902)[24] describing his confrontation with a Matabele warrior: "Then, with a swift and canny movement, he laid his arms noiselessly upon the rocks, and dropping on all fours beside a pool, he dipped his muzzle down and drank just like an animal." The native was part of an animal kingdom, a subhuman species.

Out of the violence and violation of this imaginary, two traditions of colonial dom-

Fig. 6. Proposed Consolidation of KwaZulu. (Reprinted from Jeffrey Butler, Robert I. Rotberg, and John Adams, *The Black Homelands of South Africa: The Political and Economic Development of Bophuthatswana and Kwa Zulu;* Berkeley: University of California Press, 1977, 94.)

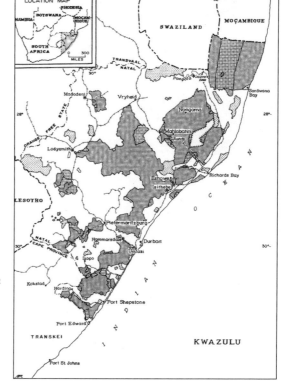

6.

Block area to remain
White area to be added
Black area to be excised
•   Town
▣   Border area town
⊛   Growth Point
◉   Present seat of government
— — — International boundary
— · — · Provincial boundary
+—+—+ Railroad
⋮⋮⋮⋮ Hulhluwe-Umolozi game reserves

0   50 miles

ination developed, characterized loosely as the Hegelian and the Bergsonian.[25] On the one hand, the native as animal could be contained through violence and domination. He/she was the property of power. On the other, the native as animal could be domesticated. In the South African case, the black body existed only "to minister to the needs of the White man."[26] A sympathizing, familiarizing, domesticating violence protected, groomed, and made him/her useful.

These two technologies of power were flattened into and permeated every aspect of daily life under apartheid. Violence and domination were enacted at the level of the banal—entering a public building, bathing on a beach, eating lunch, catching a bus, what jobs one could or could not do, whom one could or could not marry.[27] Daily acts and rituals were transformed into acts of segregation and humiliation that

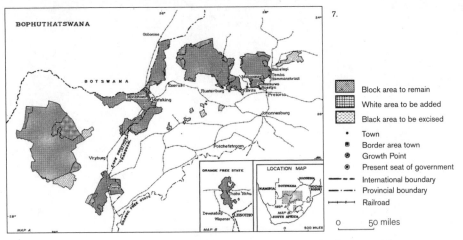

Fig. 7. Proposed Consolidation of Bophuthatswana. (Reprinted from Jeffrey Butler, Robert I. Rotberg, and John Adams, *The Black Homelands of South Africa: The Political and Economic Development of Bophuthatswana and Kwa Zulu*; Berkeley: University of California Press, 1977, 92.)

accumulated into an omnipresent violence of everyday life. In this obscene enactment of power, apartheid's walls were nowhere and everywhere. They laced every dimension of social space in a grid of legislative and ideological frontiers that overwrote all social and economic transactions with the master signifier of race.

Apartheid operated as a bio-politics of discrimination and disqualification at the level of the skin. The skin was the site where the categories of violence associated with borders were performed. At the heart of their operation lurked the figure of the "disqualified person,"[28] i.e., a vague and ill-defined person who, by virtue of appearance, was generally accepted as not being of designated group "x" and therefore not entitled to this or that right. Prosecution of apartheid offenses was required to establish that an accused was "obviously" disqualified. This was decided on the basis of skin pigmentation, often guided by "expert witnesses" such as school inspectors with years of experience in ferreting out pupils whose skin pigmentation did not match that of the educational institution concerned."[29]

Under the Group Areas Act of 1950, a white person was any person who "in appearance obviously is a white person" or "generally accepted" as a white person.[30] A white person who married or cohabited with a black person immediately became black. The black group included "any person who in fact is or who is generally accepted as a member of an aboriginal race or tribe of Africa," or any person who married or cohabited with such a person. A "colored" person was any person who was neither of these and included those of mixed race, Indian, Chinese, and Malay peoples.[31] Mobility between groups was recognized, and, in certain cases, people fell into more than one group at the same time.[32]

The skin was a moving signifier—a wall, so to speak—that located one in space, that granted or denied access, that opened or closed doors, that determined where or with whom one might socialize, work, shop, or fornicate. One carried it around with one. It regulated multiple regimes of covalent bonds and circulations and kept the moving body in its place simultaneously. As we have seen, the meaning of skin color itself shifted constantly. It meant different things at different times, in different situations, to different people. It too was a political construct, through which the multiple subjectivities necessary for the maintenance of apartheid modernity were constructed.

One of apartheid's central problems was that while, on the basis of ideology, it aimed at setting racial groups apart, it acknowledged their dependency. It designed its boundaries as moving targets or to be breached. "It is true that there are blacks working for us. They will continue to work for us for generations, in spite of the ideal we have to separate them completely ... the fact of the matter is this: We need them," said J. B. Voster, prime minister of South Africa.[33] While black and white bodies were, in theory, assigned to certain localities, fixed in space, in point of fact, they were caught up in continuous circulatory migrations and asymmetrical intimacies. Black bodies were needed to nurse white children, to clean white homes, to labor in white industry, to work on white mines. White bodies policed, regulated, and administered black space. Bodies moved through and interacted with each other's space on a daily basis. Thus, the Bantustan structure, imposed upon small and eroded reserves, was not meant to enclose or sustain its population, but was designed to force its residents into migrant labor.[34] Similarly, as industrial development was not permitted within Bantustans but just outside, in so-called border areas, workers were required to commute across borders on a daily or weekly basis. According to Christopher Hill two-thirds of the black population of South Africa was outside Bantustan boundaries at any one time. Apartheid's characteristic spatial forms were designed to be porous, to regulate the body in motion. They produced a narrative not of closure, but of hundreds of thousands of entries and crossings.[35]

Apartheid "worked," so to speak, by constructing and consolidating vague, indeterminate, and fluctuating, yet omnipresent, border zones for permanent residence. Under apartheid, borders were not things one crossed, but places one stayed in. Bantustans, townships, the body—under apartheid these were borderlands, marked by temporary boundaries, shifting locales, multiple meanings, and migrant identities.[36] Apartheid illustrated what happens when the kinds of violence that concentrate on borders (selection, separation, differentiation, confrontation, blockage) are generalized across political space as the permanent precondition for its reproduction. More than simply external, its walls became internal realities, "invisible borders ... everywhere and nowhere."[37]

It is not surprising that, in apartheid's aftermath, new signifiers, borders, and modes of discrimination between the national and the alien, between different categories of migrants, different categories of citizens, have been activated.

For instance, in 1984, as apartheid entered its emergency phase,[38] the property division of the gold-mining company Anglo American laid out a 420-erf gated residential estate in the northern suburbs of Johannesburg, the first of its kind in the country. Walled, its entrance gate manned by twenty-four-hour armed private security guards, managed by the former town clerk of a small South African town, this territorial enclave has provided the model for future suburban development in the city: enclosed, internally homogeneous zones, protected by bristling electromagnetic fields against the fluidity of the sociopolitical landscape around them.

By 2003, there were 1,127 such enclaves in the city. Walls, booms, razor wire, electrified fencing, security gates, intercoms, concealed cameras, armed guards—an entire security arsenal—had pried zones of the city from the public realm, transforming them into a patchwork of militarized borders and quasi-virtual worlds. The spaces between, the roads and highways, were networks of violent contestation, marked by frequent incidents of road rage, car highjacking, armed robbery, and cash-in-transit ambush. While Johannesburg today is a city of new fluidities and encounters, these are contained and directed by the countless, often hastily erected walls and physical barriers that score its landscape. Moving around the city involves constantly negotiating gates, booms, intercom identifications, and security checks, transforming life in the city into that of a permanent frontier zone (se Fig. 8). Like apartheid's landscape before it, these thresholds are constantly being redrawn, tugged this way and that by political agency, residents' perceptions, developers'

Lindsay Bremner

Fig. 8. Entrance to Fourways Gardens Residential Estate, Johannesburg, 2000.

intent, or criminal activity. The wall has been mobilized as a new portable instrument of control in a fluid and constantly changing political landscape.

During the last decade, the place of South Africa in the cartography of the global has been confirmed, as its diverse links to many places have been extended and as it has assembled an increasing diversity of transborder social and economic relations. Its cities are now part of a new transnational, global space, which has brought new claims on them—from international businesspeople, foreign firms, tourists, continental migrants, crossborder traders, refugees. Its spaces are being reconstituted by and in the image of these new constituencies, and new social, spatial, and political morphologies are taking shape around their demands.

Dafna Kaplan

These tend to revolve around ideas and practices of deregulation, privatization, and security, as well as various forms of privatized or semiprivatized infrastructure—hotels, offices, conference facilities, restaurants, shopping centers, etc. At the other extreme, increasing numbers of refugees or asylum seekers are reactivating the boundaries of political exclusion in disquieting new ways.

South Africa does not use camps for hosting refugees or asylum seekers. Instead they are expected to integrate into South African society. Many enter the country and seek refuge in Johannesburg's high-density inner-city residential suburbs: Hillbrow, Joubert Park, Berea. Here they have become targets of intense verbal and physical abuse, police harassment, and racial profiling.[39] Darker skin color, an unfamiliar accent or dress, signs of foreignness have become the new signifiers of political valuelessness and disqualification. Suspects are arrested and taken to the notorious Lindela Repatriation Center—a privately owned detention facility for migrants awaiting deportation, monitored by the South African Department of Home Affairs—where they are held under inhuman conditions until they are deported, frequently to return. The skin has been reactivated as a frontier, a borderland, a "limit concept" that, in the words of Giorgio Agamben "radically calls into question the fundamental categories of the nation state."[40] The body of the refugee has become the site upon which new categories of disqualification that define the limits of the postapartheid nation-state and postapartheid citizenship are drawn. Apartheid is not over; it has simply been deferred.

Notes

1. Etienne Balibar, *Politics and the Other Scene,* trans. C. Jones, J. Swenson, C. Turner (London: Verso, 2002), 107.

2. D. Dewar and R. Uitenbogaardt, *South African Cities: A Manifesto for Change* (Cape Town: Urban Problems Research unit, 1991), 77.

3. A. Mabin and D. Smith, "Reconstructing South Africa's Cities? The Making of Urban Planning, 1900–2000," Planning Perspectives, no.12 (1997): 193–223.

4. Derek Japha, "The Social Programme of the South African Modern Movement," in *Blank: Architecture, Apartheid and After,* ed. H. Judin and I. Vladislavic, 422–437 (Rotterdam: NAi Publisher, 1999).

5. Clive Chipkin, *Johannesburg Style: Architecture, and Society 1880s–1960s* (Cape Town: David Philip, 1993), 214.

6. D. M. Calderwood, *Native Housing in South Africa,* unpublished Ph.D. thesis (Johannesburg: University of the Witwatersrand, 1953).

7. Ibid., 4.

8. Chipkin, *Johannesburg Style: Architecture, and Society 1880s–1960s,* 214.

9. Calderwood, in Chipkin, *Johannesburg Style: Architecture, and Society 1880s–1960s,* 216.

10. Chipkin, *Johannesburg Style: Architecture, and Society 1880s–1960s,* 214.

11. Ibid., 216.

12. Gary Minkley, *"Corpses Behind Screens: Native Space in the City,"* in *Blank: Architecture, Apartheid and After.*

13. Jeffrey Butler, Robert I. Rotberg, and John Adams, *The Black Homelands of South Africa: The Political and Economic Development of Bophuthatswana and KwaZulu* (Berkeley: University of California Press, 1977).

14. Under the Third Reich, the Nazis aimed to take over British and French colonies in Africa and detailed a plan derived from the native reserve policy of the British in South Africa. This involved the assignment of land for black inhabitation and the support of the white supremacist Reich by black manual labor on a vast scale. The only mixing between black and white would be in the sphere of work, in Barbara Rogers, *Divide and Rule: South Africa's Bantustans* (London: International Defence and Aid Fund, 1976).

15. Gambling was outlawed in South Africa, but permitted in independent states.

16. J. Benningfield, *The Frightened Land,* unpublished Ph.D. thesis (London: University College, Bartlett School, 2003).

17. Jeffrey Butler, Robert I. Rotberg, and John Adams, *The Black Homelands of South Africa.*

18. Ibid.

19. Rogers, *Divide and Rule: South Africa's Bantustans.*

20. By 1986, 3.5 million people had been forcibly relocated into areas designated for black occupation.

21. M. Robertson, "Dividing the Land: An Introduction to Apartheid Land Law," in *No Place to Rest: Forced Removals and the Law in South Africa,* ed. C. Murray and C. O'Regan (Cape Town: Oxford University Press, 1990) 122–136.

22. Ibid.

23. Frantz Fanon, *Black Skins, White Masks,* trans. C L Markmann (London: Pluto, 1986), and Archille Mbembe, *On the Postcolony* (Berkeley: California University Press, 2001).

24. Tim Jeal, *Baden Powell* (London: Hutchinson, 1989), in "His Stories? Narratives and Images of Imperialism," in *Space and Place: Theories of Identity and Location*, ed. Erica Carter, James Donald and Judith Squires (London: Lawrence and Wishart, 1993) 200.

25. Archille Mbembe, *On the Postcolony* (Berkeley: California University Press, 2001).

26. Stallard Commision of 1922 in Christopher R. Hill, *Bantustans: The Fragmentation of South Africa* (London: Oxford University Press, 1964).

27. When writing this paper, I happened upon an article by Benjamin Pogrund, director of Yakar's Center for Social Concern in Jerusalem, which made the same point: "In South Africa pre-1994, skin color determined everyone's life: where you were born and lived, which school you went to, which bus, train, beach, hospital, library and public toilet you used, with whom you could have sex, which jobs you had and how much you could earn, and, ultimately, where you were buried," in B. Pogrund, "The Apartheid Lie," *Mail and Guardian*, Oct 22–28 (2004), 32.

28. Robertson, *Dividing the Land: An Introduction to Apartheid Land Law*, 126.

29. A. Dodson, "The Group Areas Act: Changing Patterns of Enforcement," 146–148 in *No Place to Rest: Forced Removals and the Law in South Africa*, ed. Christina Murray and Catherine O'Regan (Cape Town: Oxford University Press, 1990) 137–161.

30. Ibid., 147.

31. Ibid., 147–148.

32. Ibid.

33. Rogers, *Divide and Rule: South Africa's Bantustans*, 10. See also J. B. Voster, *House of Assembly Debates* (Cape Town: Hansard, 1968).

34. Ibid.

35. Hill, *Bantustans: The Fragmentation of South Africa*.

36. J. Benningfield, *The Frightened Land*.

37. Balibar, *Politics and the Other Scene*, 78.

38. From 1985 onward, successive states of emergency were declared in districts around the country, granting far-reaching powers to the apartheid state to contain and suppress antiapartheid activity.

39. Loren Landau, ed. *Forced Migrants in the New Johannesburg* (Johannesburg: Forced Migration Studies Programme, University of the Witwatersrand, 2004).

40. Giorgio Agamben, *Homo Sacer: Sovereign Power and Bare Life*, trans. D. Heller-Roazen (Stanford: Stanford University Press, 1998), 134.

Barriers, Walls and Dialectics: The Shaping of "Creeping Apartheid" in Israel/Palestine

Oren Yiftachel and Haim Yacobi

Dafna Kaplan

Here we shall stay
Like a brick wall upon your breast
And in your throat
Like a splinter of glass, like spiky cactus
And in your eyes
A chaos of fire.

If we get thirsty
We'll squeeze the rocks.
If we get hungry
We'll eat the dirt
And never leave.

—"Here We Shall Stay," by Tawfiq Zeyyad

We chose to open our essay on Israel's new move to transform the geography of the land with the work of this famous Palestinian poet, not only because of its obvious relation to the geography of oppression and resistance, but also due to its referral to a "wall" as a symbol of strength, persistence, and obstruction. A wall of a different kind will be the center of our short essay, in which we analyze recent changes in the political geography of Israel/Palestine, focusing on "the wall/fence" (separation barrier) now being unilaterally constructed by Israel in the West Bank, in contravention of international law.

Some 90 miles of a planned 298 miles of the barrier have already been built, consisting of a 60 to 100-meter-wide strip made of two electric fences and two track roads in the rural areas and 41 miles of high concrete wall in and around Palestinian cities. Some 51,000 acres of Palestinian land are to be affected—appropriated, cleared, or declared "out of bounds" for West Bank Palestinians.

Our main argument is that the construction of the barrier and the recent declarations of small Israeli territorial withdrawals constitute attempts to manage the growing contradictions of the state's "ethnocratic" regime. The recent adjustments, our argument continues, accelerate a process of "creeping apartheid" gradually unfolding in Israel/Palestine.

The contradictions have erupted in full force during the recent al-Aqsa intifada, which has cost nearly 4,000 lives, three-quarters of them Palestinians. This level of violence has now moved Israel to unilaterally transform the area's landscape by building the barrier and further constrain Palestinian development, rights, and movement. But in this move Israel also presents limits to its own expansion, including a (promised) voluntary evacuation of colonial Jewish settlements, for the first time in the history of the Zionist-Palestinian conflict.

Our approach highlights a point overlooked by many critical analysts: the dialectical nature of spatial and political change. It seems that a "blind spot" leads many to portray the Palestinians mainly as passive victims of Israeli aggression, both in the general unfolding of local history and in the geographical transformation of the land. Yet Palestinian agency in general and violence in particular play a major role in the reshaping of Zionist-Palestinian relations and spaces. The dialectic manifests itself in an ever-radicalizing Palestinian struggle and ever-deepening Israeli oppression, causing ever-growing levels of human misery, mainly—but not only—among Palestinians. Notably, though, this process is asymmetric, with the Jewish state mastering far greater military and economic power than its Palestinian counterparts.

The barrier's route, approved by the Israeli government in October 2003, runs within Palestinian occupied territory to include the majority of Jewish settlers on "the Israeli side," effectively annexing to Israel 16 percent of the West Bank. When complete, it may improve Jewish security, but it will have some grave consequences for the Palestinians: some 210,000 of them will be caught between the barrier and the green line, or cut off from their own lands and livelihood. Further, Israel's demand to surround many settlements by the barrier "for their security" presents an absurdity: more Palestinian land is now illegally seized to protect settlements, which was illegally seized Palestinian land in the first place!

Critically, Israel's intent to withdrawal from Gaza and small parts of the West Bank is linked to the construction of the barrier, as explicitly stated by the hawkish former prime minister Benjamin Netanyahu, who recently changed his mind about the withdrawal, like most Likud leaders:

> My change of mind about Gaza is based on the construction of the security fence which, as you know, would incorporate most West Bank settlers within the Israeli side. It's clear that American support to the fence is given due to our withdrawal from Gaza ... so strategically, this is a new situation with net benefits.[1]

Similarly, prime minister and architect of the "disengagement plan" Ariel Sharon was originally opposed to withdrawal from any parts of the occupied territories and to the construction of the barrier. How can we explain this apparent U-turn? We suggest that the contradictions of Israel's regime have grown to a point where they can no longer be reconciled or ignored without escalating international and local costs. This has now required a major tactical change in order to maintain the Israeli ethnocratic system. The recent steps represent a new phase, a new method, to pursue an age-old goal of Zionism: to maximize the Judaization of Palestine while maintaining Israel's image as a "normal," democratic nation-state.

The aim of securing Israel's control of the land through the unilateral disengagement plan was clearly apparent from Prime Minister Sharon's statements in a recent interview:

The disengagement plan and the construction of the separation fence release Israel from pressures to adopt another, more dangerous, plan. I cannot see terror ceasing, and hence we construct the fence. [Bush] . . . promised not to pressure Israel, and I cannot see the Palestinians fulfilling their part in the Roadmap. It's highly likely that after the disengagement, for a long time, there will be nothing new.[2]

Likewise, Sharon's senior advisor, Dov Weisglass, declared in a widely publicized interview:
> . . . the meaning of the disengagement plan is a freeze to the diplomatic process with the Palestinians . . . When you freeze the political process, you prevent the establishment of a Palestinian state and you prevent a discussion on the subject of refugees, borders and Jerusalem. . . . The vast majority of West Bank settlers will stay in their place forever. . . . This whole package called "the Palestinian state" has been removed from the daily agenda for an unlimited period of time.[3]

The stalling of the peace process and the unilateral withdrawal and barrier construction are intimately linked. In the absence of progress toward peace, the government will probably be "compelled" to continue its expansionist program of settlement construction and land seizure in the West Bank. While this expansionist drive has slowed in recent years, it continues to form one of the main pillars of Israel's ethnocratic regime.

Critically, wide circles in the Israeli public, including the traditional Left, now support the Gaza-barrier strategy because of the precedent of removing Jewish settlements in the land of Israel. This means that Sharon's opposition comes only from the extreme Right. But if our analysis is correct, the new plan promises little in terms of genuine progress toward peace. On the contrary, the new geography created by the limited withdrawal and construction of the barrier, and the imposing unilateral manner in which they are planned, move Israel/Palestine one step closer in the process of "creeping apartheid", typical to ethnocratic societies.

Let us take a short detour and describe the political geographic concept of "ethnocracy." The concept has been developed by Yiftachel to account for regimes found in contested territories in which a dominant ethnic nation appropriates the state to further its expansionist aspirations while keeping some features of formal democracy.[4] Ethnocratic states are typified by high levels of oppression over indigenous and (to a lesser extent) immigrant minorities. Minorities, in turn, usually develop forms of resistance typically around issues of land control and settlement, which tend to essentialize identities and polarize the spatial and political systems. Typically, gaps between the state's democratic self-representation and persisting forms of minority oppression develop into "cracks" in the ruling hegemony and often destabilize the regime. Ethnocratic regimes can be found in Serbia, Estonia, Malaysia, Latvia, pre-1989 Lebanon, pre-1999 Northern Ireland, or nineteenth-century Australia.

As in most ethnocratic projects, the Jews initially benefited greatly from the expansion strategy. Until the late 1980s, the identity, economic, and territorial goals reinforced one another. Israeli conquest of the West Bank and Gaza and their colonial settlement strengthened Jewish national identity and introduced a large pool of cheap labor and free (confiscated) land into the expanding Israeli economy. During the expansionist phase, Israel used an effective double-discourse: internally, it presented the Palestinian territories as the "eternal Jewish homeland," thereby "naturally" including Jewish settlers as full state citizens despite residing outside the official state borders. At the same time, internationally, Israel presented the same Palestinian territories as "temporarily occupied," hence excluding their Palestinian inhabitants from political participation and leaving them powerless to shape the future of their own homeland.

But like most other ethnocratic regimes, Israel began to face the increasing contradictions of the system. These surfaced with the attempt to manage the first Palestinian intifada (1987–1993), which was accompanied by growing polarization between the Palestinian minority inside Israel and the state as well as growing tensions between religious and secular Jews over the future of the territories.

The Oslo Accords constituted the first attempt to "square the circle" of democracy and colonialism. They entailed mutual recognition of Israel and the PLO, with the latter declaring a cessation of the armed struggle. They included a promise of substantial Israeli withdrawals and the establishment of an autonomous Palestinian Authority. But the "peace process" ground to halt with the outbreak of Palestinian terror in Israeli cities, the 1995 assassination of Israel's prime minister Rabin (by a nationalist Jew), and the 1996 election of the Netanyahu rightist government.[5] Israel imposed a growing system of control over the territories, built dozens of new Jewish settlements, and enforced increasing restrictions on Palestinian movement—all leading to deep economic and political crises. Notably, not one Jewish settlement was evacuated during the "Oslo period."

The al-Aqsa intifada erupted following the failed attempt to reach permanent peace. During the 2000 negotiations, Israel treated, as it does now, the occupied West Bank as an area open for negotiation, while the Palestinians believed that their 1993 recognition of Israel as a sovereign state on three-quarters of historic Palestine would allow them to be sovereign in the remaining lands—that is, the West Bank and Gaza. Israel's attempt to annex 10–15 percent of the West Bank in order to keep Jewish settlers in place, its refusal to address its role in the 1948 Nakbah (Palestinian "disaster"), the resettlement of Palestinian refugees, or its refusal to allow Palestinian sovereignty over occupied Temple Mount broke down the negotiations. While Barak's offers were indeed the most serious the Palestinians have ever received from Israel, they still fell short of anything the Palestinians could accept.

At the same time, the Palestinian Authority was seriously weakened by the paucity of Israeli withdrawals, economic decline, widespread corruption, and the rise of Islamic organizations. It could not control, and tacitly endorsed, the eruption of violence against Israel, triggered by Sharon's provocative visit to Temple Mount in September 2000. The second intifada quickly escalated into a bloodbath, with both Israel and the Palestinians using unprecedented levels of violence. Israel began a systematic destruction of Palestinian Authority facilities and launched a terrorizing military campaign against Palestinian leaders and civil society. The Palestinians widened the use of deadly suicide bombing and other forms of terror against civilians in the heart of Israeli cities, causing widespread death, disruption of daily life, and deepening economic crisis.

Given the depth of ethnocratic perception in Israel, and the fear still embedded in Jewish culture following a history of persecutions and Holocaust, the impact of renewed Palestinian violence, coupled with repeated anti-Jewish public statements, calls for the "liberation of the entire Palestine" and the return of refugees into Israel proper, has been powerful, if predictable. Most Jews closed ranks, stigmatized the entire Palestinian population as "supporting terror," legitimized a public discussion on "transferring" the Palestinians out of their homeland, and shifted politically to the nationalist Right. This was amplified by the 9/11 events and the rise of American rightist foreign policy, with Israel as a main ally in the "War on Terror."

But the "War on Terror" was not enough. The Israeli public, and especially the mainstream middle classes, demanded a major change. They sought to maintain the illusion of a "normal," democratic state while continuing the control of Palestinian areas. They demanded "security," a return to economic growth, while keeping the Palestinians voiceless and powerless. There were dissenting voices, calling for a genuine ending of the occupation and a return to sincere negotiations, but they were marginalized by the weight of the nationalist discourse.

The main response was the construction of the separation barrier. This began as an initiative of the Zionist Left (promising to combine territorial withdrawal close to the green line and protection from terror), but was cleverly hijacked by the ruling nationalist Right, which shifted the proposed route eastward into Palestinian territories. Despite the "painful ideological compromise" of withdrawing from parts of the land of Israel, the political Right could clearly see the benefits of the Gaza-barrier "package." First, it would "answer" a major demographic "headache" because without Gaza, Jews could maintain a solid majority in the area under Israeli control for another generation. Second, the barrier will take annexation of most settlers a step closer, hence ensuring the political support of many settlers despite their "official" opposition to any territorial withdrawal. The unilateral move is also likely to generate further Palestinian resistance and subsequently strengthen the political Right, whose narrative often draws on continuous ethnic hostility.

Despite the relative openness of urban areas, their development in Israel/Palestine has been strongly framed by a prevailing ethnocratic drive for Judaization. Similar to other sites shaped by the logics of settling ethnonationalism and capitalism, ethnically mixed cities are characterized by stark patterns of segregation as well as by ethno-class fragmentation within each national group. Mixed spaces are both exceptional and involuntary, often resulting from the spatial process of ethnic expansion and retreat, prevalent in contested urban spaces. We theorize this setting as an *urban ethnocracy*, where a dominant group appropriates the city apparatus to buttress its domination and expansion, often at the expense of urban minorities. In such settings, conspicuous tensions accompany the interaction between the city's economic, planning, and ethno-territorial logics, producing sites of conflict and instability, and essentializing the boundaries of group identities and the zero-sum nature of ethnic geographies.[6]

The production of ethnocratic urban space involves forceful seizure, formal legislation, cultural discourse, and invisible apparatuses of control, rooted in specific and local historical circumstances framed by the powerful logics of ethnic dominance and capital accumulation. These forces are often "softened" or concealed under the official and legal understanding of the city as an open space for mobility, residence, and political mobilization. Hence, these forces ostensibly enable, but practically undermine, the promise of the city to become a democratic arena for all citizens.

Jerusalem/al-Quds is a clear example of an urban ethnocracy,[7] which now—with the construction of the wall—is an accentuated reality. Indeed, there is a tendency to refer to the wall that is constructed these days as a clear manifestation of Israeli abuse of Palestinians' human rights. Yet, as we will suggest, the current wall has deeper roots both historically and in terms of strategic goals. It is a tangible manifestation of the ongoing urban policy characterizing Jewish-Palestinian relations in the city since 1967. Walls have existed in Jerusalem/al-Quds since then, we will argue, but were less visible, being "constructed" of the "building blocks" of urban policy, planning strategies, and a supportive legal apparatus. These enhanced the Judaization of the city and the parallel process of de-Arabization. In other words, the reality of "creeping apartheid" began in East Jerusalem very soon after it came under Israeli control.

Jordan conquered al-Quds (East Jerusalem) in 1948, which was in turn conquered by Israel in the war of 1967. In an act self-described as "unification," Israel unilaterally imposed its law over large parts of the city and surrounding villages. As documented widely, Israel used its military might and economic power to relocate borders and boundaries, grant and deny rights and resources, shift populations, and reshape the city's geography for the purpose of ensuring Jewish dominance. Two central Israeli strategies included the construction of a massive outer ring of Jewish settlements—the "satellite neighborhoods"—which now hold over half the Jewish population of Jerusalem, and a complementary containment of all Palestinian development, implemented through housing demolition and the prevention of immigration to the city.

Hence, "transparent walls" were constructed in this process; while Palestinian districts lacked many urban services and decent infrastructure, their Jewish counterparts are fully serviced. Very often, Israeli-built roads and housing were shaped in the form of segregative walls, aiming to fragment the Arab city. The results were a gradual physical decline and stagnation of the city's Arab sectors, the severance of Arab Jerusalem from the Palestinian hinterland, and the subsequent exodus of Palestinian businesses north and south of the city.

These transparent walls also emerged in Jerusalem's public and political spheres; Israel's management has meant that despite the clearly binational reality of the Jerusalem/al-Quds region, urban governance has been totally dominated by Jews. Palestinians have been excluded from the city's decision-making forums—most notably City Hall—due to their refusal to accept the imposition of Israeli law and by the distorted municipal boundaries imposed on the city. As we have argued else-where,[8] Israel wishes the Palestinian residents of East Jerusalem to see Judaization as an "inevitable fact" that should be received passively as part of the modern development of the metropolis.

Constructing the wall in Jerusalem/al-Quds represents a special case. Despite the similarity in shape and external structure between the wall in Jerusalem and that built in other West Bank cities, most segments of the wall in Jerusalem will be made of concrete segments six to eight meters high that aim to isolate inhabited areas from each other and fragment Palestinian neighborhoods. Moreover, the wall in Jerusalem and its surroundings has a significant effect on the future of the city and we propose that this is the major transformation since its occupation in 1967.

The construction of the wall marks tangibly the entire Israeli Jerusalem (that is, the area "annexed" by Israeli in 1967—illegal according to the international law) and beyond (see Fig. 1). The immediate effect of the wall is to annex de facto the settlements/neighborhoods within the municipal boundaries such as Pisgat Ze'ev and Har Homa—in total more than 4,000 dunums. The 3,200 dunums of Palestinian neighborhoods within Jerusalem's municipal boundaries, such as Shu'fat Refugee Camp, Dhahiet As-Salam, and Anata in the east, and Kufur Aqab and Samerameis in the north, will be excluded by the wall and thus their inhabitants will lose their status.

The wall will also lead to a de facto annexation of vast areas of Palestinian lands outside Jerusalem's municipal area and beyond the green line on which settlements such as Ma'ale Adumim, Givaat Ze'ev, Beit Horon, Givon HaHadasha, Efrat, Gush Etzion, and Betar Elite were built. These settlements control an area of 122 square kilometers. The

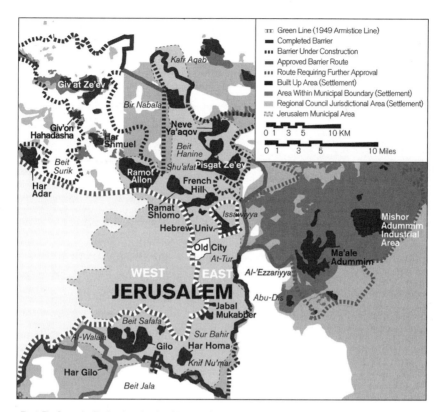

Fig. 1. The Separation Barrier—Jerusalem Area May 2005. Source: B'tselem

wall will separate around 40,000 Jerusalemite Palestinians from the city and its services, in addition to keeping in 60–90,000 Palestinian-Jerusalemites presently living in the areas surrounding Jerusalem (Ar-Ram, Beer Nabala, Al-Ezarieh, and Abu Dis) but isolated from the city. This spatial distortion is aimed at reducing the percentage of the city's Palestinian population in official publications. Last year, Palestinians reached 32 percent of the official city population (within the lines unilaterally determined by Israel as "united Jerusalem," which leave several Palestinian neighborhoods outside the official city). For the first time this approached an "acceptable" 70–30 population ratio in favor of Jews, and caused widespread concern among Israeli policymakers.[9]

For many years Jerusalem was the economic, cultural, and commercial link between the northern and southern Palestinian cities. The checkpoints and the wall force

Palestinians to use alternative roads–mainly winding Wad An-Nar Road, which cannot function as a main road. This has reduced the scope of Jerusalem's influence as a Palestinian metropolis to the point where it no longer serves some surrounding neighborhoods. The segregation and marginalization of East Jerusalem impacts negatively on the economy previously dependent on the city's central place for West Bank Palestinians.

The geopolitical and demographic reality imposed by Israel through the construction of the wall redefines the city. The "known" division of West Jerusalem (the one seized by Israel in 1948) and East Jerusalem (the part occupied in 1967) is no longer evident in reality. Moreover, the annexation border imposed by Israel in 1967 is changing as the wall is forming another border line. It appears like future Israeli "solution" for Jerusalem has been imposed before the beginning of any negotiations between the two nations who claim the city as their capital.

The wall is not simply a tangible obstacle to stop terror attacks on West Jerusalem, as perceived by most Israelis. Rather, it has a psychological, geopolitical, and demographic meaning in addition to the economic and social effects described above. The new generation of Jerusalemites will not be able to meet the "other" who is beyond the wall. This creates demonization, which is used politically to gain power through the politics of distortion, stereotypes, and fear.

Let us illustrate our argument by referring to Abu-Dis, which is located on the eastern outskirts of East Jerusalem, just two kilometers from the old city, between Al-Ezarieh to the north, Sawahrah al Sharquia to the south, and the settlement of Maale Adumim to the east. Abu-Dis has an area of 28,232 dunums. The barrier (here, literally an urban wall) will detach some 6,000 dunums of agricultural land in that area and cost the residents of the community the loss of a considerable share of their income. The case of Abu-Dis, as we will illustrate in the following paragraphs, represents, a clear example of the contradictions created by the erection of the wall in Jerusalems urban context. This is the case mainly because of the urban centrality of Abu-Dis, which has been increased in the 1990s, following its flourishing commercial activities along the main roads. Interestingly enough, some of the masonry, located at the eastern part of Abu-Dis's main road, was used by Israeli residents from the nearby (Jewish) Maale Adumim; these shops specialized in selling building materials and plants. Furthermore, even during the first period of the intifada, when Israel erected checkpoints, these commercial activities were not prevented.

Fig. 2. Al-Quds University in Abu-Dis.

But beyond Abu-Dis's economic centrality, it gained particular political-symbolic importance during the last decade of the twentieth century. All the Palestinian Authority offices dealing with Jerusalem's affairs are located in Abu-Dis. Furthermore, in some of the Israeli-Palestinian negotiations Abu-Dis was considered a potential solution to the symbolic division of Jerusalem between both parties as stated by the Israeli prime minister at the time, Ehud Barak, at a cabinet meeting regarding Abu-Dis:

> We are in the midst of a diplomatic process whose goal is to strengthen Israel and its security. In any future settlement, Jerusalem will remain united as Israel's eternal capital. They [the Palestinians] will be in Abu-Dis and we will be in united Jerusalem. We are committed to moving forward toward a peace agreement that will be 1,000 times better than any alternative.[10]

Fig. 3. Graffiti on Abu-Dis wall.

Another Palestinian urban node that is central for understanding the urban functionality of Abu-Dis is Al-Quds University, which is located at its edge. About 4,000 students study there and thus it is perceived as an important urban landmark within the Palestinian community (see Fig. 2). Yet the contribution of the university is not only symbolic; in fact, the local population of Abu-Dis (11,672) almost doubles with the daily influx of Palestinian students and employees who commute. An average of 150–200 ford (taxi) transit services transport the students every day.[11]

In the beginning of October 2003 Israel began constructing the wall from Deir Salah village southeast of Jerusalem toward the north to Abu-Dis and then eastward toward Al-Ezarieh; the length of this fragment is seventeen kilometers. As a first stage, a barrier was erected of concrete blocks to control Palestinian movement. Yet people managed to slip through or climb over these barriers, turning the ten-minute traveling time to Jerusalem into a one-hour journey.

The ongoing violence between Israel and the Palestinians, which includes on one hand violent terror attacks against Israeli civilians in West Jerusalem and on the other militaristic operations by the Israeli army in the territories, has justified the public discourse within Israel as the raison d'étre for the construction of the "security wall." It is important to mention that a few demonstrations against the wall were organized in Abu-Dis by organizations such as Ta'ayush (a joint Jewish-Arab group), the Israeli Committee Against House Demolitions, and Bat Shalom (Women's Peace Organization).

In the case of Abu-Dis, which is located on the edge of Jerusalem, the wall has been built right through the center of the neighborhood, with no consideration for the residents, creating what graffiti on the wall demands: "No to the Ghetto" (see Fig. 3). In the spring of 2004 the four-meter cement partitions were replaced by new eight-meter par-

Haim Yacobi

Fig. 4. Abu-Dis wall.

Fig. 5. Houses in front of Abu-Dis wall.

titions, making sure all access to Jerusalem is completely sealed (see Fig. 4). The majority of inhabitants in the village and the surrounding communities have Israeli identification cards (blue ID) which entitle them free access to Jerusalem. By dividing Abu-Dis into two parts, a breakdown of social structure in addition to other life aspects can be seen.

Some argue that the escalation of violent terror attacks in Israel demands a radical "solution" in the form of the "security wall." However, as we have proposed previously, the logic that stands behind the construction of the wall facilitates the process of "creeping apartheid," which unilaterally produces a new urban geopolitics in Jerusalem. In Abu-Dis this process is very visible in the daily life of its inhabitants; the actual wall separates about thirty-five families whose relatives reside on the other side of it. Ten of these families hold West Bank ID's though their houses are on the west side of the wall, and it is not clear whether they will be granted Jerusalem ID documents or will have to move to the eastern side of the wall, an act that will serve the efforts to control the official demographic balance between Jews and Palestinians. Following this line of argument, let us suggest that, from a planning perspective, other parts of the segregated area in Abu-Dis are designated for future expansion; lack of land will also lead to voluntary migration of residents to other areas, possibly on the outskirts of Jerusalem where they might be at risk of losing residential privileges.

Indeed, the wall produces a tangible segregated zone where hundreds of homes are located in very close proximity to the new structure (see Fig. 5). The wall even results in blocking out the daylight from some of these houses and other houses that have received demolition orders from the Israeli army. The Israeli army advised the home owners to take up the matter with the Israeli Jerusalem Municipality, but the municipality in its turn offered to buy the houses from the Palestinian residents. Naturally, the home owners refused to sell and submitted a petition to the Israeli court to avert the demolition order.[12] A personal testimony of Imm Amin from Abu-Dis illustrates the above:

When the military came, my two sons, the sons of my brother-in-law, and Abu Nabil, who later died, went down to the land where they were working. It was only us . . . there is nothing left of my land—only this minimal piece between us and the wall. The first day, the military kept coming and going to our house. I told them this is my land. In the evening, the Occupation Forces came and tried to take my son and his cousin, but we managed to pull them from the hands of the soldiers. The second day, I tried with my two sons to go to the land, on that day they tried to handcuff my son and stop us from reaching the land, but my son managed to escape. Yet the soldiers hit many of the boys.

I tried to argue with the soldiers and told them, "This is my land—what you are doing is illegal. There are 40 people living in this house and on this land." The Occupation Forces then came and began bulldozing, here they work every day. I had land in the middle of this hill . . . it was destroyed by the bulldozer. We sat on the land for three days, morning to evening, until the soldiers surrounded the whole neighborhood and we were no longer able to reach the lands.[13]

Important also in relation to Abu-Dis housing is the local student market. This emerging market drove up housing prices and had a significant effect on the built environment, with the construction of six to eight floor-apartment buildings to meet demand during the 1990s. However, the construction of the wall turned the situation. Land has depreciated by 60 percent and people are moving out. In January 2001 the local authority reported that 1,000 residents had emigrated from Abu-Dis. Those who were able to moved to Jerusalem even though they now live in much poorer conditions; others plan to move to Bethlehem. Moreover, housing rents decreased by 30 percent and residents expect that far fewer students will enroll at Al-Quds University because of difficulties resulting from the barrier.[14]

Beyond the effect of the wall on Abu-Dis's inhabitants, the urban dysfunctioning of Abu-Dis impinges on the surrounding Palestinian communities, now cut off from their service and commercial centers. At the same time, Palestinian Jerusalemites[15] who used to shop and do business in Abu-Dis hardly come these days. Hence shops in Abu-Dis are closing down and unemployment increases.

To sum up, it is important to highlight the tension between the explicit role of the wall as "solving" security problems and its implicit role as a mechanism of spatial control and as part of the process of "creeping apartheid." Yet, as we have noted elsewhere,[16] this claim is highly misleading. In the long term, urban ethnocracy produces a deeply flawed and unsustainable urban order, spawning further conflicts and instability. The political and economic pressure that the wall causes will contribute to the frustration within the Palestinian community in the city and thus to the escalation of the conflict.

In this article we have followed the way in which the West Banks' contested landscape has been produced. A new political geography, with its roots in the Oslo period, is now being etched into the landscape. The new political space does not resemble any of the two traditional visions for peace: (1) two national states, or (2) one (binational or secular) polity. Instead, we are witnessing the making of political space marked by *neither two states, nor one*, as Palestinians are left in the twilight zone between occupation and ghettoized self-rule.

We have conceptualized this process as creeping apartheid, whereby the vast majority of territory and resources between the Jordan and the sea are controlled by Jews, while the Palestinians who comprise nearly half the population are restricted to several "self-governing" enclaves, covering around 15 percent of the land and lacking real sovereignty, freedom of movement, military power, control over water and air, or contiguous territory. This is a natural (though not inevitable) development of ethnocratic practices, driven by fundamental assumptions regarding the "natural" right of one group to control "its" (self-defined) homeland, while controlling and marginalizing other groups residing in the same political space.

The situation resembles—though does not replicate—the pre-1994 South African apartheid system, because one's "package" of rights and capabilities is determined, first and foremost, by ethnicity (similarly to race in the former example), and because of the near total segregation between Israeli Jews and Palestinian Arabs in residential areas, workplace, politics, and culture. The Palestinian-Arab citizens of Israel form a third main group, sandwiched between the two main nations, enjoying some of the privileges granted to Jews, but being legally, economically, and politically marginalized within Israel. Unlike South Africa, most of the Palestinians do not seek equal integration into a common state but rather ethnonational self-determination. Israel has exploited the Palestinians' drive for an independent state, with partial withdrawal and partial transfer of sovereignty components to the Palestinian Authority. The limited powers and responsibilities awarded to the Palestinian Authority, and its tight control by Israel especially regarding movement and land control, resemble again pre-1994 South Africa.

This reality is only "creeping" because: (1) it is unfolding without any official declaration; (2) Jews continue to move eastward, settling the occupied territories; and (3) the ethnic stratification of civil status is "creeping" westward into Israel proper, with greater segregation and new legal controls imposed on Israel's Palestinian-Arab citizens. The separation barrier accelerates this process, driving Israel to relax its control over small pockets of territory for the benefit of reinforcing its hold on other parts, hence deepening the reality of "separate but unequal." But this new Israeli "solution" may, at best, be only short-lived, as disgruntled Palestinians are likely to mobilize against the new spaces of oppression and destabilize the new spatial order.

Finally, critical thinkers cannot but reflect on the disastrous effects of Palestinian violence against Israeli civilians. The recent success of the East Timorese and Serbian (anti-Milosevic) nonviolent struggles gives a new breath of life to this strategy, which could undoubtedly improve the moral standing of the Palestinian cause, exposing the contradictions of Israel's ethnocracy, while better reaching the substantial peace-oriented Jewish public. But this is a topic for a different debate, until which we may be inspired by the following lines from the young Israeli poet Rammi Sa'ari, who attempts to untie the violent axis knotting ethnicity and land:

We must return all—
All blood to the sores
All territories to the land
And all victims to the wars...
We must return all—
Even the globe, the entire space
We must return to the big time,
Which lies ahead.

Notes

1. "Hakol Diburim" (Israeli Radio, Channel B, April 19, 2004). Notably, the initiative to withdraw from Gaza was rejected by a referendum of Likud members on May 2, 2004, at a ratio of 6:4. Despite this, Sharon declared that the referendum was "advisory" only, relying instead on the government and the Knesset to give it political legitimacy. Hence, the plan continues to be on the agenda of most Jewish parties as a "necessary" spatial readjustment and response to international pressure to move "in the direction of peace."

2. *Yediot Ahronot*, Jewish New Year Eve, September 16, 2004.

3. *Ha'aretz*, October 8, 2004.

4. Notably, the term "ethnocracy" has been used in the literature previously but never developed into a model or a theoretical concept. For details, see Oren Yiftachel, "Ethnocracy and Its Discontents: Minority Protest in Israel," in *Critical Inquiry* 26, Summer 2000: 725–756.

5. The first act of mass violence was committed by a Jew, who killed twenty-nine Palestinians in a Hebron mosque in February 1994; this was followed by dozens of terrorist attacks on Israeli civilians, killing over 150 civilians during the 1994–1996 period.

6. For further discussion on the concept of urban ethnocracy, see Oren Yiftachel and Haim Yacobi, "Urban Ethnocracy: Ethnicization and the Production of Space in an Israeli Mixed City," in *Environment and Planning D: Society and Space* 21(6), 2004: 673–693.

7. Oren Yiftachel and Haim Yacobi, "A Shared City of Peace," in *The Next Jerusalem*, ed. Michael Sorkin, 202–215 (New York: Monacelli Press, 2002).

8. Oren Yiftachel and Haim Yacobi, "Planning a Bi-National Capital: Should Jerusalem Remain United?," in *Geoforum* 33, 2002: 137–145.

9. IPCC report, 2004.

10. Jerusalem, http://www.mfa.gov.il/mfa/mfaarchive/2000 (accessed May 15 2000).

11. UNRWA report, www.un.org/unrwa/emergency/barrier/profiles/abu_dis.pdf (accessed March 2003).

12. www.poica.org/casestudies/Abu%20Dis%2031-01-04/.

13. Personal testimony, PENGON/Anti-Apartheid Wall Campaign, www.stopthewall.org/communityvoices/318.html (accessed February 4, 2004).

14. UNRWA report, www.un.org/unrwa/emergency/barrier/profiles/abu_dis.pdf (accessed March 2003).

15. In the past, Abu-Dis local shops depended on Jerusalem clients for up to 60 percent of their monthly income.

16. Yiftachel and Yacobi, "Planning a Bi-National Capital: Should Jerusalem Remain United?"-

Spacio-cide and Bio-Politics:
The Israeli Colonial Project from 1947 to the Wall
Sari Hanafi

Dafna Kaplan

In keeping with the Zionist myth of *a land without people for a people without land,*[1] the policy of successive Israeli governments has been to appropriate land while ignoring the people on it.[2] The founding myth has been perpetuated, and, in its more modern form, can be seen in the policy of acquiring the most land with the least people (where "people," of course, refers to the Palestinians).[3] The resulting institutionalized invisibility of the Palestinian people both feeds and is being fed by Israel's everyday colonial practices. For example, parts of the Israeli West Bank wall are being constructed specifically to remove the visual presence of Palestinian villages. Moreover, this enforced invisibility sustains an Israeli system interested neither in killing nor in assimilating the Palestinians. Asking the Palestinians of Israel to be loyal to the state of Israel has never brought with it the prize of equal citizenship; while the Israeli narrative sees Jerusalem as its "eternal unified capital," it does not try to assimilate the quarter of a million Palestinians of the city.

The Israeli Left as well as the Right employs what could be called *bio-politics* to instrumentalize Palestinians, using the most sophisticated anthropological tools to divide them into categories,[4] and to place them in a state of exception for the single objective of appropriating more land. This article will argue that the Israeli state of exception should be understood as a permanent structure of juridical-political delocalization and dislocation aimed at transferring the Palestinian population, whether internally or outside of fluid state borders. I will argue that the Israeli colonial project is "spacio-cidal" (as opposed to genocidal) in that it targets land for the purpose of rendering inevitable the "voluntary" transfer of the Palestinian population, primarily by targeting the space in which the Palestinian people live. This becomes possible by deploying bio-politics to categorize Palestinians into different "states of exception" that render them powerless. In such a context, the return of refugees becomes the very point at which the entire colonial aspect of Zionism is undermined.

I. The Spacio-cide of Palestine

Compared to other colonial and ethnic conflicts (Serbia-Bosnia, Rwanda, etc.), the 1948 war did not, relatively speaking, produce a lot of casualties. The notion of "nakba" is based on losing land and on refugeehood rather than on the loss of life. Even after three years of the current intifada the number of victims is still relatively low.[5] Compare the six weeks of madness in Rwanda in which some 800,000 people were killed.

The Israeli colonial project is not genocidal but "spacio-cidal." In every conflict, belligerents define their enemy and shape their mode of action accordingly. In the Palestinian-Israeli conflict, the Israeli target is the place.[6] Different reports produced by the Jerusalem Emergency Committee, a committee set up by Jerusalem-based NGOs after the April 2002 Israeli invasion, show a systematic destruction of public places: all Palestinian ministries bar two and sixty-five NGOs were totally or partially destroyed. What was striking about this was not the confiscations but the vandalism. To steal documents and computer hard drives from the Ministry of Education can be "understood" within the framework of the culturalist and orientalist vision of a military apparatus looking for information to prove that the Palestinian education system "produced incitement and suicide bombers," but why did soldiers also smash the computer screens and destroy the furniture?[7]

During the wars in the former Yugoslavia, the architect Bogdan Bogdanovich coined the term "urbicide" to describe the destruction of cities in the Balkans. Serbian nationalism romanticized rural villages where a single community spirit predominated. The city in this context was a symbol of the multiplicity of communities and cultures, the antithesis of the Serbian ideal. In the Palestinian occupied territories the entire landscape has been targeted. The major tools are the bulldozers that have destroyed streets, houses, private cars, and dunum upon dunum of olive trees. It is a war in an age of literal agoraphobia, the fear of space as developed by Christian Salmon, seeking not the division of territory but its abolition. A trail of devastation stretches as far as the eye can see: a jumble of demolished buildings, leveled hillsides, and flattened forests. This barrage of concentrated damage has been wrought not only by the bombs and tanks of traditional warfare, but by industrious, vigorous destruction that has toppled properties like a violent tax assessor. It is "spacio-cide," not urbicide. It is more holistic, incorporating "socio-cide" (targeting the Palestinian society as a whole and its social ties between its members),[8] "economo-cide" (hindering the mobility of people and goods), and "politi-cide" (destroying PNA institutions and other embodiments of national aspirations).[9] The climax so far was the destruction of a third of the area of the Jenin refugee camp.[10]

The Israeli project during this intifada has as its objective to make a kind of "demographic transfer," or what one Israeli minister has called a "voluntary transfer" of the Palestinian population by transforming the Palestinian topos to atopia, turning territory into mere land. It is by the means of spacio-cide that Israel is preparing such a population transfer, and already, since the beginning of the intifada, around 100,000 Palestinians have left the country, some 3.3 percent of the Palestinian population in the West Bank and Gaza.[11] People have been forced to leave internally as well. In Hebron, for instance, some 5,000 people (850 families) have quit the Old City for neighboring villages because of Jewish settler activity in the Old City and the Israeli army-imposed curfew.

House demolitions form another tactic to effect this transfer. From the beginning of the current intifada in September 2000 until April 30, 2003, a total of 12,737 people have seen their 1,134 homes demolished in Gaza and the West Bank.[12] The number has since risen significantly. This destruction has mainly occurred in Rafah, Jenin, Nablus, Hebron, and Jerusalem, and the new refugees these demolitions have produced are almost all already refugees from 1948 or 1967.[13] The transfer is also effected when people become "denaturalized," as in the case of the 200,000 Palestinians who have found themselves behind Israel's West Bank barrier and are now a part of neither Palestinian nor Israeli space: de facto stateless and *space-less*.

This "spacio-cide" has been rendered easier by the division of the Palestinian Territories into zones A, B, B–, B+, C, H1, H2. In this scheme, Palestinian national infrastructure development became almost totally impossible, not only due to the fragmentation of the space, but also because of the fragmentation of the Palestinian political system. The PNA cannot, for instance, implement water reservoir projects for a set of villages if the pipeline passes through zone C. The road between Bethlehem and Hebron was stopped in 1999 because no Israel authorization was granted to pass through zone C. There was urban development in zones A and B, but these are always surrounded by Israeli zones, hindering any possible urban expansion for either industrial or residential purposes.

In addition, unwilling or unable to pressure Israel, the international community's various agencies have been reluctant to negotiate with the Israeli authority concerning funding projects in Jerusalem or areas in zone C.[14]

The Characteristics of Spacio-cide

There are many characteristics of the Israeli project's spacio-cide. First, spacio-cide is a strategic colonial ideology applied in Palestine/Israel independently of the peace process. Even after the signing of the Oslo Accords, the number of settlers increased fourfold (from 120,000 to 430,000) and the area of settlements doubled. After the signing of the Hebron Protocol in 1997, through the promulgation of six military orders, Israel stopped the work of 416 workers who were restoring Hebron's Old City.[15] The World Zionist Organization (WZO) meanwhile keeps drawing plans to conquer more land. For instance, between 1983 and 1986, the WZO prepared a regional plan suggesting an extension of the network of settlement bypass roads based on four principles: integration between the road network in Israel and in the West Bank; increasing the land allocated to the settlements; connecting the Jewish settlements with each other while separately connecting the "Arab colonies."[16] These plans have been closely followed in the development of the settlement infrastructure since.

The second characteristic of spacio-cide is to deny and ignore the demographic development of the Palestinian community. No studies have been undertaken by Israel to provide reliable demographic information concerning the Palestinian population in the Palestinian Territories. The only solid demographic studies that have been undertaken are by Israeli anthropologists working on the hamoula (tribe) system for surveillance and disciplinary power. In 1981, the Israeli Central Planning Department of the Israeli army commissioned an Israeli consultant, Shamshoni, to prepare a plan of 183 villages. The plans he came up with were not based on any survey but on information collected by the mukhtars (heads of villages).[17]

Third, spacio-cide has been justified not just on political and security grounds but also through the humanities and especially the gender fields. Tamara Neuman examined maternalism as practice and rhetoric for settlers, focusing on women's attempts during the 1970s to expand the settlement of Kiryat Arba, and on the persuasiveness of the issue of motherhood in subsequent representations of these and other contemporary events. The primary expansions into municipal Hebron include incursions into the "Tomb of the Patriarchs," the establishment of a Jewish cemetery, and the takeover of the Dabouya building. In these diverse contexts, Neuman argued, the role of maternalism in settlement expansion depends on a strategic use of the private sphere, which neutralizes the political content of women's actions.[18]

The fourth characteristic of spacio-cide is its three-dimensional nature, as Eyal Weizman elaborated in *The Politics of Verticality*.[19] As Al Najafi and Kastner also observed, the geometry of the occupation can only be apprehended in three dimensions. There are unsettled questions regarding the underground sewage, archaeology, tunnels, water reservoirs, airspace, and so on. These surface complications (it's no longer possible to draw a continuous line that separates Palestinians from Israelis) made clear to the negotiating parties during the Oslo process that a two-dimensional solution is no longer possible. The Israeli proposal was to give the Palestinians limited sovereignty on the land but to retain Israeli sovereignty of the subsoil and the airspace. In other words we have a kind of *sovereignty sandwich*—Israel, Palestine, Israel—across the vertical dimension. Peace technicians (the people who are always drawing new maps for a solution) arrive at completely insane proposals for solving the problem of international boundaries in three dimensions.[20]

The fifth characteristic of spacio-cide is that it shapes not only the place but also the borders. Israeli colonial practices entail a continuous redrawing of borders, thus creating a new type of frontier: portable, porous, and hazy, a border in motion. This border designates two spaces that are completely different: Palestinian space and settlement space. The Israeli occupation determines what will be illuminated and what will be cast into darkness, what will be rendered visible or invisible, accessible or inaccessible.[21]

Finally, the sixth characteristic of spacio-cide is that it aims to transform the Palestinian Territories into mere Bantustans, into noncontiguitious enclaves, or even, in the words of Adi Ophir and Ariella Azoulay,[22] into camps. It is very interesting to note that in August 2004, the IDF presented to the World Bank a plan of new routes, bridges, and tunnels to be constructed to be utilized by the Palestinians, requesting financing for such infrastructure. Thus Israel is no longer committed to providing the Palestinian state with territorial contiguity but merely a "pseudo-state" with transportation contiguity.

We are here looking at spacio-cide at a macro political level, but certainly researchers should in the future illustrate how this planning functions at a micro level—e.g., the interaction of the colonizer and the colonized, or how the social actor resists this planning and transgresses the power structure. On the macro political level, we must now ask which mechanisms were used by Israel to impose its colonial order and how this order interacted with the international community (the donor communities and international organizations). We will also look at how this territorial project shapes the actor and the subject.

The Wall as the Ultimate Form of Spacio-cide

In a noncolonial nation-state, Giorgio Agamben describes the sovereignty of nation-state as an exercise of state of exception. But what one feels while visiting the wall of apartheid around Jerusalem is the extent to which this state of exception can go with its incredibly bizarre and dystopian solutions. The wall is destroying the landscape and Palestinian human life and makes any political solution in terms of either one-state or two-state solutions impossible. It is not only a physical barrier but a psychological, functional, sociocultural, and geopolitical one.[23] Contrary to the stereotype of Israelis who strategize everything, we see how much the Israeli military establishment has created problems not only for Palestinian society but also for Israeli society without a vision of solving the conflict—what is called in French *fuite en avant*. Even if the wall is presented as a security solution, it hides the development of a settler society, which has the image of the certain semi-American bourgeois dream of "secure" gated communities. In fact, the wall uses identical technologies.

II. Colonial Bio-Power, Bare Life, and State of Exception

How does spacio-cide become possible in the Palestinian Occupied Territories? I argue here that there are new forms of sovereignty in the colonial governance that can be apprehended, from one side, at the point where bio-politics and "bare life" meet, and from the other, as extensive use of the state of exception. The sovereign power according to Agamben routinely distinguishes between those who are to be admitted to "political life" and those who are to be excluded as the mute bearers of "bare life."[24] It is a process of categorizing people and bodies in order to manage, control, and watch them and of reducing them to a "bare life"—the body's mere "vegetative" being—separated from the particular qualities, the social, political, and historical attributes that constitute individual subjectivity. This means that we should identify mechanisms by which the state is able to insert itself into citizen-colonized bodies as a measure of sovereign power, enacting specific forms of violence by the rule of the exception through which sovereign power is defined, turning all life and all political battles into battles, again, over bare life. These new forms of sovereignty are apparent in the way colonial power manages bodies according to colonial and humanitarian categories.

Developing an exploration of bio-power begun by Michel Foucault, Giorgio Agamben shows how sovereignty carries with it a "power over life" by the rule of the exception, being both above the law as its constituting force and also the safeguard of the law in its deployment.[25] There are two models of power for Agamben: a juridical one focused on the problem of the legitimacy of Western power (the problem of sovereignty), and a nonjuridical model centered on the problem of the effectiveness of Western power. These two models meet in the dimension of exception. The sovereign, according to the German philosopher Carl Schmit, is the one who may proclaim the state of exception. He is not characterized by the order that he institutes through the constitution but by the suspension of this order. This temporary suspension becomes a new and stable spatial arrangement inhabited by that naked life that increasingly cannot be inscribed into the order. The sovereign has the right to suspend the validity of law, a right that of course is not inscribed in the constitution.[26]

Foucault contested the traditional approach to the problem of power, which was exclusively based on juridical models ("What legitimizes power?") or institutional models ("What is the state?"). He stressed the passage from the "territorial state" to a "state of its population" and the resulting increase in importance of the nation's health and biological life as a problem of sovereign power.[27] This growing inclusion of man's natural life in the mechanisms and calculations of power becomes for the first time in history the possibility that power protects the life and authorizes holocaust.[28] In this view of sovereignty, populations are purely objective matter to be administered, rather than potential subjects of historical or social action. This does not mean the subject cannot emerge and resist this sovereignty, but that sovereignty attempts to reduce the subjective trajectories of individuals to bodies.[29] Such indistinct, displaced, localized, and colonialized bodies come to be classified and defined as refugees, the stateless, inhabitants of zones A, B, B−, B+, C, H1, H2 (Oslo categories), inhabitants of zones in front of Israel's West Bank wall, or behind it, potential terrorists (categories post–September 11), etc. Populations are thus assigned different statuses as legal subjects; individual lives are suspended in an ontological no-man's-land. The objective of this classification is primarily to exclude[30] and render possible the spacio-cidal project.

The political project of the Palestinian people (or the *political people*, as Gérard Bras has it) is thus transformed as differently categorized populations become antagonists pursuing their own particular interests vis-à-vis the conflict and its potential resolution: it is in the interest of the Palestinian population of Jerusalem to stay outside the Palestinian national project as Israel transforms it into a coalition of Bantustans; the geographical fragmentation of the West Bank and Gaza Strip creates two distinct entities with two different populations animated by their own stereotypes and power struggles. This process became possible as the exercise of the sovereign power (as actuality but also as potentiality) not only creates zones of indistinction between the inside and outside (of the nation, town, or the home), but also penetrates the whole political/social field, transforming the entire social space into a dislocated bio-political space in which modern political categories (e.g., Islamist/nationalist, Right/Left, private/public, absolutist/democratic) enter into a postpolitical zone of indistinction and dissolution.[31]

But sovereignty does not work merely according to the logic of one-way exclusion. Palestinians are denied recourse to the law but remain subject to it. Their lives are thus strictly regulated and restricted by Israeli laws and military orders which apply even to the private sphere: marriage, for instance, is subject to many restrictive laws. Palestinians from Israel can no longer marry their counterparts in the West Bank and Gaza Strip since an Israeli High Court ruling legalizing a 2003 government order not to allow the family reunification of such couples. The case of the Palestinians of Jerusalem is the archetype of the game of exclusion/inclusion. They are included (by the Israeli act of annexing and proclaiming a unified Jerusalem) while being excluded (they receive few services; there is no master plan for construction; the city is effectively segregated). They are excluded from having citizenship while being included as Jerusalem ID holders.

The international community's inability to see Israel as a constitutional colonial state comes from the fact that its practice regulating the "white" majority living in a "normal" zone (the Jewish population inside the green line) overshadows its practices for the minority living in the state of exception: the Palestinians of Israel; the Palestinians of Jerusalem; the Palestinians of the different zones of the occupied territories; the refugees inside the camps and outside.

With these categorizations, which correspond to different regimes of exception, Israel is able to restrict residential construction in East Jerusalem and then "legally" destroy housing built without permits.[32] And, with the same state of exception, residential construction for the Palestinians of the different zones in the occupied territories is constrained.

Military Order 418, "Order for the Planning of Towns, Villages and Buildings (Judea and Samaria)," outlines the requirements to obtain construction permits. One of the last articles (no. 7), called "Special Powers," gives the High Planning Council the power to "amend, cancel or suspend for a specified period the validity of any plan or permit; to assume the powers allocated to any of the committees mentioned in articles 2 and 5; to grant any permit which any of the committees mentioned in articles 2 and 5 are empowered to grant, or amend or cancel a permit; to dispense with the need for any permit which the Law may require."[33] In other words, the sovereign can use these exceptions to cancel the very order that was promulgated to regulate the construction permit.

This is a regime of exception that renders conceivable the idea according to which passage to action is possible in certain "legal" circumstances to the extent that one can even be killed without the mediation of the courts or judges. In this way we can say that the Palestinian is a *homo sacer*: one who may be killed without due process and without the killer being punished.[34] The very frequent extrajudicial killings committed by Israel[35] are possible since Israel constitutes and exercises its sovereignty in a manner in which it is permitted to kill without committing homicide or without celebrating a sacrifice. This is killing that is neither capital punishment nor sacrifice but simply the actualization of a "capacity to be killed" inherent in the condition of the colonized people—i.e., the Palestinians.

The international community, with its silence and/or timid protestations, by default encourages Israel to continue in this direction.[36] During an invasion of a Palestinian town, the Israeli occupation forces declare it a military zone prohibited to foreigners and journalists. In the regime of exception, it is important to keep the exception invisible and to hinder the media from witnessing it. For that reason, at one time or another almost all Palestinian cities and especially refugee camps have been transformed into military zones.

The logic of bio-power affects not only the colonized but also the colonizer itself: there is much differentiation between Jews. In the 1980s, the "impure" blood of the Falash Jews (of Ethiopian origin) was designated as nontransmissible to other Jews; Mizrahis (Oriental Jews) were deprived of avenues to express their oriental culture, etc. Oren Yiftachel has described these "ethnocratic" politics and the emergence of the ethno-class stratification and polarization as a system of "creeping apartheid." According to him, a systematically stratified citizenship has developed from the combination of "Judaization policies and religious-legal control. Several types of citizenship have emerged, differentiated by the combination of legal and informal rights and capabilities. Each category, especially among religious groups, is also divided internally on gender lines, with men enjoying a superior position. The groups include: (1) 'mainstream' Jewish citizens, (2) ultra-Orthodox Jews, (3) 'pseudo-Jews' (mainly Russian immigrants recognized as Jews under the Israeli law of return, but not recognized as such by the religious establishment), (4) Druze, (5) Palestinians holding Israeli citizenship, (6) Bedouins, (7) East Jerusalem and Golan Arabs, (8) Palestinians in the rest of the West Bank and Gaza, and (9) immigrant labor."[37]

In addition, the regime establishes a certain presentation of the conflict and obstructs any alternative versions. Witness the unprecedented symbolic and physical violence directed at anticolonialist Israelis; witness the repression of the Arab-Israeli group (Tayoush); the imprisonment of refuseniks; and the serious harassment of Israeli academics that question the orthodoxy (such as Ilan Pappé).

The states of exception and suspension are activated geographically. In the Occupied Territories, this juridical state is triggered especially in disaster areas like Nablus or in the refugee camps as a heterotopic place disconnected from the local environment. Suspension is the rule of the game. Israel and the United States have insisted, since the second year of this intifada, on a cease-fire rather than an end to occupation; and negotiations have been security-related rather than political. This exception is established by the colonial in the name of "security," "planning against the terrorism," "emergency," and "humanitarian crises."

However, Agamben's notion of the state of exception is not only a juridical-legal concept but also a concept that stems from actions on the ground and what is de facto. Thus the possibility arises for the colonial state to act by proclaiming a state of exception to construct the apartheid wall.[38] Nevertheless, Agamben did not take sufficiently into account the extent to which the exception becomes structured and consequently structuring and institutionalizing of life. Sidi Mohammed Barkat[39] observed more structure in colonial and postcolonial systems: the erection of a body of exception (corps d'exception) for the colonized. Drawing from the French colonial experience in Algeria, Barkat noted an essential fact: the submission, from the beginning of the colonization, of the entire colonized civil population to a legal regime of exception, e.g., in the case of Algeria, the construction of a category called "French citizen with personal title" (citizen français à titre personnel) where nationality is not passed down. For Barkat, "the submission of the colonized population to a regime of exception is the origin of the image of this body of exception with which they confound them in the social presentation. The body in which the colonized is reduced is precisely a body of exception, because s/he submits to a parallel penal law different from the common law, unique to the colonized. This law is established in the heart of the democratic system."[40]

"Spacio-cide" becomes possible through three mechanisms. . . . The first mechanism is the bio-politics deployed by Israel; the second, the capacity of this power as sovereign to proclaim the state of exception; and the third, by enforcing a state of suspension. However, the colonized are not passive within these three mechanisms.

They act using violent and nonviolent modes of action, encircling the settlers after being encircled by them, constructing home and society, creating visibility, mobilizing an international movement. The Palestinian "voluntary" transfer cannot pass with an Israeli one. Many indicators show Israeli populations quitting Israel, and the year 2003 had the lowest migration to Israel since 1975.

III. Resisting the Colonial Order: Subjectivity of Colonized

Bio-politics renders possible spacio-cide and spacio-cide creates a *de-territorialized* body—e.g., Palestinians without place in this territory or refugees literally without land. Spacio-cide leaves the body without space. This body then becomes a subject again by exploding him/herself against an enemy that is also classified biologically and ethnically (the concept of Jews as a biological category emerges strongly at the discursive level, guiding different modes of action especially since the beginning of the second Intifada). Spacio-cidal politics is in itself a suicidal politics. The uprooted body it creates is a body ready to explode. The uprooted body is a body without relationship to a territory; it is a body in orbit, a satellite. In the unipolar era of total imperialism under the hegemony of the United States, the body becomes an uncontrollable and unsupervised object that will exercise its revenge. These satellites are the objects to control but are hard to control, and the result is a *Ground Zero*, whether produced by individual terrorists (the World Trade Center) or by state terrorism (the Ground Zero at the Jenin refugee camp).

But violence is not the only form of resistance. To counter the Israeli spacio-cidal project, Palestinians attach particular importance to transgressing the regime of exception by constructing their habitat without permit even if there is always the risk of demolition. A survey I conducted about the investment of the Palestinian diaspora in the Occupied Territories shows clearly a heavy investment in construction.[41]

The bio-politics deployed and the regime of exception that the sovereign proclaims are reinforced in the case of the Israeli and Palestinian actors because of the chain of victimization. In a mirror of interactions and projections, Israelis look at themselves as the exceptional victims, an exceptionality which stems from the exceptionality of the Holocaust. The Palestinians also perceive themselves as the ultimate victims (the last colonized and the more numerous refugees in a very long protracted situation) and they construct this exceptionality starting with the Nakba. In the same

vein, as the Israeli "spacio-cide" is informed by the Zionist myth of land without people for people without land, the Palestinian refugees have created a dream of a land
without people for refugees without land. The Palestinian refugees in the West Bank
and Gaza Strip as well as in the diaspora have greater attachment to the land of
Palestine than to the people of Palestine. In interviews, I find refugees insist on talking about property, the land, the Mediterranean Sea, Al-Aqsa Mosque, Deir Bor'om
Church, etc., and avoid the question of how they would live and with whom. I am not
suggesting here the impossibility of the cooperation between Palestinian returnees
and their Jewish neighbors but the necessity of thinking of the return not only in
terms of geography but also in terms of society.

Notes

1.   The "land without people" statement was used occasionally by early Zionists to refer to the fact that the Arab residents of Turkish-ruled Palestine did not consider themselves to be a "people" or "nation" separate from the Arabs of surrounding countries; in those days, the Arab residents of Palestine usually referred to themselves as "Southern Syrians." The term was actually coined by a British Christian, Lord Shaftesbury, in 1853; the first time it was used in print by a Zionist was in 1901. For more details about this term, see Adam M. Garfinkle, *On the Origin, Meaning, Use and Abuse of a Phrase* (Middle Eastern Studies: October, 1991).

2.   According to Julie Peteet, citing Meron Benvenisti, the Arab communities were "white patches—terra incognita" in the mental map of Jews and goes on to acknowledge that the settlers were aware of the Arab presence but that it "had no place in the Jew's perception of the homeland's landscape. They were just a formless, random collection . . . viewed through an impenetrable glass wall" and had meaning only "as the objects of their perceptions and political concerns, but not as subjects in their own right." See Julie Peteet, *Landscape of Hope and Despair: Place and Identity in Palestinian Refugee Camps* (Philadelphia: University of Pennsylvania Press, forthcoming).

3.   For a recent espousal of this policy, see the November 14, 2003, *Haaretz* interview with Israeli deputy prime minister Ehud Olmert entitled "Maximum Jews, Minimum Palestinians."

4.   For more about the role of Israeli anthropologists in categorizing people, see the thesis of Cedric Parizot, *Le mois de la bin-evenue: réappropriations des mécanismes électoraux et réajustements de rapports de pouvoir chez les Bédouins du Néguev* (EHESS, Paris: Thèse de Doctorat nouveau régime, 21 décembre, 2001).

5.   The number of victims in these three years is 2,785 deaths and more than 41,000 injured on the Palestinian side and 909 deaths and 6,077 injured on the Israeli side. Statistics indicate casualty rates from September 2000 to January 11, 2004. For Palestinian figures, see www.palestinemonitor.org, and for Israeli numbers, see www.idf.il/daily_statistics/english/1.doc.

6.   Israel used what Amira Hass called weapons of light construction, which do not make a lot of noise, like killing people, at least for the Western media. See Amira Hass, "Weapons of Light Construction," *Ha'aretz*, January 28, 2003.

7.   See Rema Hammami, Elisabeth Tylors, and Sari Hanafi, "Destruction of Palestinian Institutions," *Preliminary Report*, April 13, 2002, and Sari Hanafi, "Report on the Destruction to Palestinian Institutions in Nablus and Other Cities (Except Ramallah), Caused by IDF Forces between March 29 and April 21", 2002.

8.   Socio-cide, which is developed by the Palestinian political scientist Saleh Abdel Jawad, is a concept that denotes policies used by one political entity for the total destruction of another, not only as a political national entity, but also as a society in all of its economic, social, and cultural dimensions. Its final objective is the complete replacement of one society by another. Israeli policy in Palestine can be usefully understood as an example of socio-cide. See Saleh Abdel Jawad, "Sociocide: The Zionist Scheme for the Destruction of the Palestinian Society," printed in 3 parts in *Palestine Report of Jerusalem Media Center*, October 1997, and Saleh Abdel Jawad, *Genese et Evolution d'un Movement de Liberation National: Le Fath*, Doctoral Dissertation in Political Science (University of Paris: X–Nanterre, 1986).

9.   For instance, the destruction of the port in Gaza as a symbol of autonomy, or the canceling of the Palestinian international phone code (970), etc. See also Baruch Kimmerling's book *Politicide*, in which he claims that the primary goal of the Israeli government is the destruction of the PNA in particular and any Palestinian polity in general. Baruch Kimmerling, *Politicide: Ariel Sharon's War Against the Palestinians* (London: Verso Press, 2003).

10.   The invasion of this camp resulted in the destruction of 1,846 habitats, from which 680 were completely destroyed and 1,166 partially.

11. Sari Hanafi, "The Impact of Social Capital on the Eventual Repatriation Process of Refugees. Study of Economic and Social Transnational Kinship Networks in Palestine/Israel," in *The Predicaments of Palestinians and Jews: The Meanings of Catastrophe, Historical Knowledge, and the Return of Exiles*, ed. Ian Lutsic and Ann Lesch (Philadelphia: University Press of Pennsylvania, forthcoming).

12. This is according to a May 13, 2003, United Nations Relief and Works Agency (UNRWA) report. Often, the Israel Military Forces Spokesman's Office reports why a house was demolished: it was the family of an arrested terrorist, a wanted terrorist, a dead terrorist, the house was used to shoot at soldiers, the neighborhood sheltered armed men or tunnels, the house was built without a permit. But in many cases there are no explanations.

13. For more details about the destruction, we can note that "during the first 15 months of the intifada physical damage amounted to US $305 million. During the month-long invasion in March-April, the Israeli army destroyed and looted US $361 million worth of property. Since the beginning of the intifada until February 2002, shelling and demolitions destroyed 720 homes completely and damaged 11,553; 73,600 people, 30 mosques, 12 churches, 134 water wells; cemeteries were affected; 34,606 olive and fruit trees were uprooted; 1,162.4 dunums of land confiscated, 14,339 dunums of land bulldozed or burned. During the March-April invasion, 881 homes were destroyed, 2,883 houses in refugee camps were damaged affecting 22,500 people. In the Gaza Strip, more than 601 houses were completely demolished and approx. 16,000 dunums of land, mostly agricultural, was razed by the Israeli army." See http://www.palestinemonitor.org.

14. Sari Hanafi and Linda Tabar, "NGOs, Elite Formation and the Second Intifada," in *Between the Line* vol. II, 18 (Jerusalem: October 2002).

15. Anita Vitullo, "People Tied to Place: Strengthening Cultural Identity in Hebron's Old City," *Journal of Palestine Studies* XXXIII, 1, fall 2003, 68–83.

16. Meron Benvenisti, *The West Bank Data Project—A Survey of Israel's Policies* (Washington, DC: American Entreprise Institute for Public Policy Research, 1984).

17. Anthony Coon, *Town Planning Under Military Occupation: An Examination of the Law and Practice of Town Planning in the Occupied West Bank* (Hants: Darmouth, 1991), 94. In 2003, Daniel Seidmann, one of the Israeli lawyers who works with the Palestinian population to stop the separation wall, noticed that the military officers who defined the itinerary of the wall use maps for the Jerusalem area dating from 1967.

18. Tamara Neuman, "Maternal 'Anti-politics' in the Formation of Hebron's Jewish Enclave," *Journal of Palestine Studies* 33(2), Winter 2004 (Berkeley: University of California Press) pp. 1–20.

19. Eyal Weizman, *The Politics of Verticality*, 2000, www.opendemocracy.net

20. Sina Najafi and Jeffrey Kastner, "The Wall and the Eye," *Cabinet magazine online*, issue 9, Winter 2002/03.

21. Christian Salmon, "The Bulldozer War," *Le Monde Diplomatique*, May, 2002.

22. Communication in conference, "Political of humanitarism," Van Leer Institute (March 2004).

23. Rassem Khamaisi, "From Centrality to Fringe: Jerusalem/Al-Quds Planning and Development Space between Two Walls," paper for *Cities in Collision* (Jerusalem: Van Leer Institute, November 2004).

24. Derek Gregory, "A Whole Geography Remains to be Written. The Colonial Present and Space of Political Violence," paper for *Cities in Collision* (Jerusalem: Van Leer Institute, November 2004).

25. Agamben recognizes this as a position of danger when, under modern conditions, ideas of the sacred are entwined with sovereign power, when the sacred is shattered into all aspects of bare biological life, making life itself the sacred terrain for all forms of governance, including the right to kill or to make.

26. Gerard Bras, lecture at Shaml Center, Ramallah, May 2003.

27.　Michel Foucault, *Dits et Écrits, tome II* (Paris: Gallimard, 1994).

28.　Giorgio Agamben, *Homo Sacer: Sovereign Power and Bare Life* (Stanford: Stanford University Press, 1998).

29.　Mariella Pandolfi, "Moral Entrepreneurs, Souverainetés Mouvantes et Barbelé: Le Bio-politique Dans les Balkans Post-communistes," Anthropologie et Sociétés numéro spécial, 2002.

30.　As Giorgio Agamben noted, bio-politics is the original exclusionary function of Western politics.

31.　Agamben, *Homo Sacer: Sovereign Power and Bare Life,* 4.

32.　See the analysis of Sylvaine Bulle in this respect.

33.　Anthony Coon, *Town Planning Under Military Occupation: An Examination of the Law and Practice of Town Planning in the Occupied West Bank* (Hants: Darmouth, 1991), 280.

34.　Agamben, *Homo Sacer: Sovereign Power and Bare Life*

35.　According to human rights organizations, there were 297 extrajudicial killings; 149 of those were bystanders or "unintended" victims, killed as they were with the victim; 374 were children; and 25 were women. B'tselem report, "Illusions of restraint: Human Rights Violations during the Events in the Occupied Territories 29th September–2nd," December 2000.

36.　Communication by Adi Ophir at the MADA conference in Nazareth, 2003.

37.　Oren Yiftachel, "The Shrinking Space of Citizenship: Ethnocratic Politics in Israel," *Middle East Report*, no. 223, Summer 2002.

38.　Personal communication with May Jayiusi.

39.　Sidi Mohammed Barkat, "Le corps d'exception et la citoyenneté intransmissible dans l'Algérie coloniale" papier présenté au Collège international de philosophie, September-October 2002.

40.　Barkat developed his ideas on the body of exception. He wrote: "On ne saurait penser la condition des colonisés sans la référence à l'image du corps d'exception. Un corps représenté ainsi non pas simplement comme une réalité objective sur laquelle porteraient les coups de la répression coloniale, mais bien comme ce corps imaginé et institué par l'Etat et qui porte en lui, comme sa condition spéciale d'existence au sein de la nation, le principe qui régit la domination coloniale, c'est-à-dire le principe de subversion du rapport d'égalité au cœur des agencements et du dispositif démocratiques eux-mêmes. Ce principe qui colle donc à la peau du colonisé est ce que l'on pourrait appeler le principe d'arbitraire, le principe indiquant que le corps en question est susceptible d'être réprimé et brutalisé, sans possibilité sérieuse de recours légal. Ainsi, l'affaire ne consiste pas seulement en une classification, en un rangement des composantes de la société. Elle suppose l'inscription de l'exception à même le corps du colonisé, de sorte que ce corps fonctionne dans le système institutionnel comme un symbole, le symbole de la division inégalitaire de la société." In Sidi Mohammed Barkat, "Le corps d'exception et la citoyenneté intransmissible dans l'Algérie coloniale," papier présenté au Collège international de philosophie. See also Sidi Mohammed Barkat's paper "Le 17 octobre 1961 ou la haine de la vie," *Revue Drôle d'époque*, printemps, 1999, 27–36.

41.　To gain a foothold in Palestine, some of the Palestinians abroad buy or build an apartment or a house to be used for vacationing. Others build for the family remaining in Palestine. The PCBS carried out an "Existing Building Survey" and a study of "Expenditure and Consumption Levels," estimating the individual transfers from the diaspora to private construction in Palestine to be approximately US $169.5 million in 1996 and US $197.1 million in 1997. See Sari Hanafi, "Contribution de la diaspora palestinienne à l'économie des Territoires: investissement et philanthropie," *Maghreb-Machrek*, no. 161, Novembre 1998.

How to Really Tear Down the Wall Between Blue and Red

Slavoj Zizek

Miki Kratsman

The enigmatic spectacle of a large-scale collective suicide is always fascinating—
recall hundreds of Jim Jones's cult followers who obediently took poison in their
Guyana camp. At the level of economic life, the same thing is going on today in
Kansas. Thomas Frank[1] aptly described the paradox of today's populist conservatism
in the United States whose basic focus is the gap between economic interests and
"moral" questions. That is to say, the economic class opposition (poor farmers and
blue-collar workers versus lawyers, bankers, and large companies) is transposed/coded
into the opposition of honest, hardworking, Christian, true Americans versus the deca-
dent liberals who drink latte and drive foreign cars, advocate abortion and homosex-
uality, mock patriotic sacrifice and the simple "provincial" way of life, etc. The enemy
is thus perceived as the "liberal" who, through federal and state interventions (from
school busing to ordering the teaching of the Darwinian evolution and perverse sexual

practices), wants to undermine the authentic American way of life. The main economic interest is therefore to get rid of the strong state that taxes the hardworking population to finance its regulatory interventions; the minimal economic program is thus "fewer taxes, fewer regulations." From the standard perspective of enlightened rational pursuit of self-interest, the inconsistency of this ideological stance is obvious: the populist conservatives are literally *voting themselves into economic ruin*. Less taxation and deregulation means more freedom for the big companies that are driving the impoverished farmers out of business; less state intervention means less federal help to small farmers; and so forth. In the eyes of the U.S. evangelical populists, the state stands for an alien power and, together with UN, is an agent of the Antichrist: it takes away the liberty of the Christian believer, relieving him of the moral responsibility of stewardship, and thus undermines the individualistic morality that makes each of us the architect of our own salvation. How to combine this with the unheard-of explosion of the state apparatuses under Bush? No wonder large corporations are delighted to accept such evangelical attacks on the state, when the state tries to regulate media mergers, to put strictures on energy companies, to strengthen air pollution regulations, to protect wildlife, and limit logging in the national parks. It is the ultimate irony of history that radical individualism serves as the ideological justification of the unconstrained power of what the large majority of individuals experience as a vast anonymous power that, without any democratic public control, regulates their lives.[2]

As to the ideological aspect of their struggle, it is more than obvious that the populists are fighting a war that simply *cannot be won*: if Republicans were effectively to ban abortion, if they were to prohibit the teaching of evolution, if they were to impose federal regulation on Hollywood and mass culture, this would mean not only their immediate ideological defeat, but also a large-scale economic depression in the United States. The outcome is thus a debilitating symbiosis: although the "ruling class" disagrees with the populist moral agenda, it tolerates their "moral war" as a means to keep the lower classes in check—to enable them to articulate their fury without disturbing their economic interests. What this means is that *culture war is class war* in a displaced mode; so much for those who claim that we live in a post-class society.

This, however, makes the enigma only more impenetrable: How is this displacement *possible*? "Stupidity" and "ideological manipulation" are not the answer; it is clearly not enough to say that the primitive lower classes are brainwashed by the ideological apparatuses so that they are not able to identify their true interests. If nothing else, one should recall how, decades ago, the same Kansas was the hotbed of progressive populism in the United States—and people certainly have not gotten stupid in recent decades. Neither would a direct "psychoanalytic" explanation do, in the old Wilhelm Reich style (people's libidinal investments compel them to act against their rational interests): it confronts too directly libidinal economy and economy proper, failing to grasp their mediation. It is also not enough to propose the Ernesto Laclau solution: there is no "natural" link between a given socioeconomic position and the ideology attached to it, so that it is meaningless to speak of "deception" and "false consciousness" as if there is a standard of "appropriate" ideological awareness inscribed in the very "objective" socioeconomic situation. Every ideological edifice is the outcome of a hegemonic fight to establish/impose a chain of equivalences, a fight whose outcome is thoroughly contingent, not guaranteed by any external reference like "objective socioeconomic position." In such a general answer, the enigma simply disappears.

The first thing to note here is that it takes two to fight a culture war: culture is also the dominant ideological topic of the "enlightened" liberals whose politics is focused on the fight against sexism, racism, and fundamentalism, and for multicultural tolerance. The key question is thus: Why is "culture" emerging as our central life-world category? With regard to religion, we no longer "really believe," we just follow (some of the) religious rituals and mores as part of respect for the "lifestyle" of the community to which we belong (e.g., nonbelieving Jews obeying kosher rules "out of respect for tradition," etc.). "I do not really believe in it; it is just part of my culture" effectively seems to be the predominant mode of the disavowed/displaced belief characteristic of our times. What is a cultural lifestyle, if not the fact that although we do not believe in Santa Claus, there is a Christmas tree in every house and even in public places every December? Perhaps, then, the "nonfundamentalist" notion of "culture" as distinguished from "real" religion, art, etc., *is* in its very core the name for the field of disowned/impersonal beliefs: "culture" is the name for all those things we practice without really believing in them, without "taking them seriously."

The second thing to note is how, while professing their solidarity with the poor, liberals encode culture war with an opposed class message: more often than not, their fight for multicultural tolerance and women's rights marks the counterposition to the alleged intolerance, fundamentalism, and patriarchal sexism of the "lower classes." The way to unravel this confusion is to focus on the mediating terms whose function is to obfuscate the true lines of division. The way the term "modernization" is used in the recent ideological offensive is exemplary here: first, an abstract opposition is constructed between "modernizers" (those who endorse global capitalism in all its aspects, from economic to cultural) and "traditionalists" (those who resist globalization). Into this latter category of those-who-resist are then thrown all, from the traditional conservatives and populist Right to the "Old Left" (those who continue to advocate the welfare state, trade unions, etc.). This categorization obviously does comprise an aspect of social reality—recall the coalition of church and trade unions which, in Germany in early 2003, prevented the legalization of stores staying open on Sunday. However, it is not enough to say that this "cultural difference" traverses the entire social field, cutting across different strata and classes; it is not enough to say that this opposition can be combined in different ways with other oppositions (so that we can have conservative "traditional values" resistance to global capitalist "modernization," or moral conservatives who fully endorse capitalist globalization); in short, it is not enough to say that this "cultural difference" is one in the series of antagonisms that are operative in today's social processes. The failure of this opposition to function as the key to social totality does not only mean that it should be articulated with other differences. It means that it is "abstract," and the wager of Marxism is that there is one antagonism ("class struggle") that overdetermines all others and that is as such the "concrete universal" of the entire field. The term "overdetermination" is here used in its precise Althusserian sense: it does not mean that class struggle is the ultimate referent and horizon of meaning of all other struggles; it means that class struggle is the structuring principle which allows us to account for the very "inconsistent" plurality of ways in which other antagonisms can be articulated into "chains of equivalences." For example, feminist struggle can be articulated into a chain with progressive strug-gle for emancipation, or it can (and it certainly does) function as an ideological tool of the upper-middle classes to assert their superiority over the "patriarchal and intolerant" lower classes.

The point here is not only that the feminist struggle can be articulated in different ways with the class antagonism, but that class antagonism is doubly inscribed here: it is the specific constellation of the class struggle itself that explains why the feminist struggle was appropriated by upper classes. (The same goes for racism: it is the dynamics of class struggle itself that explains why direct racism is strong among the lowest-class white workers.) Class struggle is here the "concrete universality" in the strict Hegelian sense: in relating to its otherness (other antagonisms), it relates to itself—i.e., it (over)determines the way it relates to other struggles.

The third thing to take note of is the fundamental difference between the feminist/antiracist/antisexist struggle and class struggle: in the first case, the goal is to translate antagonism into difference ("peaceful" coexistence of sexes, religions, ethnic groups), while the goal of the class struggle is precisely the opposite—i.e., to "aggravate" class difference into class antagonism. So what the series race-gender-class obfuscates is the different logic of the political space in the case of class: while the antiracist and antisexist struggles are guided by striving for the full recognition of the other, the class struggle aims at overcoming and subduing, annihilating even, the other. Even if not a direct physical annihilation, class struggle aims at the annihilation of the other's sociopolitical role and function. In other words, while it is logical to say that antiracism wants all races to be allowed to freely assert and deploy their cultural, political, and economic strivings, it is obviously meaningless to say that the aim of the proletarian class struggle is to allow the bourgeoisie to fully assert its identity and strivings. In one case, we have a "horizontal" logic of the recognition of different identities, while in the other case we have the logic of the struggle with an antagonist. The paradox here is that it is the populist fundamentalism which retains this logic of antagonism, while the liberal Left follows the logic of recognition of differences, of "defusing" antagonisms into coexisting differences: in their very form, the conservative-populist grassroots campaigns took over the old leftist-radical stance of the popular mobilization and struggle against upper-class exploitation. Since in the present U.S. two-party system, red has come to designate Republicans and blue Democrats, and since populist fundamentalists, of course, vote Republican, the old anti-Communist slogan "Better dead than red!" now acquires a new ironic meaning—the irony residing in the unexpected continuity of the "red" attitude from the old leftist grassroots mobilization to the new Christian fundamentalist grassroots mobilization.

This unexpected reversal is just one in a long series. In today's United States, the traditional roles of Democrats and Republicans are almost inverted: Republicans spend state money, thus generating a record budget deficit, and they de facto build a strong federal state and pursue a politics of global interventionism; Democrats pursue a tough fiscal politics that, under Clinton, abolished the budget deficit. Even in the touchy sphere of socioeconomic politics, Democrats (as with Blair in the UK) as a rule accomplish the neoliberal agenda of abolishing the welfare state, lowering taxes, privatizing, etc., while Bush proposed a radical measure of legalizing the status of millions of illegal Mexican workers and made prescription drugs more accessible to the retired. The extreme case here is that of the survivalist groups in the western United States: although their ideological message is that of religious racism, their entire mode of organization (small illegal groups fighting the FBI and other federal agencies) makes them an uncanny double of the Black Panthers from the 1960s. According to an old Marxist insight, every rise of Fascism is a sign of a failed revolution. No wonder, then, that Kansas is also the state of John Brown, the key political figure in the history of the United States, the fervently Christian "radical abolitionist" who came closest to introducing a radical emancipatory-egalitarian logic into the U.S. political landscape:

> John Brown considered himself a complete egalitarian. And it was very impor-
> tant for him to practice egalitarianism on every level. African Americans were
> caricatures of people, they were characterized as buffoons and minstrels,
> they were the butt-end of jokes in American society. And even the majority of
> the abolitionists, as antislavery as they were, did not see African Americans as
> equals. The majority of them, and this was something that African Americans
> complained about all the time, were willing to work for the end of slavery in
> the South but they were not willing to work to end discrimination in the North.
> John Brown wasn't like that. For him, practicing egalitarianism was a first step
> toward ending slavery. And African Americans who came in contact with him
> knew this immediately. He made it very clear that he saw no difference, and he
> didn't make this clear by saying it, he made it clear by what he did.[3]

His consequential egalitarianism led him to become engaged in the armed struggle against slavery: in 1859, Brown and twenty-one other men seized the federal armory at Harpers Ferry, hoping to arm slaves and thus create a violent rebellion against the South. However, after thirty-six hours the revolt was suppressed and Brown was taken to jail by a federal force led by none other than Robert E. Lee. After being found guilty of murder, treason, and inciting a slave insurrection, Brown was hanged on December 2, 1859. Even today, long after slavery was abolished, Brown is the dividing figure in American collective memory—this point is made most succinctly by Russell Banks, whose magnificent novel *Cloudsplitter* retells Brown's story:

> The reason white people think he was mad is because he was a white man and he was willing to sacrifice his life in order to liberate black Americans. Black people don't think he's crazy, generally—very few African Americans regard Brown as insane. If you go out onto the street today, whether you are speaking to a schoolkid or an elderly woman or a college professor, if it's an African American person you're talking to about John Brown, they are going start right out with the assumption that he was a hero because he was willing to sacrifice his life—a white man—in order to liberate black Americans. If you speak to a white American, probably the same proportion of them will say he was a madman. And it's for the same reason, because he was a white man who was willing to sacrifice his life to liberate black Americans. The very thing that makes him seem mad to white Americans is what makes him seem heroic to black Americans.[4]

For this reason, those whites who support Brown are all the more precious. Among them, surprisingly, was Henry David Thoreau, the great opponent of violence. Against the standard dismissal of Brown as bloodthirsty, foolish, and insane, Thoreau[5] painted a portrait of a peerless man whose embrace of a cause was unparalleled; he even goes as far as to liken Brown's execution (he states that he regards Brown as dead before his actual death) to Christ's. Thoreau vents at the scores of those who have voiced their displeasure and scorn for John Brown: the same people can't relate to Brown because of their concrete stances and "dead" existences. They are truly not living; only a handful of men have lived.

When talking about the Kansas populists, one should bear in mind that they also celebrate John Brown as their saint.[6] We should thus not only refuse the easy liberal contempt for the populist fundamentalists (or, even worse, the patronizing regret of how "manipulated" they are); we should reject the very terms of the culture war. As to the positive content of most of the debated issues, a radical leftist should of course, support the liberal stance (for abortion, against racism and homophobia, etc.), but one should never forget that it is the populist fundamentalist, not the liberal, who is, in the long term, our ally. In all their anger, they are not radical enough to perceive the link between capitalism and the moral decay they deplore. Recall how Robert Bork's infamous lament about our "slouching toward Gomorrah" ends up in a deadlock typical of ideology:

> The entertainment industry is not forcing depravity on an unwilling American public. The demand for decadence is there. That fact does not excuse those who sell such degraded material any more than the demand for crack excuses the crack dealer. But we must be reminded that the fault is in ourselves, in human nature not constrained by external forces.[7]

In what, exactly, is this demand grounded? Here Bork performs his ideological short-circuit: instead of pointing toward the inherent logic of capitalism itself—which, in order to sustain its expanding reproduction, has to create newer and newer demands—and thus admitting that, in fighting consumerist "decadence," he is fighting a tendency that exists in the very core of capitalism, he directly refers to "human nature," which, left to itself, ends up in wanting depravity and is thus in need of constant control and censorship:

> The idea that men are naturally rational, moral creatures without the need for strong external restraints has been exploded by experience. There is an eager and growing market for depravity, and profitable industries devoted to supplying it.[8]

This, however, throws an unexpected light onto the Cold Warriors' "moral" crusade against Communist regimes: the embarrassing fact is that the Eastern European Communist regimes were overthrown by forces that "represented the three great antagonists of conservatism: the youth culture, the intellectuals of the '60s generation, and the laboring classes that still favored Solidarity over individualism."[9] This feature returns to haunt Bork: at a conference, he "referred, not approvingly, to Michael

Jackson's crotch-clutching performance at the Super Bowl. Another panelist tartly informed me that it was precisely the desire to enjoy such manifestations of American culture that had brought down the Berlin wall. That seems as good an argument as any for putting the wall back up again."[10] Although Bork is aware of the irony of the situation, he obviously misses its deeper aspect.

Recall Jacques Lacan's definition of successful communication: in it, I get back from the other my own message in its inverted—i.e., true—form. Is this not what is happening to today's liberals? Are they not getting back from the conservative populists their own message in its inverted/true form? In other words, are conservative populists not the symptom of tolerant, enlightened liberals? Is the scary and ridiculous Kansas redneck exploding in fury against liberal corruption not the very figure in the guise of which the liberal encounters the truth of his own hypocrisy? We should thus—to refer to the most popular song about Kansas, from *The Wizard of Oz*–definitely reach *over the rainbow*: over the "rainbow coalition" of the single-issue struggles favored by radical liberals, and dare to look for an ally in what often appears as the ultimate enemy of multiculti liberalism.

There is a further irony that Bork is missing in his reference to the Berlin Wall. On September 11, 2001, the twin towers of the World Trade Center were hit. Twelve years earlier, on November 9, 1989, the Berlin Wall fell. November 9 announced the "happy '90s," the Francis Fukuyama dream of the "end of history," the belief that liberal democracy had, in principle, won, that the search was over, that the advent of a global, liberal world community lurked just around the corner, that the obstacles to this ultra-Hollywood happy ending were merely empirical and contingent (local pockets of resistance where the leaders did not yet grasp that their time was over). In contrast to this, 9/11 is the main symbol of the end of the Clintonite happy 1990s, of the forthcoming era in which new walls are emerging everywhere, between Israel and the West Bank, around the European Union, on the U.S.-Mexico border.

The case of Europe is less known but more instructive here. In 2003, an ominous decision of the European Union passed almost unnoticed: the plan to establish an all-European border police force to secure the isolation of the EU's territory and thus to prevent the influx of immigrants. *This* is the truth of globalization: the construction of *new* walls safeguarding the prosperous Europe from the immigrant flood. One is tempted to resuscitate here the old Marxist "humanist" opposition of "relations between things" and "relations between persons": in the much celebrated free circulation opened up by global capitalism, it is "things" (commodities) that freely circulate, while the circulation of "persons" is more and more controlled. This new racism of the developed is in a way much more brutal than the previous one's: its implicit legitimization is neither naturalist (the "natural" superiority of the developed West) nor any longer culturalist (we in the West also want to preserve our cultural identity), but the unabashed economic egotism—the fundamental divide is the one between those included into the sphere of (relative) economic prosperity and those excluded from it. What lies beneath these protective measures is the simple awareness that the present model of late capitalist prosperity *cannot be universalized*—an awareness formulated with a brutal candor more than half a century ago by George Kennan:

> We/the U.S. have 50 percent of the world's wealth but only 6.3 percent of its population. In this situation, our real job in the coming period ... is to maintain this position of disparity. To do so, we have to dispense with all sentimentality ... we should cease thinking about human rights, the raising of living standards and democratisation.[11]

And the sad thing is that, concerning this fundamental awareness, there is a silent pact between capital and (whatever remains of) the working classes: if anything, the working classes are more sensitive to the protection of their relative privileges than the big corporations. This, then, is the truth of the discourse of universal human rights: *the wall separating those covered by the umbrella of human rights and those excluded from its protective cover.* Any reference to universal human rights as an "unfinished project" to be gradually extended to all people is here a vain ideological chimera—and, faced with this prospect, do we in the West have any right to condemn the excluded when they use any means, inclusive of terror, to fight their exclusion?

Miki Kratsman

Notes

1.	See Thomas Frank, *What's the Matter with Kansas? How Conservatives Won the Heart of America* (New York: Metropolitan Books, 2004).

2.	Why is it that conservative evangelicals who, against Darwinism, like to insist on the literal truth of the Bible are never tempted to read literally Christ's "Sell all that you have, and give to the poor" (Mark 10:21)?

3.	Professor of history Margaret Washington interviewed in *American Experience: John Brown's Holy War*, PBS, 2000, www.pbs.org/wgbh/amex/brown/filmmore/reference/interview/washington05.html.

4.	Russell Banks interviewed in *John Brown's Holy War*, www.pbs.org/wgbh/amex/brown/filmmore/reference/interview/banks01.html.

5.	See Henry David Thoreau, *Civil Disobedience and Other Essays* (New York: Dover Publications, 1993).

6.	Some antiabortionists draw a parallel between Brown's fight and their own: Brown acknowledged blacks as fully human. They were people who, for the majority, were less than human and as such denied basic human rights; in the same way, antiabortionists acknowledge as fully human the unborn child.

7.	Robert H. Bork, *Slouching Toward Gomorrah* (New York: Regan Books, 1997), 132.

8.	Ibid., 139.

9.	Quoted from www.prospect.org.

10.	Bork, *Slouching Toward Gomorrah*, 134.

11.	George Kennan in 1948, quoted in John Pilger, *The New Rulers of the World* (London: Verso Books, 2002), 98.

Twenty-three Steps Across the Border and Back
Rebecca Solnit

Rene Peratta

1

In the United States, or at least my part of it, "The Border" means the U.S.-Mexican border, not the other one we share with Canada. That's one semantic oddity located somewhere in the nebulous borderlands, like monotheism, monomarginality. God, not the gods; the Border, not the borders.

2

In the 1984 indy punk-rock movie *Repo Man*, set in Southern California, there's a character driving around in a Chevy Malibu with a trunkful of aliens who are apparently radioactive. I failed to understand much of the movie because I thought the trunk contained undocumented immigrants—Mexicans or Central Americans who maybe picked up some radiation at a border military base, like Yuma Proving Grounds—not nonhumans from outer space. After all, trunks of cars are one of the places coyotes—smugglers—hide people attempting to cross the border illegally. It's a telling linguistic overlap, this migration of meaning back and forth from outer space and outside national boundaries, an other-ization of neighbors and people who aren't even always from there but from here, when here was there. The border, the aliens, the makings of a theology.

Still, my friend Guillermo, who is from Mexico City but has been here most of his adult life, has a penchant for collecting glow-in-the-dark outer-space trinkets, of which there is a copious supply. A few of them conflate the two kinds of aliens: bug-eyed monsters in sombreros. Was there ever a fifties horror movie in which the flying saucer disgorged mariachi bands? You'd think so.

3

That is the unspeakable background to this premise that the border is some kind of great natural division and brown people are some kind of outer-space creatures who belong on the other side of it. That, and the war Mexico never forgot and that the United States can never quite remember the 1846–1848 war that Thoreau went to jail to oppose but that U.S. history books hardly mention, the one whereby Mexico was cut in half and the United States was increased by a third to become its current sea-to-shining-sea self, the war some Latinos reference when they say, "We didn't cross the border, the border crossed us." The border is also a migrant. Texas had already been taken, but New Mexico, southern Colorado, Arizona, Utah, Nevada, and California were added to the spoils pile of Yankee expansion. Its arbitrariness is everywhere—in the fact that there are two Californias, Alta and Baja; in tribes such as the Tohono O'odham, whose homeland (like that of the Mohawks on the other border) is on both sides. The border is a strictly western phenomenon, going from the Gulf of Mexico to the Pacific, and everywhere north of it the influence of Mexico is evident, down to the outfits cowboys wear and the food we eat and the Spanish place-names everywhere.

4

In California, the Mexican-American War began as the Bear Flag Revolt on June 16, 1846, when some trigger-happy Yankees illegally started a little shooting in the beautiful Spanish-style plaza in Sonoma, from which General Mariano Vallejo governed the northern half of Alta California. These Yankees wouldn't know for months that Polk had declared war on Mexico much farther southeast, but the United States's anxiety to grab Mexican territory was so powerful the two wars would soon become two fronts of one war. Their acts carried all the moral authority of a convenience store holdup, and the bear on the flag they raised was so poorly drawn Californios thought they were flying an image of a pig. (It became the California state flag, but the California grizzly it represented was hunted into extinction over the next several decades.) Lieutenant John C. Frémont of the U.S. Army came to their aid, various North Bay Californios were killed or taken hostage, and the squabble joined the war being fought in other scattered locales across the west.

The war begun in Texas in 1846 was a more serious business, and a third front opened up when the U.S. Army landed in Veracruz and invaded Mexico City. More soldiers died of disease than of combat in this war, and, like the Gulf War, it was largely won by the United States's superior technology. Mexicans still annually commemorate "los niños heroes," the teenage military cadets who fought bravely and mostly died defending their academy, but the U.S. military record in this war is made up more of squabbles, insubordinations, and desertions. The people wading and swimming across the Rio Grande then were U.S. soldiers seeking more civilized conditions than their army camps. The first aggressive border patrol was instituted to stop this leak of U.S. troops to Mexico; Major General Zachary Taylor gave orders to shoot all deserters. Keep those deserters in mind; they will return in the twenty-first century.

5

I went to the sesquicentennial celebration of the Bear Flag Revolt on June 16, 1996. It was during the heyday of Pete Wilson's demonization of Latino immigrants (and by extension of Latinos generally), not long after Proposition 187 attempted to deny basic services—education and health care, including emergency health care—to undocumented immigrants. Now, when terrorists so neatly occupy the bogeyman niche vacated by communists, few remember that many other groups tried out for the role, most particularly immigrants. In fact terrorists—if you ignore Timothy McVeigh—and immigrants share the basic status of "outsider"—or, if you prefer, "alien"—so that antiterrorism rhetoric has continued to focus on the border, particularly on The Border, even though some of the September 11 terrorists came over the Canadian border and none over the other one. Proposition 187 explained away California's sagging economy by blaming it on illegal immigrants, who were siphoning off social services without paying taxes, though actually it was more the other way around: they were failing to collect major social services—unemployment, disability, social security—while working hard, sometimes under the table, sometimes with taxes taken out of wages, which they would never file to recoup. Then, too, the notion that they were stealing jobs never looked very carefully at how many gringos were hoping to break into dishwashing and strawberry-picking careers.

Anyway, the sesquicentennial celebration in Sonoma Plaza was beautifully staged. The parade seemed to consist almost entirely of white people, including adult men in the Davy Crockett outfits of their youth toting rifles. A group of young Latinos protesting the celebration—which was by no means merely a commemoration—arrived in the plaza first, so that it had to be taken all over again, with a certain amount of conflict, or at least anxiety. Governor Wilson, who the great émigré artist Enrique Chagoya once depicted as a cannibal in an Aztec codex, spoke, and the Latino kids shouted and drummed while he did so. "I don't know *what* they're so angry about," an elderly lady clucked to her husband, so I told them. He said to me, at this celebration of the seizure of Mexico's northern half, "Young lady, California was never part of Mexico. You should go to college and study some history."

6

Thus the border, which is not so much a line drawn in the sand of the desert as one drawn in the imagination, is a line across which memory may not travel, empathy may be confiscated, truth held up indefinitely, meaning lost in translation. The West is cast as nature, not culture, which is part of why we are not supposed to have to remember anything that happened here. If the border is natural, it must not have a history, since despite the realm called natural history we consider those two terms to describe exclusionary territories. "Naturalness" is justification in a nation that has long cast itself as nature against European culture, and requires forgetting the displacement and devastation of Native Americans—an easy omission for all the nativist groups opposed to immigrants at least since the Irish began to arrive in quantity after the Great Potato Famine of the 1840s. It may have been their homeland, but it was our Eden; we were Adam and Eve and they were just a trailer for another movie or the cartoon running before the main feature. And the defense of nature has become another semiautomatic weapon in the arsenal of exclusion.

7

Some might consider the fact that fences are unnatural a slight problem here, a little blight on the landscape or at least on the ideology of nature wielded on the border's northern side. I wrote once before, "To put up a fence is to suggest difference when there is none (though there will be), and to draw a border is much the same thing." Paradise means a walled garden, and only when Adam and Eve are expelled from Eden do its walls first appear in the narrative, because they only matter from outside. Adam and Eve are the first refugees, the fig leaves the first canceled passports, paradise the first immigration-restricted country. And, of course, the angel with the flaming sword is a border patrolman, like the ones with their flaming guns and night-vision goggles who kill people in California as part of the stepped-up border-patrol program called Operation Gatekeeper. In the last decade the wall, the guard, and the gate have become increasingly popular devices for maintaining difference, the difference between the garden and the world. They show up at every scale, from the domestic to the national front, and though they are usually seen separately, it makes sense to look at them together. Whatever is inside the wall, past the gate, protected by the guard is imagined as some version of paradise, but only paradise so long as its separateness is protected. Which means that paradise is a violent place.

On the smallest scale, these dividers are nothing more than incongruous little garden ornaments I noticed on a recent visit to the highlands of West Hollywood and then started to notice in affluent zones everywhere. In the more plush parts of Southern California, every house has a garden in front of it, a garden that seems to be a sort of no-man's-land, since nobody ever diverges from the driveway to tread upon it but the gardener. It provides a certain amount of private property between the house and the street, and it proclaims, in lawn and bougainvillea, a certain pastoral attainment and affluence. In the midst of each one is a little medallion on a steel stick promising some security company's "armed response." A flaming sword for every paradise, and an armed response for every garden (or perhaps the medallions are more like fruit of the tree of knowledge of good and evil, as long as we're going to allegoricize). Visually, these medallions are akin to the fire extinguishers, bathroom signs, and so forth, one is not supposed to notice as part of the wall furnishings of museums. Symbolically, they proclaim the same message as the garden, albeit to a different audience: that the goods herein are both coveted and secured. Politically, these gardens seem to be constructed for two distinct audiences: for those who are meant to admire the plants and ignore the medallion, and for those to whom the medallion speaks—the former being a majority audience of friends, neighbors, and those who belong, and the latter being those who do not belong (and seldom show up, making them something of an imaginary audience). To a third audience—to me, anyway—the medallion and the garden cancel each other out: what kind of serenity can a garden promising gunmen provide?

Anti-immigration rhetoric portrays the entire United States as a kind of garden and imagines the border as intrinsic a part of the terrain as mountains, rivers, forests. The border has become, like the flag, a kind of sacred object in the cult of nationhood. Often described as an object or a fact rather than a concept, the border is nothing more than a line on a map drawn by war, only occasionally imposed on the actual landscape. It can be imagined as a kind of blueprint for a largely unbuilt public work of art, like a 3,000-mile Christo *Running Fence* with just a few chunks completed in places like Tijuana/San Diego. It exists largely as a line running through the national imagination now. Sometimes the map is the territory, or at least it fuels the territorial imperative. But since there is no border, armed response is supposed to keep people out of our garden.

8

In fact, putting a fence across nature has been pretty actively destroying it in one respect: Operation Gatekeeper, which stepped up security in urban areas, forced more and more people to cross the border in remote places, and, by defecating, littering, making fires, and otherwise messing around in fragile desert territory, they created unfortunate environmental impacts, as did the government's all-terrain vehicles sent out to hunt them. A lot of immigrants began to die in the desert too, hundreds every year, and the hunts became in part search-and-rescue missions, hydrating and cooling down the undocumented who were dying of heat and dehydration. In Arizona, however, vigilantes began joining the hunt with considerably less empathy than some of the border patrol agents.

In his novella *Heart of Darkness*, Joseph Conrad depicts his Kurtz living with human skulls as ornaments outside the house deep upriver; if the United States is to be pictured as a garden out of which aliens must be kept, imagine it with skulls and skeletons and mummies, not garden gnomes or pink flamingos, as its lawn ornaments, along with those death-threat lawn plaques and angels with flaming swords. A very crowded garden, withal—not crowded with immigrants but with props and weapons to guard the boundaries of empathy and imagination.

9

The fantasy of the nationalist garden wall emerged in 1998 as Amendment A, the Sierra Club ballot measure, which for a while threatened to fracture the organization and even the environmental movement. The measure stated that restricting immigration was key to protecting the domestic environment. It implied that immigrants were to blame for the deterioration of the environment, as though those huddled masses were rushing out to buy Jet Skis and ten-acre Colorado ranchettes, as though sheer numbers alone, rather than habits of consumption and corporate practices, were responsible for the degradation of the U.S. environment. It reeked of American isolationism—the idea that our garden could be preserved no matter what went on outside its walls, though many ecological issues are transnational: migratory birds, drifting pollutants, changing weather—and it implied that we live in a garden and they do not. Amendment A was meant to be a kind of garden medallion to be read by politicians as well as potential intruders. It harkened back to the unattractive origins of one part of the environmental movement, the Save the Redwoods League. Historian Gray Brechin recently unearthed the organization's turn-of-the-century origins in a eugenicist linking of preserving native species with preserving "native"—i.e., white Protestant old immigrant-culture and majority. Saving the environment is usually imagined as being inherently moral and apolitical, but neither condition is necessary: think of the greenness of the Nazis postulating their forests as a nationalist landscape and their mountains as an Aryan zone. Hate and suspicion are not uncommon garden crops.

Amendment A was signed by nature romantics rather than central players in the Sierra Club's environmental work, by the (Canadian) nature writer Farley Mowat, by eco-reactionary Dave Foreman, by neon-sunset-photography superstar Galen Rowell, and opposed by most of the club's past and present leadership. Entertainingly enough, San Francisco's Political Ecology Group demonstrated that Amendment A had been introduced by people who were themselves largely outsiders to the Sierra Club, which is to say that the club itself could be imagined as a kind of garden of shared belief which had been invaded by hostile raiders seeking to transform its nature (and as one of their tactics urged members of anti-immigration and population-control groups to join the club en masse to vote for Amendment A). Fortunately the proposal lost, but it left in its wake a renewed vision of the United States as a garden that could be sequestered from the world. The winning alternate amendment proposed that drawing such lines between nations and people would alienate important allies for fighting the real issues.

10

Having been blamed for every other sin under the sun, immigrants were now to be scapegoated for our environmental problems as well. By the time the club's membership had voted Amendment A down, a lot of participants were embittered and the environmental movement was tarnished in the eyes of many onlookers. The 1990s saw the rise of the environmental justice movement, which addresses environmental racism—i.e., who gets poisoned by dumps and incinerators, among other things—but the mainstream environmental movement is not always so good at the racial politics within its own priorities and assumptions. The very white-collar premise that nature is where you take your recreation belies the possibility that some people toil in nature or its agricultural edges and would rather do something less rugged on the weekend.

Still, this is a long way from the politics of the anti-immigration activists who attempted an openly hostile takeover of the Sierra Club in the spring of 2004, with three candidates for the March board elections looking to form a majority with some of the more dubious current board members and various outside organizations—some clearly racist and white supremacist—encouraging their members to join the club and sway the vote. (That the name of the Sierra Club is half Spanish, a souvenir of when California was Mexico or Spain, recalls a history no one in these debates seems to have examined, or perhaps the exclusionary British term *club* trumps it.) "Without a doubt, the Sierra Club is the subject of a hostile takeover attempt by forces allied with ... a variety of right-wing extremists," said the Southern Poverty Law Center in a warning letter. "By taking advantage of the welcoming grassroots democratic structure of the Sierra Club, they hope to use the credibility of the club as a cover to advance their own extremist views."

The three were Frank Morris, David Pimentel, and Richard Lamm. Former Colorado governor Lamm is a longtime board member of the Federation for American Immigration Reform (FAIR), which receives funding from the pro-eugenics and "race betterment" Pioneer Fund. Lamm, who has apparently spent little time in Switzerland, has said, "America is increasingly becoming, day by day, a bilingual country, yet there is not a bilingual country in the world that lives in peace with itself," and was quoted by the Cato Institute as saying, "[T]he rash of firebombings throughout the Southwest, and the three-month siege of downtown San Diego in 1998, were all led by second-generation Hispanics, the children of immigrants." He spoke in 1984 of the "duty to die" of the elderly and believes in rationing medical care. The garden is the pretty metaphor employed by anti-immigration activists; the more ferociously paranoid imagination of characters like Lamm imagines it instead as a lifeboat with limited supplies, which is why you have to clobber the fingers of those swimmers clinging to the boat.

11

The vision of a homogenous place overrun by disruptive, destructive outsiders is a better picture of the Sierra Club under siege than the United States in relation to immigration. Outside groups such as the National Immigration Alert List encouraged their members to join the club to force it to endorse an issue rejected six years before and so perhaps permanently warp its identity and image; further, most candidates for a seat on the club's board are active longtime members, but the three outsiders who were trying to break in this time seem to have become members specifically to stage the nonprofit equivalent of a hostile corporate takeover. This was underscored by the fact that they filed, then petulantly dropped, a lawsuit against the club, various club personnel, and three other board candidates (including longtime club activist Phil Berry and civil rights activist Morris Dees, who called attention to their links to racist groups). Thirteen past presidents of the club came out in opposition to the coup; eleven of them issued a statement that included these remarks: "These outsiders' desire is to capture the majority of seats so as to move their personal agenda, without regard to the wishes or knowledge of the members and supporters of the Sierra

Club, and to use the funds and other resources of the Club to those ends. . . . We believe that the crisis facing the Club is real and can well be fatal, destroying the vision of John Muir and the work and contributions of hundreds of thousands of volunteer activists who have built this organization." (Of course, John Muir was a racist too—he said some pretty astounding things about Native Americans–but that's another story, and era.)

A lot of leftists have already written off the 112-year-old Sierra Club, and though I've occasionally thought its slogan should be Earth First!'s "No compromise in the defense of Mother Earth" without the "No," it remains what it has been for so many decades: the flagship of the environmental movement dealing with everything from clear-cutting and global warming to endangered species and water pollution. Discrediting it would drain credit and potency away from much of the movement. And it seems that the goal of these anti-immigration activists has little or nothing to do with the protection of the environment. After all, the links between immigration and environmental trouble are sketchy at best.

12

During the 1990s, the border was always talked about as though it was a tangible landform, a divinely ordained difference. I grew up with a clear picture of the Iron Curtain too, since it was spoken of as though it were as coherent an artifact as the Berlin Wall. But the Berlin Wall was made out of concrete, while the Iron Curtain was not made out of metal, despite the vision I'd had of a continental cyclone fence. Like the U.S.-Mexican border, it was a political idea enforced by a variety of structures, technologies, and people with guns.

During the spring of Amendment A, I actually spent several days on the border, or rather in the place where the border is supposed to be: along the lower canyons of the Rio Grande where the left bank is named Texas and the right bank is Chihuahua. The river, which divides nothing at all on its long run through New Mexico, has been an international boundary since the signing of the Treaty of Guadalupe Hidalgo ended the United States's territorial war on Mexico 150 years ago and transferred a million square miles of Mexico to this country. Yet rivers are capricious, and this one has a habit of throwing out oxbows that put some bewildered farmer and his land in a new country. So, in the 1960s, the border was designated as the deepest part of the river during the years of the survey, wherever the river should go afterward. This means that the phantom river of thirty years ago is now the international border—not the most solid object for nationalism to rest upon. After all those years of fiery rhetoric about the border, it was strange to float down the place it was supposed to be and find nothing but water, rock, and prickly pears. The possibility that "the border" didn't exist was a stunning one.

As our raft floated downstream, crossing songbirds and cattle seemed indifferent to the idea that the Chihuahuan desert was really two countries. The slow river along the banks of which all this life clustered and bloomed was not a boundary but an oasis where the toxins from American agriculture and Juarez maquiladoras mixed indiscriminately. Not quite a Berlin Wall, even if you're not a swallow or a cactus wren.

Borders don't exist in nature. I learned that again in northern Canada, up where British Columbia meets the Northwest Territories. I was traveling by raft again, and the ornithologist with us would get up at dawn to identify, band, and free the song-birds that she caught in her mist nets. She liked to point out that a lot of them wintered in the tropics of Central America and so conservation efforts needed to be transna-tional. Canada's remotest wilderness was not a place apart; it was intimately tied to the tropics. Weather, toxins, species all move without regard to borders, which is one of the reasons why environmental politics don't work as nationalist politics.

13

There were, of course, people to enforce the concept of the border and to profit from it: during my ten-day rafting trip I watched as what appeared to be a drug smuggler—a picturesque old man with a heavily laden burro—was confronted by a Mexican army commandante and his machine-gun-carrying soldiers, and met on my last day an armed Immigration and Naturalization officer who was there to patrol a stretch of river that even livestock crossed regularly. Like the front yards of Angelenos, the international border is usually just an expanse with a few threats and armed-response guards scattered along it. But the conceptual line running down the river didn't mark a garden off from the world; the river was instead a different kind of garden, an oasis around which flourished birds and plants that couldn't have survived elsewhere in the arid desert spreading far in all directions. Birds and seeds and air pollution emigrated across the river without passports; contaminants from upriver agriculture, sewage, and industry flowed down it without visas. Amendment A, it seemed to me there, was wishful thinking, a fantasy that spaces could be truly sequestered, could have happy fates independent of the unhappiness all around. This is not to deny that environmental devastation and crime are bad things—they are unquestionably bad. The questions, however, are all about the way they are imagined and addressed.

14

When the Mexican army with their machine guns arrived at Hot Springs Rapids, two of the river guides and several passengers were drinking wine in the hot spring and hooting out lurid speculations about guide anatomy. The commander and his three stolid Mayan-faced soldiers were first seen by someone napping in a tent who did little more than hope it was a bad dream; the second went to tell the trip leader in the springs; and I must have been the third. My primitive Spanish regressed further under the circumstances, but I figured that being female, fully dressed, and impressed with the gravity of the situation made me the best person around to take on the job of soothing diplomatic liaison anyway (besides, the one Spanish speaker in the group was off hunting red-eared slider turtles, unsuccessfully—"el buscar las tortugas," I said, or something to that effect, and my interrogator laughed). We were camped on the Mexican side of the river, of course, on one of the few spots where a road leads all the way to the river, twelve miles down a long canyon from the nearest ranch, and the road was used periodically by people coming to bathe in the springs.

I never ascertained why the Mexican army had arrived—whether we were interrupting their bathing schedule, or whether it had something to do with the old man we'd seen the day before, who, with his heavily laden burro, perfectly fit the bill for a drug smuggler. It seemed unlikely to be a routine patrol, in this remote place bordered by cliffs. I did ascertain that the commander, who seemed to be in a good if unrelenting mood, preferred "la costa–Acapulco y Puerto Vallerta" to "el desierto" and wouldn't mind being transferred soon. I was just trying to put in a good word for the desert—though I myself live in "la costa," as he had seen when he inspected my papers—when the trip leader came along and found out that he didn't want to stay for a drink.

The Canadians were horrifically clueless about where they were, regarding the desert with all its intrinsic dangers (dehydration, flash floods, rattlesnakes, and scorpions) and manufactured ones (drug dealers and other armed desperados, intensely toxic water) as some sort of underequipped version of Club Med. Only an older man who had spent time in Africa comprehended the possibilities of the situation; he and I seemed to be on one trip, the rest of the crew on another one, down a pleasantly meaningless river I couldn't recognize as the borderlands Rio Grande, let alone what it is called from its right bank, the more ominous Rio Bravo.

15

On the last day of my journey down the river, a long parade of goats trotting by the dusty riverbank made me think of Ezekiel Hernandez, who lived and died not far upriver, in Redford, Texas. His story seemed at last to make the ominous ambience of the border real to the people I was traveling with. A high school senior and a U.S. citizen, Hernandez was herding his goats near the river one evening when he was shot in the back by U.S. Marines wearing camouflage and night-vision goggles. They claimed he threatened them with his .22 rifle, which he apparently carried for rattlesnakes (and because he was a West Texan; even the fisherman I saw on the Rio Grande had six-guns on either camo-clad hip). The circumstances, however, make it seem unlikely that he even saw them. Who knows why they shot him, except that he looked like a Mexican, a stranger in the garden? Hernandez's story reads like a pastoral eclogue—not one of Theocritus's cheerful Greek ones, but one of Virgil's sad pastorals, where Arcadia is always under siege and where shepherds are the principal spokesmen for a vision of tranquility in the deterritorialized pastures. Sometimes their songs are of Daphnis, the ideal shepherd who died in the fifth eclogue. The men with arms win the battles, but those with the shepherd's crook win the war of representation, as Cain and Abel demonstrate. What is so peculiar about these new wars of meaning in the American West is that the imagery is so rustic, full of appeals to the beauty of the mountains and the fields. But the dead young goatherds are on the other side: not of the border, but of the cult. We have reversed Virgil's terms, or perhaps Virgil himself distinguished between the eclogues' Arcadia and the georgic paradise. After all, it was Cain who was the gardener (along these lines, one can trace the moral reversal of Jews become Israelis as that of nomads become gardeners; since goats walk and crops don't, agriculture requires territoriality in ways pastoral nomadism does not. Or note that country boy Timothy McVeigh used a truckload of fertilizer to blow up the

Oklahoma Federal Building). Gardens are portrayed as serene spaces, but perhaps it is time for the guards to be incorporated into the iconography of gardens.

16

Borders don't exist in nature, but they can be made. In San Diego and Tijuana shortly after the devastating October 2003 fires, friends pointed out to me how a single bioregion had sharply diverged because of distinct human practices. On the Baja side, the resources to put out fires never really existed, the fire cycle had never been seriously interrupted, and so the colossal fuel loads that would incinerate so much around San Diego had never accumulated. Besides, Mexicans are less interested in moving into locations remote from their fellows. The upshot is that not only didn't they have such devastating fires but they also tend not to have mansions in canyons and on mountaintops for which firefighters must risk their lives and the state squander its dwindling funds. Sometimes the ecology is better preserved south of the border than north of it. Consider the case of the nearly extinct Sonoran pronghorn on the Arizona-Sonora border. About ten times as many survive on the Mexican side, while on the U.S. side, they're pretty much confined to the Barry Goldwater Bombing Range—not the healthiest habitat for the last couple dozen of their kind in the country. I traveled there too, amid signs warning of live ordnance and the sound of distant bombing operations.

17

The takeover of the Sierra Club would only have succeeded if the invaders convinced people to believe again that the border marks a coherent environmental divide. The official idea is that immigrants are bad for the environment, but you can reframe that several dozen ways. One is to point out that we don't need help being bad for the environment. The United States consumes the world's resources in huge disproportion to its percentage of the global population, and most of us work overtime to do our bit for global warming. (My mother got caught up in the same arguments the last time the immigration issue roiled the Sierra Club waters and exclaimed to me, "But what if they come here and live like us?" to which the only possible reply was, "What if we stay here and live like us?") If you care about the environment, there are more relevant issues you might choose to take up before immigration. If you care about stopping immigration, on the other hand, the environment is a touchstone of conventional goodness, or at least of liberalism, that you can hide behind.

The poor nonwhite immigrants who are the real targets of this campaign are generally building and cleaning those big houses in remote places and mowing the lawns and fueling up the snowmobiles, but they tend not to own them, or to make the decisions to delist an endangered species, or defund the Superfund cleanup program, or lower emissions standards. (We elect people to do that, actually.) In fact, if sprawl and resource consumption are the immediate threat that population growth poses, then the new immigrants who live frugally, densely, and rely on public transport are a rebuke to the suburbanite majority in the United States.

The fantasy that the United States can be sealed off from the world like a walled garden in a slum overlooks dozens of other inconvenient facts, like the role of our country, with tools such as agricultural dumping and the World Bank, in making those other nations slummier, or the fact that they too have their gardens and we too have our slums. (Sometimes it's the destruction of their gardens that set them on the immigrants' path in the first place—certainly that's the case with the Mexican farmers bankrupted by NAFTA.) But it's also dismaying because setting gardens apart is how the conservation movement began, back at the turn of the twentieth century when it was far more closely affiliated with racist, nativist, and eugenicist movements. Behind the early national parks and wilderness areas was the idea of scenery segregation—that it was enough to save the most beautiful and biotically lush places, a few dozen or hundred square miles at a time.

18

The implication of setting one piece apart is that the rest of the environment was up for grabs, and into the 1960s the Sierra Club's basic strategy was doing exactly that. They fought a nuclear power plant in California's Nipomo Dunes but agreed it was okay to put one in Diablo Canyon instead; club activists like David Brower eventually came to regret that they had secured protection of Utah's Dinosaur National Monument from damming by letting Glen Canyon Dam go forward. Now most environmentalists are against big dams and nuclear power, so that the debates are about policy, not just geography.

Back then, Rachel Carson had only recently brought the bad news about pesticides—that they didn't stay put but moved through the environment into both wild places and our own bodies, and with that it began to become clear that you couldn't just defend places. You had to address practices; you had to recognize systems; you had to understand that, in John Muir's famous aphorism, "When we try to pick out anything by itself, we find it hitched to everything else in the universe." When he said that, of course, he wasn't imagining plastic detritus being ingested by seabirds in the center of the Pacific Ocean, or polar bears far beyond the industrialized world becoming hermaphroditic from chemical contamination, but we can.

More and more things come under the purview of environmentalism these days, from what we eat to where our chemicals end up. Immigration, unless it's part of a larger conversation about consumption, birthrates, reproductive rights, trade, international economic policy, sprawl, and dozens of other issues, isn't really one of them. It seems instead that environmentalism is a cloak of virtue in which anti-immigration activists are attempting to wrap themselves. But they're better looked at naked.

19

And those portrayed as invaders are in fact maintaining the garden. Throughout this century various "bracero" programs have brought in Mexicans to do the work citizens don't want—namely, to toil in the garden, not only the gardens of the wealthy, but the agricultural fields as well. Despite all the rhetoric around immigrants as assailants of the economy, the vast agricultural economy of California and much of the rest of the country is propped up by farmworkers from south of the border, documented or not (including many fleeing the economic collapse of small farms brought about post-NAFTA by the sale of cheap U.S. corn in Mexico; NAFTA opened the borders to goods but not to people). Think Virgil, think wetback georgics. And the desire to secure cheap labor has created an alternative boundary around some of these agricultural gardens, ones that the workers cannot get out of. In 1990 a Southern California flower grower was given a small jail sentence and fine for enslaving undocumented Zapotec Indian immigrants from Mexico (fear of the border patrol keeps many undocumented inhabitants of the Southwest not as outsiders, but as insiders afraid to leave the house or the private-property boundaries of the farms they work on garden captives). It is part of the murderous poetry of these garden wars: slaves on a flower farm. Who thought, while picking up a dozen roses for love's sake, that one man's bed of roses was another's wall of thorns?

20

"A people who would begin by burning the fences and let the forests stand!" exclaimed Thoreau. America was founded on a vision of abundance, on enough to go around for all. The relatively open immigration policies of past eras were based on this assumption, as was the homesteading act, which until the 1920s gave away western land to anyone willing to work it—a vision of privatized land but universal ownership that would have put everyone inside some garden or other. On a smaller scale, city parks were founded on the interlocking beliefs that nature was uplifting, that open space was democratic, that it was possible and even important for all members of society to find literal common ground. The great irony of Central Park in its early years was that public money and democratic rhetoric were used to make a place most notable for its concessions to the rich, who promenaded there in carriages, while the poor took to private pleasure gardens where less aristocratic pleasures such as drinking beer and dancing the polka were acceptable. Elizabeth Blackmar and Ray Rosenzweig wrote in their magisterial history of the place, "The issue of democratic access to the park has also been raised by the increasing number of homeless New Yorkers. Poor people—from the 'squatters' of the 1850s to the 'tramps' of the 1870s and 1890s to the Hooverville residents of the 1930s—have always turned to the park land for shelter.... The growing visibility of homeless people in Central Park posed in the starkest terms the contradiction between Americans' commitment to democratic public space and their acquiescence in vast disparities of wealth and power."

21

This is the same park that New York City Republican mayor Michael Bloomberg banned activists from in August 2004, saying that they would be bad for the grass if they gathered on the Great Lawn as a million antinuclear activists had some twenty-two years before. New York, in this scenario, became pristine nature to be protected from an invasion by activists. Despite the overwhelmingly Democratic majority in New York City, the media reassured viewers that the anti-Bush contingent were "outsiders." One of them carried a photograph of his son, Jesus A. Suarez, who had died in Iraq, on a pink sign labeled, "Bush lied, my son died (and 1000s more)," and his face was filled with an unabashed, infinite sorrow. One of the peculiarities of the current war is that the economic draft brought in thousands of young people who were not citizens;

those who died fighting the "War on Terror" were given retroactive citizenry. In death, but only in death, did these young Mexicans, Salvadorans, and Guatemalans become Americans. One could rearrange the old western saying about Indians to go something like, "The only naturalized immigrant is a dead immigrant."

22

But when I flew East for the event, the airline screened the film *The Day After Tomorrow*, in which global warming convulses the Northern Hemisphere with a boomerang cold snap that buries and freezes most of the United States and Europe so fast that millions become frozen like Popsicles. In the most interesting scene in the movie, groups of gringos wade across the Rio Grande carrying luggage, trying to flee the ecological destruction of El Norte, while the Mexican border patrol tries to keep them out. Finally, in return for a blanket forgiveness of Latin American debt, the gringos are welcomed in, and the Dick Cheney look alike president admits that the United States had been wrong in its environmental and its social policy and would try to do better.

23

In August 2004, a life-size statue of Jesus Christ was found in the Rio Grande, near Eagle Pass, Texas. Border patrol agents spotted it from the air and thought it was a body—Jesus as an unsuccessful border crosser, a dead alien. They launched a rescue attempt and retrieved the statue, which no one subsequently claimed as lost property. It was regarded by Catholics in the area as a message from God. On the south side of the border, in Piedras Negro, the statue was regarded as the Christ for the undocumented. "He's telling us he's alive and he is here with us," Veronica de la Pena told a newspaper reporter. "He's trying to tell us that there is hope."

Border Spaces/Ghettospheres

Daniel Bertrand Monk

1. "Dot/Bomb"

We have a saying around here: . . . Nasdaq has been more detrimental to Israeli investment than Nablus has.[1]

—Fitz Haney, senior associate, Israel Seed Partners

A hundred years from now, when the first serious histories of the dot-com bubble are written, its connection with a series of seemingly unrelated political ideas will probably take center stage. Future interpreters of bubble culture will not fail to relate its characteristic visions of a borderless world of information to contemporaneous visions of peace and security in the new millennium. Just as the Web gurus of a waning twentieth century suggested that barriers to information would give way to the inherent democracy—and even anarchy—of a virtual public sphere, political gurus predicting the imminent demise of long-standing conflicts spoke of a world in which the demarcated frontiers of the nation-state would go the way of the five-and-a-quarter-inch floppy drive. Linking the notion of the "avatar"—a virtual persona/identity—to that of a post-Westphalian concept of sovereignty, the visionaries of a peaceful new world order suggested that borders would dissolve in favor of tracked bodies in motion. Ours was to be a new political landscape, a society of "netizens,"[2] in which "cookies" would become the paradigm for the obligations of the new citizenship and "servers" the functional models for the role of the state. According to this understanding of our future, in the Middle East, Ireland, and Bosnia, the degree of peace afforded by the "virtualization" of *physical* borders—that is, by their passage to insignificance—would exist in inverse proportion to their "smart" status. As one cyberthusiast stated in 1996:

> . . . there are cities, states and nations that have been founded and built in cyberspace; these territories seem to fall into two major categories: They either try to recreate a digital version of an existing locality, or to reconfigure and experiment with existing notions of cities, states and nations in the *essentially borderless digital space.* . . .[3]

2. Absurdistan

We need soft borders, not rigid, impermeable ones. . . . At the threshold of the twentieth century, we do not need to reinforce sovereignty. . . .[4]
—Shimon Peres

Clearly, events have conspired to stain this progressive vision of techno-politics with the quaint patina of the implausible. In today's cyberspace, utopia is more commonly recognized as an already anachronistic MUD—Web-based multi-user dungeon—than as a virtual "paradise of association" for geek-libertarians in cyberspace.[5] *And some people appear to like it this way.* In our present, the scowling adherents of a "new realism" in world affairs are quick to indict the border theories of a burst and exhausted bubble culture as dangerous and impractical, even as they commandeer many of the principal features of these "Absurdistans" in their own attempts to reconceptualize political frontiers.[6] (Where peace and security are seen as the opposite poles of a zero sum, the technologies of deterrence regularly trump the efforts of "sensitive" statecraft, which is itself dismissed as the pastime of diplomatic "girlie men," to paraphrase the governor of California.)[7] For example, today the U.S. Department of Homeland Security (DHS) maintains a Science and Technology Directorate (S&T), which is in turn advancing a "smart borders action plan" (SBAP) in coordination with Mexico and Canada. Testifying before a congressional oversight committee in 2004, the DHS undersecretary heading the SBAP "portfolio" explained that "the objective [of the smart border action plan] is to govern S&T activities that address protection of the nations' mutual critical infrastructure and of their air, land, and sea perimeters so as to achieve a secure flow of people and goods."[8] Foreign nationals traversing U.S. passport control already experience the SBAP's effects firsthand: as they surrender their fingerprints to a digital touchpad, they *permanently* exchange biometric identifiers for *temporarily* unrestricted movement within the United States. Performing the classic liberty/security conundrum with their thumbs, these travelers also stamp themselves as the authentic netizens of the twenty-first century.

3. Wired

The continuous obstacle is not only a fence, but rather a security concept.[9]

–Benjamin (Fuad) Ben-Eliezer

Most conspicuously, in Israel—where many of the ideas about "smart" borders and "flexible" sovereignty were first seriously broached in the context of the 1994 Oslo Peace Accords—the same politicians who once dismissed as science fiction the peacemakers' ideas concerning new technologies of political normalization now advance the same type of proposals in their own fantastic efforts to create a high-tech membrane between Israelis and Palestinians.[10] Calling it the "separation fence," this project's apologists explain that the Sharon government's policy of unilateral separation marks Israel's return to a realistic and commonsense approach to the Middle East's harsh realities. They suggest that this structure will remain a tactical necessity for as long as the Palestinian Authority does little to abate terror attacks emerging from its territory, despite Israel's ongoing blockade of the West Bank. For their part, Palestinians and Israeli critics of the fence alike refer to it as an instrument of "apartheid."[11] Despite the vehemence of these opposing claims, one fact is certain (even if it advances no one's perceived interests to admit it): the so-called separation fence that Ariel Sharon is currently building is not a nostalgic return to Berlin or to Bantustan. It is something new and potentially far more ominous. Eschewing old paradigms of security and segregation alike, this border-that-is-not-a-border exists solely to guarantee that no one will ever again be able to relate to the demarcation lines of this conflict *except as an avatar.* Developed by the Israeli high-tech firm Magal Security Systems (NASDAQ: MAGS), the fence is actually a continuous sensor so effective that it is reportedly capable of detecting "the difference between a breeze and a squirrel."[12] (There are no squirrels in Israel or Palestine.) Magal's "TWIDS" technology (taut wire intrusion detection system) combines with a series of other devices to create a comprehensive data network that has simply made the horizons of sovereignty and of human identity virtually indistinct. Hence, its sublime effect: as a "conceptual" border between humans *in particular* and humans *in the abstract,* the fence elicits the "negative pleasure" that accompanies the inadequacy of imagination to total reason.[13] Considered universally valid, this sublime frontier paradigm and its attendant "security concept" are now equally popular in eastern Europe, where the newest members of the EU are reviewing ways to stem the flow of unregistered workers from post-Socialist republics into the West.

4. Auschwitz Borders

Sovereign is he who decides on the exception.[14]

—**Carl Schmitt**

Think of it this way: with this latest reconceptualization of frontiers, we cross a border by denying a border even exists. Content to advance what R. B. J. Walker has called a "new exceptionalism" in world affairs, the advocates of smart barriers now unthinkingly ratify means as ends.[15] In the process they evaporate the authority they believed themselves to have usurped from contingency by virtue of their so-called realist stance. Here, EZ Pass becomes the paradigm of the new citizenship, just as the unmanned toll plaza introduces itself as the model of the state. In the process, the nature of the sovereign who "determines the exception" is himself now reciprocally determined by the exception to be little more than a function, not even a functionary. The twentieth century had a name for this curious amalgam of reformist technology and popular tyranny at the limits of the state (popular, in the sense that anyone who has ever been stuck in traffic loves EZ Pass as much as the Italians loved the trains Mussolini caused to run on time). Calling it "fascism," those who first experienced this fabulously modern form of populist inhumanity would not have failed to recognize in our smart fences and avatars the triumph of what their tormentors first advanced in crude fashion with barbed wire and tattooed human flesh. One cannot help but suspect that from their standpoint the future that is our present would certainly appear borderless, but only because it betrays an incomprehensible nostalgia for a space so confined that it becomes its own world: the ghetto.

5. AATW: Anarchists Against the Wall

Pseudo-activity is generally the attempt to rescue enclaves of immediacy in the midst of a thoroughly mediated and rigidified society.[16]

–Theodor Adorno

A coda: to suggest that in our present practices we evince an incomprehensible nostalgia for the foundry of our own dehumanization is not, however, to confirm the view that artifacts like the security fence embody the universal logic of a "carceral" society, or a "bare life."[17] Quite to the contrary, as a "thing," the fence can only corroborate a ghetto *effect* (that is, the perverse identification of a barbed-wire universe as an irreducible given, rather than as a tenuous historical artifact of our own construction).[18] And, where frontiers are assigned the character of totality in this fashion, apparent criticism—or, more properly, *virtual* criticism—and *actual* resignation swap places.

This suggests that our "now" is not only confirmed as a shameful ghetto by the fate of those who first experienced with horror what would eventually become our present's normative forms of inhumanity. The exact character of our "now" is also disclosed in the frisson (and there's no other word for it) evinced by those "virtual" critics who love to hate artifacts like Israel's security fence. (Virtual, once again, because in their pseudo-activity they need to be distinguished from actual anarchists against the wall, who practice civil disobedience in the service of justice.) Giving priority to their own indignation over the demands of authentic political analysis, the harshest virtual critics of our new frontiers lay proprietary claim to intellectual praxis while avoiding it studiously. Confusing the material for the conceptually concrete (or, in other words, fences with their own political significance), virtual critics of the barrier present their own cogitative ghetto as the horizon of cognition per se. These indignation junkies make a fetish of architecture as instantiated politics and of geography as transparent war, arguing that construction constitutes a cruel territorial logic in and of itself. In their spontaneity, they thus leave that logic unexplained and, for that reason, unchallenged. (This, perhaps most of all, explains our current infatuation with the small sections of Israel's barrier that are actually opaque and solid, instead of the forty-five square kilometers of habitable land—an area fifty times larger than the old city of Jerusalem—that is lost to a linear installation of concertina wire and the TWIDS stuff.) The current oppositional chatter of Tel Aviv architects has become the popular jargon of political authenticity in matters concerning Israel's dominative spatial practices, but it offers little more than a mockery of critique, valid only by virtue of its status as sanctioned controversy.

The logic of which the smart fence is a part cannot be conveniently "embodied" in a vulgar geometry of conflict that would make a brutal historical process contiguous with its apparent morphology. This is a kind of argument that has been abandoned by intelligent students of war from Jomini to Schelling for the simple reason that strategy, like the threat of war itself, cannot be hypostatized into its forms or "without leaving something to chance"—a something, moreover, that confirms the original hypostasis as dangerously affirmative to begin with because nothing can signify in the absence of mediation.[19] Even in pragmatic terms, it would be impossible to see the boundary as an icon—that is, as the immediately discernible shape of the occupation—precisely for the same reason that it is impossible to say that a celebrity is famous for anything other than being famous. Where tautologies rule, slogans become the shameful plenipotentiaries for critical reflection on the nature of the borders we cross each time we claim to have seen through them.

Notes

For R. B. J. Walker and Mike Davis.

1. Fitz Haney, as cited in Emily Benedek, "Antiterror Inc," *Newsweek* (November 12, 2001), 66.

2. According to those who identify themselves as "Netizens," the term describes two types of participants on the Internet: (1) someone who uses the Internet as a form of political action (blogs, discussion boards, etc.), and (2) a user who participates in the development of the Internet itself. "The implication is that the Internet's users, who use and know most about it, have a responsibility to ensure that is used constructively while also fostering free speech and open access." See,TeachTarget.com, "Definition of Netizen," 2004, http://whatis.teachtarget.com/definition/0,,sid9_gci212636,00.html.

3. "Call it the colonizing of cyberspace. Forget surfing: Today, people of like minds and interests are establishing Internet communities faster than any construction company in the brick-and-mortar world. According to a new *Business Week*/Harris Poll, 57 percent of those hopping on to the Net today go to the same sites repeatedly instead of wandering like nomads from one to the next. And of the 89 percent of Netizens who use E-mail, nearly one-third consider themselves part of an online community. 'We're at the beginning of an explosion,' says Andrew Busey, chairman and chief technology officer of ichat Inc., an Internet startup in Austin, Tex., that makes software for online chats." From "Cybercities/Cybernations" (Hyperactive Co, 1996), http://web.archive.org/web/20010119171500/intelligent-agent.com/july_cyber.html, emphasis added.

4. Shimon Peres with Ayre Naor, *The New Middle East* (New York: Henry Holt, 1993), 171–172.

5. On the history of MUDS, see Sherry Turkle, *Life on the Screen: Identity in the Age of the Internet* (New York: Simon & Schuster, 1995). For a neat example of a MUD, log onto http://games.swirve.com/utopia/. For the concept of "techno-libertarians" see Francis Fukuyama, "Bring Back the State," *Observer* (London), July 4, 2004. Finally, for a brilliant history of the first and probably last great paradise of association, see Martin Philip Johnson, *The Paradise of Association: Political Culture and Popular Organizations in the Paris Commune of 1871* (Ann Arbor: University of Michigan Press, 1996).

6. Although the term "Absurdistan" refers to "the first virtual country on the planet," I introduce it here to designate the confluence of technology and progressive politics that is now treated as utopian. See, http://www.hradec.org/.

7. "America has been in too many wars for any of our wishes, but not a one of them was won by being sensitive. President Lincoln and General Grant did not wage sensitive warfare, nor did President Roosevelt, nor Generals Eisenhower and MacArthur. A 'sensitive war' will not destroy the evil men who killed 3,000 Americans. . . . The men who beheaded Daniel Pearl and Paul Johnson will not be impressed by our sensitivity." U.S. vice president Dick Cheney, as cited in Judy Keen, "Cheney Slams Kerry's 'Sensitive' War Plea," *USA Today*, August 12, 2004 http://www.usatoday.com/news/politicselections/nation/president/2004-08-12-cheney-war_x.htm.

8. Statement of Charles McQueary, undersecretary, Directorate of Science and Technology, U.S. Department of Homeland Security Committee: "On Senate Commerce, Science, and Transportation," *Lexis/Nexis*: Federal Document Clearing House, Inc., June 17, 2004.

9. Benjamin Ben-Eliezer, as cited in Ellis Shurman, "Construction of Security Fence Criticized as Setting Political Border," *Israel Insider*, June 17, 2002, http://web.israelinsider.com/Articles/Security/1137.htm.

10. On the kind of flexible sovereignties floated during the Oslo Accords, see Ian Ward, "The End of Sovereignty and the New Humanism," *Stanford Law Review*, 55, May 2003, 2091-2112. See also Helen Stacy, "Relational Sovereignty," *The Stanford Law Review* 55, May 2003, 2029–2059.

11. Following the example of Israel's justice minister Tommy Lapid, the less angry and more cynical of the project's critics refer to it as *hagader hakoalitzioni,* or the "coalitional" fence. Pointing to its indefensible course, they argue that the purpose of the barrier is to preserve the life of the current government, and not the safety of the average Israeli citizen. It bears stating, however, that Lapid would eventually join the ranks of those who called the barrier an "apartheid fence." See Herb Keinon, "Lapid Recalls Apartheid," *Jerusalem Post*, January 5, 2004.

12.   David Rosenberg, "Playing It Safe?," *The Jerusalem Report*, April 8, 1993, 49.

13.   "It is a greatness comparable to itself alone. Hence it comes that the sublime is not to be looked for in the things of nature, but only in our own ideas. [I]t is the disposition of soul evoked by a particular representation engaging the attention of the reflective judgment, and not the object, that is to be called sublime. In a metaphysical sense, this negative feeling is the disposition of soul evoked by a particular representation engaging the attention of the reflective judgment, and not the object [or fence itself], that is to be called sublime." Immanuel Kant; translated by James Meredith, *The Critique of Judgment*, §25 (Oxford: Clarendon Press, 1961), 25.

14.   Carl Schmitt, *Political Theology* (Cambridge: MIT Press, 1985). The term "Auschwitz Borders" was coined by Israeli foreign minister Abba Eban to describe the indefensibility of the nation's borders prior to the Arab-Israeli war of June 1967. See David Essing, "Transcript of Abba Eban's Speech, 1967," *Israel and Their Territories* (IsraCast.com, 2004), http://www. isra-cast.com/Transcripts/territories_trans.htm. But the same term has recently been taken up by members of the "Yesha Council" (the West Bank settlers' leadership) to describe the potential effects of the separation fence on the "Greater Land of Israel."

15.   R. B. J. Walker, "Sovereignties, Exceptions, Worlds," in Jenny Edkins and Michael Shapiro, eds., *Sovereign Lives: Power in Global Politics* (New York: Routledge, 2004).

16.   Theodor Adorno, "Resignation," *Critical Models: Interventions and Catchwords* (New York: Columbia University Press, 1998), 291.

17.   Michel Foucault, *Discipline & Punish: The Birth of the Prison* (New York: Random House Inc., 1995), 216–217; see also, Giorgio Agamben, *Homo Sacer* (Stanford: Stanford University Press, 1998).

18.   Foucault, *Discipline and Punish*, 217.

19.   Thomas Schelling, "The Threat That Leaves Something to Chance," in *The Strategy of Conflict* (Cambridge: Harvard University Press, 1960), 187–-203.

Transparent Wall, Opaque Gates
Ruchama Marton and Dalit Baum

Miki Kratsman

A. Transparent Wall

In a recent conversation, one of our friends, a prominent Israeli artist and designer, Professor Ziona Shimshi, commented that the concrete wall was quite ugly, and suggested it could have been built from a transparent material, like a polycarbonate silicone, Lexan, that is extremely strong and used in the construction of spacecraft. We found this suggestion intriguing—it was a way of calling into question the existence of the wall, but on aesthetic grounds. It conveyed a need to see the other side—but only through Lexan. Why *is* the wall so ugly? What is it supposed to block from our view? What does it expose while concealing?

The Gilo Wall

The suggestion of a transparent wall immediately brought to mind the famous picture of the Gilo wall, by the Israeli photographer Miki Kratsman. Gilo is a Jewish settlement on the outskirts of Jerusalem. Its main street is lined by an odd assortment of concrete slabs, erected at the beginning of the Al-Aqsa intifada as a shelter from sniper fire from the neighboring Palestinian town of Beit-Jalla. In the picture, the pastoral view of the Beit-Jalla hills is continued in painted form along the concrete slabs. A pine tree and some stones behind this wall are portrayed on it as if[1] it were transparent. The painting is meant to conceal the wall itself by reconstructing the concealed view by concealing the concealment. The reconstructed view serves as a second concealment, since the painted houses on the painted hills are devoid of people. They were supposed to portray the houses of Beit-Jalla, but they look like those of a little eastern European village, maybe because the artists were immigrants from the former Soviet Union.

ZIC

Kratzman's picture is an artful illustration of some basic assumptions, deeply held by Israelis, or, more precisely, by members of the imagined collective of Zionist Israelis, or what we will call the Zionist Israeli Collective, the ZIC. The collective is organized around these unchallengeable basic assumptions, and most aspects of life in Israel are affected by them.

Such underlying basic assumptions are that "We are pure, we are right, we have high moral values, we don't do evil, we are victims, and we are united." In the ZIC's eyes, its army conducts itself with "purity of arms," meaning that it uses only unavoidable force only for the defense of the ZIC. According to the ZIC, Israeli moral values are dominant and exemplary.

The ZIC is held together by a common feeling of victimhood: Jews carry a long history of being victims in different places and times; and behind Israeli military might, the ZIC still maintains the identity of a victim, always preparing for the inevitable catastrophe. In Palestine, the ZIC has always viewed itself as being under mortal threat from "Arabs." These mortal fears have shifted over the years between fears of invasion and defeat in war, of becoming a Jewish demographic minority again, and, most lately, of suicide bombings. Closely connected to the victim identity is the deterministic belief that "the whole world is against us." "The Arabs" too become part of this ahistorical enemy entity, focused wholly on Jewish destruction, always intent on "throwing us into the sea."

Another extremely important Zionist axiom is that Palestine was an empty land ("a land without people to a people without a land" in the well-known early Zionist slogan, attributed to Israel Zangwill in 1892). This belief was very much needed at the time: it allowed Zionists to maintain their self-image as righteous people, avoiding the notion of taking another people's land. But the land was not empty; therefore, the ZIC implemented an active nonseeing mechanism: its members actually saw an empty land.

This has all worked quite well for years, but the Palestinian uprising, the intifada, made it much harder not to see Palestinians. In order to protect itself, the ZIC has built a wall that conceals the Palestinians. Of course, the stated reason for the wall was defense: defense from bullets (overt), defense from seeing (covert). The self-image remained as it should be: pure, good, righteous. The wall maintains the illusion that on the "other side" is the empty land we have come to inherit: we cannot see over it, we cannot see through it; we see nothing but it, and the land continues to be empty.

Discussing the wall as a defense mechanism[2] of the ZIC, it seems appropriate to discuss it in psychological terms, especially since one of us is a practicing psychiatrist. The wall has many psychological advantages: what one doesn't see actually doesn't exist.[3] As one knows from the theater, when the curtain falls, the world we have experienced on stage seems to have come to an end. It is "as if" this world does not exist any more. The curtain, like the wall, is all we see. Moreover, seeing means acknowledging the existence of the seen; it is a form of understanding. This serves as a very convenient way out of inner conflict: not seeing, therefore not understanding, ensures psychological blindness. This way, there is no danger of achieving an insight.[4]

Splitting

A useful way of understanding some of the psychological mechanisms involved in the wall is the concept of splitting. The power and magic of the splitting mechanism lies in its simplicity. It permits only two extremes: the whole world is split into "good" and "bad," with nothing in between. According to Melanie Klein, splitting is the psychological defense mechanism that separates good from bad, both in oneself and in the Other: "Splitting is caused by a high level of anxiety, which offers no options or choice and is considered to be the most primitive kind of defense against anxiety: the object (the Other), with both erotic and destructive instincts directed towards it, splits into 'good' and 'bad'.... The splitting of objects is accompanied by a parallel splitting of the ego (the subject or oneself) into a 'good' ego and a 'bad' one."[5] In this manner, the splitting mechanism splits both the inner self and the Other into the same extremes, pure and good versus bad and evil.

Fright activates the most immediate of mechanisms, a primitive mechanism of brute force. As such, the splitting process requires continuous maintenance and an ever-increasing investment of energy. Eventually, it is not an effective mechanism. It does not reduce the anxiety, only blocks it; it does not enable working through the causes of the anxiety, but just distances them. The wall separates the contents of the inner space into two parts: the "bad," unwanted parts, which are hard to deal with, and the "good" parts, which are in accord with the self-image. The "bad" parts are externalized—in other words, projected onto the Other. Thus, the ZIC self is preserved as good and pure.

Projective Identification

Projecting an unwanted part of the self outward onto the Other serves two goals: relief from the unwanted part and legitimacy to despise this part in the Other. Moreover, this mechanism enables the fantasy of control and possession of the projected parts–in this case, the "bad" parts. Klein defines projective identification as a "mechanism revealed in fantasies in which the subject inserts his self–in whole or in part–into the object to harm, possess or control it."[6] The wall allows the ZIC self not to see itself as aggressive, violent, cruel, possessive, a violator of human rights, by projecting all these traits on the Palestinians beyond the wall.

The wall is not perceived by the ZIC as an aggressive act; it is perceived as a protective act, an act of self-defense, protecting itself from aggression associated only with the Palestinians. It takes a complex psychological mechanism to facilitate such a reversal. This way, the wall achieves its goal: protecting the ZIC from seeing its own aggression and thus preserving its basic assumptions that it is the "good," "just" victim.

Looking at the Wall

The concrete wall is an anachronistic splitting device; it is both ugly and opaque, and as such it is highly suitable for its role in the psychological mechanisms described here. The formidable concrete wall seems out of place and time, a "simple" physical "solution" to a historically, politically, and psychologically complex question. The ZIC views itself as postmodern, high-tech, up-to-date, sophisticated as a fashionable

Westerner in the wild (Middle) East. "Israel is the only democracy in the Middle East," the tourist ads proclaim. In the ZIC's mind, the wall functions as a space/time machine, a tool to separate the ZIC from primitive regions of the world that surround it. The wall helps to locate the primitive, simpleton, backward, and savage aspects of the Palestinians behind it. Thus it preserves the ZIC's own self-image as advanced, civilized, sophisticated, high-tech on the other side of the same wall.

It is ugly—because it serves the need to create the illusion of an evil, ugly monster on the other side, rather than ordinary people. The Palestinian existence within the wall is considered inferior, ugly, dirty, violent, and dangerous. A recent illustration of these ideas and concepts can be found in the court testimony of Professor Rafi Israeli (The Hebrew University, Middle Eastern Studies) as state expert in the trial against the leaders of the Islamic movement in Israel: "The Arabs are neglecting their hygiene. Their villages are dirty. They are criminals in high percentage. They are noisy."[7] The wall thus becomes both a symbol and realization of the impossibility of identifying with Palestinians.

It is opaque in order to prevent the sight of misery and suffering on the other side. If it were transparent, we could actually see the troubling suffering of the people on the other side. We might see the child who must go through the hills to school and cannot; or the father who cannot reach his farm to cultivate his olive trees; or the sick person who cannot make his or her way to the hospital; or the pregnant woman who cannot deliver her child in safety or, worse, is forced to give birth in the dirt next to the checkpoint. Seeing this misery and suffering might trigger compassion for those people, might develop identification with them. This must be avoided at all costs, because otherwise the question might arise: Who caused this suffering?

Walls and Fences

Farther away from urban population centers, the concrete wall gives way to a system of fences, razor wire, and various surveillance mechanisms-sensors, watch stations, and watchtowers. Some forms of seeing are to be avoided, but others are considered valuable. The ZIC does not want to see the Palestinians, but it finds it necessary to oversee them, to watch them with nonhuman sight, through a gun sight.

"It is easier to shoot through a fence than it is through a wall," remarked one Israeli activist in the Mas'ha Peace Camp. The camp consisted of two tents on the outskirts of the West Bank Palestinian village Mas'ha, near the construction site of the wall. Dozens of Palestinians, Israelis, and international activists shared the camp for almost five months in 2003, in protest against the wall. Six months later, during another protest at the same site, Gil Na'amati, an Israeli activist from the same group, was shot through the wire fence and severely injured.

B. Opaque Gates
Security

The wall, in some places made of gray concrete three stories high, snakes across the West Bank. The ZIC notes its ugliness but blames it on the Palestinians. The wall is justified as a necessary security measure. The ostensible reason for the wall is very concrete; it supposedly exists in order to physically prevent a Palestinian youth with explosives strapped to his or her body from reaching the ZIC body and harming it. Potential terrorists should be prevented from reaching our territory, driving on our roads, sitting at our cafés, shopping at our markets, riding our buses. But all Palestinians are potential terrorists in the ZIC's mind. In other words, for it to achieve its main goal, the wall aims to prevent all suspicious Palestinians—i.e., all Palestinians—from reaching the ZIC's body, anywhere.

As repeatedly claimed by its planners, the wall does not delineate the ZIC's borders, since Israel has never defined its own borders and is still refusing to do so. It is a security apparatus designed to defend the ZIC from various threats. As Ehud Barak, the former Israeli prime minister, said, "Israel is a villa in the jungle." In the ZIC's mind, the wall functions as a space/time machine, a tool to separate the ZIC from primitive regions of the world around it. In this image the world is full of dangers that threaten the white man living in the villa. The wall is conceived as a part of the villa and, as such, not surprisingly has come to symbolize the ZIC body itself. Army firing regulations have been changed to permit a response to any attack on the wall as if it were an attack on Jewish lives. The shooting of Israeli activist Na'amati was justified by the fact that he and his group, Anarchists Against the Wall, were attempting to open a gate in the wall. Palestinian residents who wander too close to the wall have been shot at and killed and their deaths later justified by army regulations.

Movement

In recent years there has been a vast intensification in the erection of fortifications and fences, roadblocks and checkpoints, walls and watchtowers throughout the West Bank. All of these physical barriers, including the wall in all its forms, are part of an elaborate system controlling Palestinian movement, a system that includes regimens like sieges and curfews, bureaucratic and legal inventions, technological innovations and brute force. This is not only an attempt to control all forms of movement, but in fact a mechanical attempt to control all aspects of Palestinian life. When viewed as a system for controlling life and movement, a system with dynamic functions, the wall is, in fact, no more then a frame for its openings, a series of gates and checkpoints that control and regulate all movement flow.

The Amers' House

One example of the fantasy[8] of total control over Palestinian life by controlling movement can be seen in the Amer family's house on the outskirts of the Palestinian village Mas'ha. This was the last site of the Mas'ha Peace Camp in August 2003, and after the camp was torn down and all the activists arrested, one segment of a twenty-five-foot-high concrete wall was erected between the house and the rest of Mas'ha. For miles and miles in both directions, the wire fence cuts through the olive groves; it encircles the house on all sides, but the only place where the wall takes its concrete form is between this house and its village. When the Amers look through their windows, they see either the neighboring Jewish settlement of Elkana or they see the wall.

The wall around the house locks the family in. On three sides there are four gates. One huge gate separates Mas'ha from the Jewish settlement of Elkana; two vehicular gates for army patrols connect this wall segment to the rest of the wall; and one small gate allows family members supervised access to their village. The ominous yellow gates are formidable, equipped with motion and touch sensors. No one can come and go without the approval of the army.

Buffer Zone

Just like the Amers, thousands of Palestinian residents are cut off from the rest of the West Bank, from their fields, workplaces, from neighboring towns and vital services. "The seam area" is the Israeli name given to areas locked between the wall and the

1949 cease-fire border of the state of Israel. Immediately after the completion of the first stage of the wall in October 2003, the seam area was declared a closed military zone: no Palestinians are allowed in this area without a special permit.

For Palestinians living in this area, an extensive permit system was devised by the Israeli authorities. They are required to apply for permits to continue living in their own homes. Other residents of the West Bank have to obtain special permits to enter the seam area through special gates. There are twelve different kinds of permits, based on the purpose of entry. Each permit indicates a certain gate through which the permit holder must cross, as well as the times of day during which the holder is allowed to pass. Sleeping over in the seam area, bringing a vehicle into the area, or transporting merchandise into the area require additional permits. A long list of forms, certificates, and documents are necessary for applying for different permits. The criteria for obtaining permits are not stated anywhere, and the Israeli authorities have almost complete discretion to grant or deny them. Permits may be denied on the grounds of secret security concerns by the Military Appeals Committee. The permits have arbitrary expiration times, and have to be constantly renewed.

The permit system is designed to incorporate the entire seam area into the control mechanism. The total control of minute aspects of Palestinian lives in this area secures it as a buffer zone, an added volume to the physical obstacle, a living wall.

Control

This system is not merely bureaucratic and Kafkaesque. Again, a psychological explanation can be useful: in an obsessive disorder,[9] fear of death plays a central role and there is a deeply held belief that certain actions prevent impending death of the self and of loved ones. The body's orifices are conceived as danger zones, through which hostile agents may penetrate, infect, and cause disease or death. In fantasy, total control of the orifices is achievable, preventing all penetrations and thus protecting the self from fear of disease, death, and feelings of helplessness. The fantasy of keeping orifices clear of germs is well illustrated by the military concept of controlling the openings along the wall.

The obsessive control of the body's openings is a typically modern control mechanism, associated with metaphors of hygiene, purity, and defense from bacteria infection. Rituals are created with the aim of self-preservation from contamination, diseases, and death. These rituals are constantly refined in arbitrary ways. The person knows deep down that there is no total control; thus, the anxiety is ever present, reinforcing these rituals, which may take over an obsessive person's life, achieving precedence over all other aspects of life, requiring an ever-growing investment of resources.

Sphincters

The openings of the wall function like sphincters, which are voluntary round muscles that one is trained to control. In the wall case, the sphincters or openings are controlled by the army.

In the development of a child, control of the sphincters is used not only for the purpose of hygiene, but also in a struggle for independence from parents and in the attempt to demonstrate autonomous power in front of bigger, more powerful others.[10] A child will refuse food or stop defecating as a display of control in front of worried or angry parents. Opening and closing the sphincters at will, despite outside pressures (international critique, international law) as well as strong pressures from within (economic necessities, state laws), indicates a fear of powerlessness in front of big and powerful parents, and a need to display basic and crude control of the situation.

The need for control finds its realization at the openings. This is where control is expressed. If the wall conceals and obfuscates, its openings become clear foci of pressure—the conflict points where the powerful occupier exercises power over the weak occupied.

In spite of the great investment in denial, there is always some inner knowledge that the control system is imperfect, that there can be no total control. The relation between the methods employed and the actual protection achieved always remains unclear. Therefore, the obsessive person has to constantly invent more and more elaborate rituals of "control." After each elevation to another supposedly "secure" level, there is temporary relief and self-assurance that the method is working; but these rituals offer no permanent relief because they require continuous refinement. The price constantly gets higher and higher and, because the limitations are never considered, the fantasy has to be constantly maintained by an ever-greater investment of resources.

Transparent Wall, Opaque Gates Ruchama Marton and Dalit Baum

Concrete

The wall is a formidable human-made construction, and it is easy to see it as symbolizing the Zionist Israeli Collective's basic assumptions and fears, standing twenty-five feet tall as a manifestation in concrete of security itself for the Jewish state, its yellow metallic gates realizing obsessive control fantasies. However, in its concrete form, the wall is just a wall, and, like other human-made constructions, when its symbolic worth shifts, when the beliefs and values that sustain it falter, it can disappear almost overnight.

In August 2004 we joined a mass rally against the wall in Abu-Dis, a Palestinian neighborhood of Jerusalem. Thousands of Palestinians, Israelis, and internationals gathered to hear Arun Gandhi, the grandson of Mahatma Gandhi, speak about non-violent resistance to the wall. During the rally, one young man started free climbing onto the great concrete slabs. The audience gasped in awe as in just a few seconds the courageous climber was standing up on the wall, waving a Palestinian flag at those on both sides of the wall, which cuts through this Palestinian neighborhood. After a moment of silence, dozens of people lined up below him and quickly followed his example. Suddenly stripped of a whole layer of beliefs and psychological investments, the massive concrete construction flickered and shifted meaning before our eyes. For that brief moment, the wall was just a wall.

Notes

The authors wish to express their gratitude to Dorothy Zellner for her assistance in the preparation of this article.

1. "[The] 'As if' personality belongs to the group of borderline personality disorders. 'As if' characters used to be called 'pseudologia fantastica.' ... [It] goes hand in hand with an insufficiently developed superego, predominance of aggression against the objects...." Otto Kernberg and Jason Aronson, *Borderline Conditions and Pathological Narcissism* (New York: Jason Aaronson, 1975).

2. "*Defense Mechanism*: A process whereby the ego protects itself against demands of the id. More generally, it is a pattern of feeling, thought, or behaviour arising in response to a perception of psychic danger, enabling a person to avoid conscious awareness of conflicts or anxiety-arousing ideas or wishes," *Oxford Dictionary of Psychology, ed.* Andrew M. Colman (New York: Oxford University Press, 2001) 189.

3. "*Denial*: A defense mechanism involving a disavowal or failure consciously to acknowledge thoughts, feelings, desires, or aspects of reality that would be painful or unacceptable, as when a person with a terminal illness refuses to acknowledge the imminence of death," Colman, *Oxford Dictionary of Psychology*, 194.

4. "*Insight*: (3) The capacity to understand oneself, especially the abnormal or pathological nature of aspects of one's behaviour or mental experience that result from a mental disorder. ... In psychoanalysis, conscious understanding of unconscious reasons for maladaptive behaviour is believed to be curative in itself," Colman, *Oxford Dictionary of Psychology*, 368–369.

5. J. LaPlanche and J.-B. Pontalis, *The Language of Psychoanalysis* (New York: Norton, 1973), 430.

6. LaPlanche and Pontalis, *The Language of Psychoanalysis*, 356.

7. *Ha'aretz*, December 23, 2004.

8. "*Phantasy* (Fantasy): An imaginary scene in which the subject is a protagonist, representing the fulfillment of a wish in a manner that is distorted to a greater or lesser extent by defensive processes." LaPlanche and Pontalis, *The Language of Psychoanalysis*, 314.

9. "*Obsessive-compulsive personality disorder*: a personality disorder characterized by a pervasive pattern of preoccupation with orderliness, perfectionism and control, at the cost of flexibility, openness and efficiency, beginning by early adulthood and indicated by such signs and symptoms as excessive preoccupation with details, rules and order ..." Colman, *Oxford Dictionary of Psychology*, 503.

10. "*Anal Sadistic Stage*: Freud's second stage of libidinal development, occurring between the ages of two and four. The stage is characterized by an organization of the libido under the primacy of the anal erotogenic zone. The object-relationship at this time is invested with meanings having to do with function of defecation (expulsion/retention) and with the symbolic value of faeces. The anal-sadistic stage sees the strengthening of sado-masochism in correlation with the development of muscular control." LaPlanche and Pontalis, *The Language of Psychoanalysis*, 35.

Hollow Land: The Barrier Archipelago and the Impossible Politics of Separation

Eyal Weizman

Tom Kay

An Impossible Line

The discontinuous line of fences, ditches, concrete walls, and high-tech sensors that the Israeli government refers to as the "seam-line obstacle," the general Israeli public as the "separation fence," and those Israelis and Palestinians opposing it (and recently the International Court of Justice) as the "wall" or sometimes the "apartheid wall"[1] isn't the only barrier in the frenzy of fortification taking place in the region, but it is the most definitive.

A recent opinion poll suggested that more than 83 percent of the Israeli public supports the barrier.[2] For those on the political Left in Israel, it is the physical embodiment of the territorial compromise implicit in a two-state solution, while for the settlers' movements and their supporters it reflects the consolidation of some territorial gains. Although the settlers initially rejected the idea of the barrier for fear it might concede parts of the West Bank to the Palestinians, they have since grown to accept it, and even learned to try and manipulate its route to serve their aims.

Indeed, except for a few Israelis and Palestinians who challenge the very idea of a politics of separation and the necessity of barriers as such, each of the different strands within the Israeli political spectrum promotes an "own path" that runs somewhere between the green line (the closer to the green line the more left-leaning the promoter is) and a fragmented patchwork of territory around Palestinian demographic centers.[3]

The fantasy of separation seeks to create a defensible and homogeneous Israeli political space that will guarantee, if not protection from Palestinian attacks, at least a space of Jewish demographic majority and control. Why fantasy? Because although preparations for the voluntary evacuation of settlements are already under way, no government to date has had either the political ability or the wish to dismantle the large settlement blocks of the West Bank.[4] President Bush's letter to the Israeli government further guarantees it will never have to do as much. The result is a fragmentation of the West Bank, mainly around Jerusalem and in the western slopes of the West Bank mountains near the metropolitan area of Tel Aviv, into an intertwined patchwork of non-contiguous and noncontinuous enclaves. Through this fragmented geography, no geometrical gesture, as elegantly meandering as it may be, could achieve separation and place Israelis and Palestinians on two sides of a single line. For anyone looking at the hundreds of maps and partition plans suggested lately, it is apparent that this line is either impossible to achieve or too arbitrary to offer a viable separation.

Although, and perhaps because, the barrier project is unable to create a political border, it attempts to display the reassuring iconography of one. In its different components—eight-meter-high concrete walls, electronic fences, barbed wire, radars, cameras, deep trenches, observation posts, and armed patrols[5]—of an abundance and cost that have made it the largest and most expensive project in the history of the state,[6] the barrier seeks to appear as a heavily fortified, absolute border. The illusion that—with the sweep of a unilaterally fortified line and for the cost of some concrete, barbed wire, and electronic gadgets—Israel could become an ordinary, territorially defined nation-state is easily enough conjured up to disguise the reality of the shifting colonial frontier.

Left Line, Right Line–Sharon's "Politicide"

The construction and fortification of a solid line between Israel and the areas to be handed over to a future Palestinian state was the central component of Ehud Barak's politics of separation during the days of the peace process, months before the outbreak of the second intifada in 2000. But effective decisions to implement a uni-lateral separation was conceived only after the collapse of Labor's political project at Camp David and when reciprocal attacks brought the conflict into the streets of all major Israeli and Palestinian cities.

The project's initial identification with the Israeli Left, and the territorial conces-sions that it implied, made Ariel Sharon reject it out of hand upon assuming power in the election of 2000. Most of the members of Sharon's cabinet, its coalition Knesset members, and the Likud central committee also strongly opposed the project. But in April 2002, while Israel Defense Force bulldozers were carving their way through the refugee camp of Jenin and with all other major Palestinian cities firmly in IDF hands, Sharon "surrendered" to the demands of the Labor ministers in his unity government, as well as to growing public pressures, and announced his decision to construct the "seam-line obstacle."

But if it appears that Sharon was reluctantly bowing to military contingencies and political pressures, and had miraculously transformed his entrenched territorial policies, the decisions over the route of the barrier were to demonstrate otherwise: he only ever intended to exploit the public enthusiasm for the idea of separation to execute his long-standing geopolitical agenda.[7] After attempting in April 2002 what Baruch Kimmerling calls "politicide"[8]—the eradication of a unified Palestinian polity by mili-tary means—Sharon has used the barrier to attempt a territorial version of the same thing. Without a contiguous territorial basis, the ability of a united Palestinian polity to operate as a single entity would be severely limited.

Sharon wanted the barrier to run not only in front (west) of the Palestinian-populated mountain region of the West Bank, but also behind it (east) through the Jordan Valley. According to this plan—already drawn up in various different versions as the "H Plan" at the time Sharon was a minister in charge of settlements from 1977 to 1981–several east-west corridors, the main one running through Jerusalem, would further carve up the Palestinian mountain strip into several isolated cantons, each around a major Palestinian city, producing a number of (very approximate) H-forms.

The Palestinians would be not only surrounded on the surface, but enveloped on all sides. Sharon announced that he would keep effective sovereignty over the mountain aquifer below Palestinian areas and over the airspace above them. So, instead of the ground-level separation effected by a border-like device, the barrier was designed to complete a project of containment. In fact, as far as the Israeli security establishment was concerned, the IDF should keep effective control over the airspace above the West Bank and Gaza as a precondition for any territorial compromise. The more territory it conceded, and the more it had to fortify behind a series of land barriers, the more dependent it would become on the airspace. Thus a new type of territorial compromise is achieved along the vertical dimension: an archipelago of isolated bits of terrain would be handed over to Palestinian control under a variety of security arrangements, while the occupation would be transferred to the skies, policed by Israeli UAVs and attack helicopters.

If Sharon's original plan were to be followed, the Palestinian state would effectively become a series of unstable pockets, completely surrounded by a Zionist body-politic that would cover the entire territory between the Mediterranean Sea and the Jordan River.[9] In this geographic arrangement, the Palestinians would be simultaneously inside and outside: landlocked within a territorial envelope, without any border save the very long and fragmented one to Israel, but—and here recalling the geography of apartheid-era South African Bantustans—outside the Israeli state system.[10] This archipelago of isolated territories would gradually turn, when political and security circumstances allowed, into what would be defined as the "Palestinian state within temporary borders"—something that the George Bush-sponsored "roadmap" has as a stated objective.

Flexible Line

But, as the government gradually realized, constructing the barrier along a predrawn route was not an easy task.

The physical reality of the barrier has given international and local opposition a clear target. If the images of mundane, almost benign, red-roofed suburban settlements were not shocking enough to mobilize a global opposition, the images of barbed-wire fences and especially those of high concrete walls resonated strongly within a Western historical imagination still dealing with unresolved memories of its colonial and world war legacies.

Moreover, the incremental approach to the implementations of the barrier, whereby different segments are planned, authorized, and constructed in succession,[11] has provided the opposition with an opportunity to influence the path of its as-yet unbuilt segments. As the months go by and as the horrific influence of the barrier on the daily lives of Palestinians is exposed, a truly global campaign waged via the UN, the Israeli High Court of Justice, local and international NGOs, the International Court of Justice, the media, and scores of foreign governments acting along visible or back channels has, in some cases, managed to deflect the gestural sweep of the lines drawn in Sharon's original plan, and currently looks likely to cancel the implementation of the eastern part of the barrier altogether. No longer simply a reflection of the political vision of Sharon's master plan, the folds, deformations, stretches, wrinkles, and bends in the barrier path have now started to plot the influences of all political forces in the region.

Flexible Territories

Against the familiar binary opposition that posits place-bound stability—defined as a hard and fixed material reality—versus a spatial mobility, which is composed of the soft "actions of mobile bodies of various speeds and directions," as suggested by Michel de Certeau,[12] the concept of flexibility allows for these seemingly dialectical categories to be synthesized into a single liquid continuum. Far from describing the relation between space and action as a rigid container for soft performance, flexible territories may incorporate processes by which spaces are constantly transformed, morphed, and claimed by action. Space and actions are no longer be distinguished as two separate categories.

Flexible territories flatten the difference between scales of action through a variety of gearing effects, of which the international media is a prominent one. Actions of individuals, the work of micro-political or armed organizations, the mediatized action of humanitarian and human rights groups, geopolitical pressures, changing strategic, economic, or technological realities all physically challenge the envelope of political space and transform it. In the dynamic ecologies of these liquid geographies—embracing the relation between action, flows and material organizations—the built environment is both performed and transformed by human action. Sometimes individual action

Miki Kratsman

could be more effective than government action: flexible territories describe a mobile, transformable complex of feedback-based relations between habitat and inhabitants. Because flexible boundaries undergo constant and continuous transformation in response to external influences, space can be understood as the embodiment of all forces that are applied on it.

Such flexible territories do not imply a benign environment, of course. Highly liquid political space can be even more dangerous than static and rigid space. This is ever more true of frontier regions, where everything is temporary and shifting. Although in frontier geographies, an asymmetrical power balance means that the colonizer may pour across and arrange the environment to suit its aims and impose unilateral actions, in many contemporary frontiers, the seemingly stronger side, with its volatile "conqueror" status, could well be the losing one.

Palestinian agency is manifested in its success in holding steadfast to the ground, mobilizing world opinion through diplomatic channels and international institutions as well as through political violence, and thus playing a major part in the shaping of the spaces of the conflict.

Consider the following typical "flexible" scenario. A mobile home is bought by a large suburban settlement in order to house an extension for its kindergarten. The day after it arrives, the mobile home is "stolen" by a group of young settlers and taken to a barren hilltop. There they lay out other such mobile structures in a circle and inaugurate a new outpost. The new outpost is provided with infrastructure and receives IDF protection. A roadblock is placed at the exit of the next Palestinian village. The outpost location redefines the border of conflict and the limit of the settlers' controlled area. The scout of a Palestinian information group spots the outpost and posts maps and images of it together with the narrative of its construction on the group's home-site on the Internet. The international media pick up the story. European governments apply pressure on the United States. The United States applies pressure on Israel to remove the outpost. The military arrives to remove the outpost. After a short and violent clash with the settlers, a compromise is reached: the mobile homes are placed on tracks again and relocated to another hilltop, beginning the whole process again. Within this typical example of frontier life, all the actions described do not happen within the fixed envelope of space but act to challenge and transform it.

Political Vectors

On its Web site, the Israeli Ministry of Defense claims that the path of the barrier responds to tactical defensive needs and local geographical singularities—primary among them topography—rather than to an all-encompassing political strategy. Seeking to generate what they call "topographical command and control," the military claims to have drawn a path from which armed patrols could visually dominate the Palestinian towns and villages located on its other side.[13] This "ideal" path—conceived to undo some of the perceived tactical limitations of the green line, has however been influenced by other considerations as well.

As the barrier's construction site nears their region, settlement councils have started applying as much political pressure as they can for the path to "loop around" and absorb them into the safer, western side they refer to as "Israeli" even though it is in effect within the Occupied Territories. This pressure is most often applied by intense lobbying with the minister of defense or with other cabinet ministers, but has a territorial component as well. The logic behind the current frenzy in construction of outposts lies in the settlers' wish to influence the path of the barrier by seeding the terrain with "anchor points" around which the barrier should loop.[14] Appearing to be wary of settlers' pressure, but actually using it as an excuse to perform what has been planned in advance, the government seeks to include as large a number of settlement points as possible and leave as few Palestinians as possible within the "Israeli" side of the barrier.[15]

A particularly strong outcry came from the settlement of Alfei-Menashe, a relatively wealthy suburban community of five thousand. It was the first settlement to lobby with the government and has encouraged a number of other settlements to do the same. According to the first phase, the northern path, authorized in June 2002, Alfei-Menashe was to be left "outside." The local panic about being "abandoned," mediated through political pressures and ultimatums from the right-wing ministers in the government, forced a revision of the path and the extension of a loop to incorporate the settlement back "inside." This loop meant, however, that the road connecting Alfei-Menashe with Israel proper had to be rerouted through the Israeli suburban community of Matan (pop. 2,500).[16]

Wanting to "protect" their cul-de-sac gated community from becoming a thoroughfare, however, the residents of Matan assembled an impressive legal team that managed to force on the government another rerouting of both the barrier and the road. As a result, the neighboring Palestinian towns of Qalqilyah and Habla, a few hundred meters apart as the crow flies, were cut apart by the barrier's extension. The settlers now have a road that passes safely between the two towns. The Palestinians, on the other hand, have to travel some twenty kilometers and pass several checkpoints to make use of the joint economic infrastructure of the two towns.

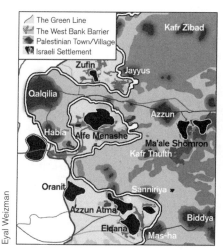 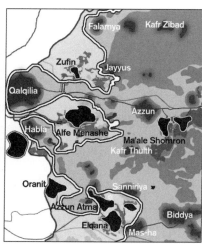

Eyal Weizman

Barrier path approved by the government in August 2002.

Barrier path after the rerouting gererated by pressure from the residents of Matan. Approved in March 2003, completed in July 2003.

There were further outside influences affecting the path of the barrier. Religious parties applied pressure to government ministers to alter the path of the Jerusalem envelopment (the Jerusalem metropolitan part of the barrier), which was duly extended to form a small concrete loop a few hundred meters long that broke through the urban fabric of Bethlehem and secured for metropolitan Jerusalem an archaeological site believed to be the biblical-era tomb of Rachel. This construction has also blocked the ancient Jerusalem-Hebron Road and turned the area into another protected Israeli cul-de-sac.

Ten other archaeological sites, including one complete ancient Egyptian city, were discovered during the digging for this segment of the barrier and in some cases the path was rerouted to incorporate these sites within the "Israeli" side. In the northern part of the West Bank, the path recommended by the Ministry of Defense was rerouted to respond to pressure from Israeli environmentalists who thought that the protection of a nature reserve of rare Iris flowers would be guaranteed only if it were to remain under Israeli control.

The desire to match the path of the barrier with subsurface interests meant the incorporation of the water extraction points of the mountain aquifer, while the desire to serve Israel's aerial interests led to the attempt by the Ministry of Defense to include those areas located within shoulder-missile range of the landing paths of international flights directed at Ben-Gurion airport.

It seems that the only consideration absent from the vectors of push and pull were those relating to the human rights and daily lives of the Palestinian residents of the seam area. Along the built and proposed paths of the barrier, the fabric of Palestinian life is completely torn apart and the economy of the area is already grinding to a standstill. People will be separated from their farmland and water sources, from their families, friends, and places of work, hospitals, schools, recreation areas, and universities. The human rights organization B'tselem estimated that the barrier would negatively affect the livelihood of at least 300,000 Palestinians and irreversibly damage the economic prospects of a Palestinian state.[17]

But Palestinian and Israeli activists have managed, sometimes by risking their lives in perilous demonstrations along the path or by directly appealing to various global institutions, to put the barrier and its path at the top of the international agenda. European leaders have demanded the cancellation of the project and

American officials have proposed significant reroutings. The American administration was particularly "worried" by the loop designed to encapsulate the city settlement of Ariel and has even threatened to reduce loan guarantees as a penalty if construction goes ahead.[18]

Responding to petitions submitted by Palestinians through Israeli civil rights groups, the Israeli High Court of Justice (HCJ) ruled in June 2004 that the state must reroute some thirty kilometers of the barrier northwest of Jerusalem to take into account the impact on Palestinian livelihood. Further cases concerning other sections of the barrier are still pending with the HCJ.

Almost simultaneously, the International Court of Justice (ICJ) in The Hague has given an advisory opinion to the UN stating that the sections of the barrier built beyond the green line, as well as the barrier's associated regime, were in contravention of international law. It rejected out of hand the Israeli government's claim for "tactical necessity" in routing the barrier around settlements. In their ruling, the judges noted that: "The infringement of Palestinian human rights cannot be justified by military exigencies or by the requirements of national security or public order," because the Palestinian lands over which Israel constructed the barrier were expropriated in order to secure settlements which were themselves illegal according to international law. The judges have called on the Israeli government to stop the construction, tear down the sections of the barrier already built, and compensate the Palestinians directly affected. With a majority of 13 to 2, they furthermore advised the UN's Security Council to consider its options for "further action"–diplomatic code for a variety of possible sanctions–to enforce this.[19] Such legal pressure on both a national and an international scale (officially, the government contends that it disregards the ruling of the ICJ and heeds only those of its HCJ) prompted the Israeli Ministry of Defense to redraft the entire path of the as-yet-unconstructed barrier and to order the rerouting of some segments it considered vulnerable to further petitions. Although this was later to become a Pyrrhic victory for the opposition, never before had the concentrated action of international diplomacy been so visibly effective in transforming the "flexible" geography of Israeli domination.[20] Encouraged by the rulings, Azmi Bishara, Israeli-Palestinian member of the Knesset, has recently proclaimed that the conflict over the barrier "is a winnable case."[21]

"Islands"

In a strange and grotesque role reversal, after the court cases were won and the barrier route changed, the settlers themselves started appealing to the Israeli HCJ with a wave of petitions that protested against route changes. Using language similar to that which won the Palestinian cases, they claimed that the new path would now leave them—the settlers—landlocked within isolated enclaves, "separated from their land, work and services."[22]

But the settlers' pressure to include as many settlements within the western side of the barrier as possible and the military intention to run the barrier through "strategic ground" were at odds with the diplomatic and legal pressures to place the barrier as close as possible to the green line. So, unable to accommodate contradictory political pressures while maintaining its graphic coherence, the path of the barrier has reached its breaking point.

The more forces in the vicinity of a line, the more complex its path. The modernist painter Wassily Kandinsky thus set the basis for the formal organizations of lines across a canvas in his book *Points and Line to Plane*. When the force field around a line contains intense contradictions, the line can no longer maintain its graphic coherence and shreds into fragments and discontinuous vectors. Like sliced worms taking on renewed life, the fragments of the barrier started to curl around isolated settlement blocks and Palestinian towns and along the roads connecting them. Each of the separate elements, termed by the Ministry of Defense "depth barriers," contained a sequence of fortifications similar to that of the main barrier, and was laid out to provide a particular material response to "local security problems." With the multiplication of the "depth barriers," the constantly updated maps of the barrier grew to resemble layouts typical of Scandinavian coasts, where fjords, islands, and lakes make an inconclusive separation and break the coherent contiguity of both water and rock.

Paradoxically, the more success that local and international opposition has had in pushing the barrier closer to the green line, the more "depth barriers" have been planned and built on its eastern side and the more Palestinian life has been disrupted.[23]

The fragmentation of the barrier led the government to release in September 2004 an apparently contradictory statement, according to which "Ariel, Emanuel, Qedumim and Karnei Shomron [major settlements on the western slopes of the West Bank, where about fifty thousand settlers live] would be on the 'Israeli' side of the barrier . . .

but the barrier would not be connected to the main section."[24] If this proposal is real-ized, the large settlement blocks may become Israeli exterritorial islands within Palestinian space, strung together by protected corridors.

With public attention directed mainly to the visible, linear part of the barrier, its offspring "depth barriers" remain largely invisible to international politics and criti-cism. And thus a pact of convenience has been conceived: Israel will move the main barrier closer to the green line but will not be reproached for the series of politically invisible barriers it places in depth. The settlers will be both inside and outside, con-tent to be encircled by shards of the barriers composed of the same system of forti-fication and sensors as the main, linear section. The Palestinians would be left to pay the price, as usual, with the fabric of their lives further severed by this exponential increase in the total length of barriers.

Indeed, with the projects for fortifications in depth merely beginning at the time of this writing, an estimate published in *Ha'aretz* claimed that since the start of the intifada about 500 kilometers of fence have already been built around settlements throughout the West Bank—more than current estimates regarding the total length of the main barrier.

The settlements earmarked to remain east of the main section of the barrier have also been fenced in and are already defined as "special security zones." In them, the area within the fenced perimeter, which extends 400 meters out from the last ring of homes, has been declared by the IDF as "sterile." Beyond the hygienic neurosis sug-gested by the term, its real meaning is that the military and the settlements' civil security guards may shoot to kill any Palestinian present there without warning.[25]

A similar geography of fortification exists in the yet to be dismantled Gaza Strip settlements. There the geographer Michael Romann has identified five different systems of fencing, ranging from one which borders the entire Gaza Strip to another which surrounds each one of the settlements within, and another which criss-crosses the area between settlements in an effort to stop penetrations.[26]

The Palestinians, for their part, have found themselves trapped in the several dozen enclaves that lie in the seam area between the barrier and the green line. The number of people living in these enclaves currently stands at about 12,000, but, according to present estimates, more then 100,000 Palestinians—about 5 percent of

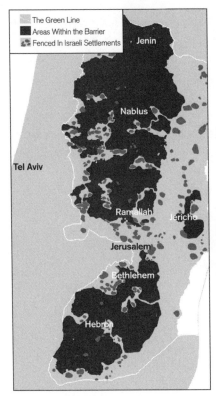

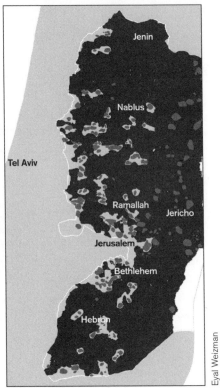

The Green Line
Areas Within the Barrier
Fenced In Israeli Settlements

Eyal Weizman

Isolated Palestinian enclaves within the barrier as planned in summer 2003.

Isolated Israeli islands within the barrier after ICJ and HCJ rulings in summer 2002 (estimated path).

the total population of the West Bank—may be trapped in this interborderline zone, mainly around Jerusalem, when the barrier project is completed.[27] In October 2003, the IDF declared the enclaves "closed military zones" and enforced this status with extra barriers between them and the green line. Simultaneously, IDF orders have coerced their residents into a new legal status: "temporary residents." Without moving, physical reality has been shifted around these communities, rendering their presence west of the wall "temporary"—a prelude perhaps to their future relocation to the east of it. "Temporary residents" are currently forbidden to enter either Israel or the occupied area without special permits.

The settlements in the "special security zones" and the Palestinian communities in the "closed military zones" are both spaces of exception—islands that are physically and legally estranged from their immediate surroundings—but their functions must not be confused. The settlements' fences are meant to protect the lives of settlers and exclude a "threatening" outside. Gates within the fences lead out to protected fast and wide traffic corridors that effectively integrate the settlers economically and politically with Israel. Palestinians, on the other hand, according to a recent report from B'tselem, have restricted access on more than 700 kilometers of West Bank roadways because of forty-one "sterile" roads reserved for the use of Jews only.[28] Fortifications (fences, walls, ditches, dikes) around Palestinian enclaves are meant to imprison those inside and to exclude them physically and legally. Their gates, when opened, lead out through crowded checkpoints into narrow dust roads.

The net result of the barrier's fragmented path is a condition of double enclosure: "Israeli islands," where Israeli law applies, which will be fenced in east of the barrier for their "self-protection," and Palestinian islands remaining west of the barrier, which will be sealed off to prohibit "security threats" from leaking out and remain subjected to Israel's military-legal regime. Under this arrangement, the traditional perception of political space as a contiguous territorial surface, delimited by continuous borders, is no longer relevant.

More than merely a fortification system, the barrier is a bureaucratic-logistical device that seeks to create and maintain a demographic separation. By designating and limiting habitats, by physically marking out the limit of different legal statuses, the barriers are administrative apparatuses of population control. Their convoluted paths create an archipelago of exclusion that separates out zones of democracy where civil liberties are exercised from those where no rights fully apply, and thus between two types of lives: one protected and precious, comprising a modern political public, and the other an imagined premodern tribal society that is seen as an alien and hostile component of the landscape and natural environment. Without common humanity between the settler and the native, understood and accepted, there is no limit to the violence that members of the former are willing to apply to those of the latter for the protection of their lives and superiority.

A Temporary-Permanent Line
The Web site of the Israeli Ministry of Foreign Affairs claims that "the anti-terrorist fence is a passive, temporary ... measure, not a permanent border," and that decisions

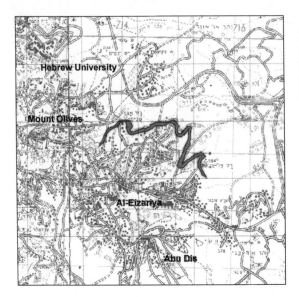

Expropriation Order 53/03:
An expropriation order for temporary
military necessity around Jerusalem.
The dark stain is land taken for the
construction of the barrier (place
names have been translated to
English and do not appear in the
Hebrew/Arabic original.)

regarding its nature and path are designed to address "urgent security needs."[29] As such, its path may be amended in the context of a final status political resolution.

Barriers are indeed different from borders in that they do not separate an "inside" and an "outside" of a sovereignty-based political and legal system, but merely act as contingency apparatuses to prohibit movement across territory. The claim for the "temporariness" of the barrier attempts thus to position it as an instrument of contingency in a temporary state of emergency. Here, the famous warning of Italian philosopher Giorgio Agamben becomes relevant. Following Carl Schmitt's analysis on the state of emergency—a state defined as a "temporary" exception to the law in which the juridical order is suspended or eased—Agamben warns that this state may in fact, while camouflaging itself as temporary, continue indefinitely, and thus that "temporariness" should itself be rejected as a justification for the suspension of the law.[30]

The use of the term "occupation" for the forty-year-old Israeli military control and administration of the West Bank and Gaza Strip may also be misleading. An "occupation" is associated with a transitional state, one in the process of being resolved through political or military means and during which contingency measures that would not be tolerated otherwise may be applied. Israeli philosophers Adi Ophir and Ariella

Azoulay claim that the very logic of the military rule in the West Bank and Gaza perpetuates itself through ever-new, seemingly "temporary" facts, and that it is the definition of the "temporality" of the state of conflict that allows this presence to continue: "Temporariness is now the law of the occupation ... temporary encirclement and temporary closures, temporary transit permits, temporary revocation of transit permits, temporary enforcement of an elimination policy, temporary change in the open-fire orders ... This occupier is an unrestrained, almost boundless sovereign, because when everything is temporary almost anything, any crime, any form of violence is acceptable, because the temporariness seemingly grants it a license, the license of the state of emergency."[31] When temporariness is both the method and the law, the military can portray every action as a response to emergency and Israeli civilian society can ignore every evil.

Temporariness as a principle is enshrined in international law. The Hague convention of 1907 allows for the suspension, during times of war, of some civilian rights. Similarly, an occupying force may, in times of combat, temporarily seize private property and land in order to construct the temporary fortifications and installations that serve its momentary military necessities.[32] Problematic here, though, for the situation under discussion, is the idea of war and peace as separate and defined states. Symmetrical wars between state actors can be long but tend to have clear beginnings and ends. In contrast, the Israeli-Palestinian conflict, like other past and present colonial conflicts, is an ever- and always present asymmetrical, low-intensity conflict between a state and quasi-state actors. It is a conflict that persists throughout time rather than one which abruptly disrupts time's flow. In it, war and peace are no longer dialectical opposites, but are intertwined in a single extended "no war/no peace" continuum. Resistance is violent, constant but sporadic; pacification missions are sometimes brutal and at other times bureaucratical; total peace is not possible and war has no end.

Indeed, throughout Zionist history, pre-state authorities and later the state itself often used arguments concerning temporary security needs in order to create permanent political facts on the ground. The "relocation" of Palestinian communities throughout the war of 1947–48 was initially argued as a "temporary" security measure taken in order to protect the traffic arteries. The expulsion of many other Palestinian villagers was argued as "temporary" for a variety of other security reasons.[33]

Almost sixty years later, those refugees left in Israel are still considered "present absentees," and those who left the borders of the state still live "temporarily" in refugee camps.

In the first twelve years following the 1967 occupation, when Israeli governments were called upon to respond to Palestinian petitions in the High Court of Justice (HCJ) against the seizure of their private lands for the construction of settlements, military officers were invited as expert witnesses to testify, along the principles laid out in the Hague Convention, that there was an "essential, urgent and temporary military necessity"[34] in setting a particular settlement there and then. Settlements were argued for as security measures, undertaken for the protection of the state from invasion as well as in the task of antiterrorist control. Until the settlers themselves, fearing that this legal defense might threaten the continuation of the settlement project, replaced their argument of "temporary" security necessity to the "permanence" of their divine right, the HCJ accepted expert military opinion and allowed the seizure of Palestinian land for the establishment of settlements.[35]

Two seemingly contradictory conditions maintain the "temporary" state of the Israeli military regime: the persistence of violence and the presence of initiatives for political resolution. The fact that some degree of violence exists justifies the continual application of "urgent security measures." Violence allows "security" to be invoked as a legal argument to justify what would otherwise be illegal.[36] For security to go on fulfilling this role, insecurity must persist, as the Palestinian scholar Samera Esmeir claims: "Security-rituals must not bring about absolute security" because that would mean the loss of the rationale for their further application. Instead, they "must always engage in redefining what security means."[37] The definition of all military activities as responses to "security threats" seeks similarly to perpetuate the conditions that justify its further deployment. The logic of "security" is thus employed beyond the narrow military sense of the word—as protection from bodily harm or damage to property—as a political-ideological concept that promotes itself through the configuration of the built environment, resource allocation, and freedom of movement.

In this context the popular belief that suicide bombings could be stopped by the construction of a barrier has been employed to achieve a new political-territorial reality. This belief completely ignores the fact that most suicide bombers do not smuggle themselves into Israel across open borders, but pass most often through manned checkpoints.[38] If the barrier were solely responsible for the reduction in bombing, we would expect to see far more attacks take place on its eastern side, which is still full of civilian and military targets.

The other condition, the constant presence of a political initiative on the diplomatic table (there have been proposals for conflict resolution from day one of the post–1967 war era right through to the present day) has made the conflict seem always on the brink of being resolved. The very possibility of such a tantalizing prospect enables the justification of the inconveniences and suffering of the present.

In the context of such continuing (mis)use of the notion of temporariness, it is hardly surprising that the Israeli government is currently attempting to apply the same formula—of "essential, urgent and temporary" need—to defend, in the High Court of Justice, the seizure of private Palestinian land for the construction of the barrier, and moreover that the same category of temporariness is again proposed to the Palestinians in the context of the roadmap—a soft sovereignty within temporary, flexible borders that the Palestinians would be free to call a state.

The recurrent use of this legal measure exposes the underlying paradox behind the system of Israeli domination and control: in order to pacify the territories, "temporary" security measures must be employed. But, since the population now rebels against the very security measures (the settlements) originally placed to pacify it, the state of conflict must be extended and further "temporary" measures (now, the barrier) must be erected to engage the ever more radical hostilities. This situation precisely repeats the nightmare scenario offered by Agamben: the Occupied Territories are trapped in a time loop where temporariness becomes permanent and exception becomes the rule, where no reality is fixed, no rules are clear, and no legal definition is stable.

In terms of the transformation of the built environment, what the temporary state of emergency is to time, flexibility may be to space. The Israeli planning system in the Occupied Territories has learned to use the ever-developing and fast-transforming security environment to create temporary security measures that at "every stage," as Amira Hass claims, "can be explained as an ad-hoc reaction, or the whim of this or that government or pressure group. . . ."[39] but in effect all add up to form a general strategic reality.

Enclaves, Exclaves

The open frontier has made the "politics of separation" spread into the entire Israeli political body, blurring the border even further. On both sides of the green line, manned checkpoints and guarded entrances have been erected to protect bus stations, shopping malls, and inner-city residential neighborhoods. Physical and manned fortifications (electronic surveillance alone is no longer seen adequate in face of the intensity and immediacy of threats) are "sold" to the Israeli public as product on the market, recalling Mike Davis's observation that, in Los Angeles, security has turned into a lifestyle.[40]

Within Israel, proper barriers between Jews and Palestinians camouflage their real objectives. The high earth rampart that was recently raised between the poor Palestinian coastal village of Jisr al-Zarqa and Caesarea, a town of the extremely wealthy, was planted with trees and flowers, a supposed innocent landscape feature, in order to disguise its function. Following this example, the wealthy, previously agricultural—and presently suburban—Moshav Nir Ziv demanded the government to construct a 1.5-kilometer-long and 4-meter-high "acoustic" concrete wall that would in effect separate it from the predominantly Palestinian-Israeli, drug-plagued Lod-city neighborhood of Pardes Snir that, as members of the Moshav claim, bothers them and disturbs their quality of life.[41] These apparatuses form mainly visual barriers—creating a series of scopically defensible spaces and blind zones. The visual exclusion of Palestinians from the Israeli space obviously mirrors their increasingly political exclusion.

This is not surprising given the fact that Israel's own Palestinian minority, comprising more then 20 percent of the citizens of the state, has been repeatedly cast out as second-class citizens. They are included within the Israeli economy as laborers and service providers but are increasingly excluded from other spheres of the Israeli state and have even been described by Finance Minister Benjamin Netanyahu as a "demographic problem"[42] that upsets rather than forms part of an Israeli public. The territorialization of this demographic phobia has meant more barriers, planned and built, between Jewish and Arab communities in neighboring villages or shared cities and the further fractalization and fragmentation of the terrain into a peninsula of enmity and alienation.

The multiplicity of overlapping territorial claims, the presence of fortifications across the entire terrain, and the evolving landscape of permanent low-intensity conflict reflect the free-frontier mentality of the Israeli state, one which seeks to blur borders

A barrier between the Palestinian-Israeli village of Jisr al-Zaqa and the town of Caesarea as a landscape feature.

rather than fix them.[43] And thus, floating in a perpetual state of physical and social fermentation, uncertain in its identity, with its inconsistent behavior and self-destructive impulses, Israel—in the words of Israeli architect Zvi Efrat—goes on affirming its unresolved "borderline disorder."[44]

Ruling in Three Dimensions

With the solidification of the territorial strategy embodied by the barrier, and the specter of a permanent "Palestinian state in temporary borders" scattered on land-locked sovereign islands and without control of its subterranean water resources below or its airspace above, yet another territorial paradox will have to be resolved. The fragmentation of jurisdiction will not be compatible with Sharon's public pledges that, with the implementation of the Bush-sponsored "roadmap," he will carve out a "contiguous area of territory in the West Bank that would allow the Palestinians to travel from Jenin [the northernmost city in the West Bank] to Hebron [the southernmost] without passing any Israeli roadblocks." When bewildered reporters asked how continuity could be resolved with such intense territorial fragmentation, Sharon responded (probably with one of his notorious winks) that this would be accomplished by "a combination of tunnels and bridges."[45]

This type of continuity, as Sharon first realized in 1996—when, as minister of national infrastructure under Benjamin Netanyahu, he inaugurated the first "tunnel road"—can be achieved not on the surface but in three-dimensional space. The tunnel road connects Jerusalem with the southern settlements of Gush Etzion and, further, with the Jewish neighborhoods of Hebron. To accomplish this, it performs a double contortion: spanning as a bridge over a Palestinian-cultivated valley and diving into a tunnel under Beit-Jalla, a Palestinian town adjacent to Bethlehem.

The Israeli writer and activist Meron Benvenisti, who first spotted the phenomenom, describes the effects of this project as the "crashing of three dimensions into six: three Israeli and three Palestinian."[46] Both the valley that the road spans and the city it dives under are areas under limited Palestinian control. The physical separation of traffic infrastructure cuts through the legal labyrinth created by the Oslo Accords. The tunnel and bridge are under full Israeli control (zone C), the valley below the bridge is under Palestinian civilian control (zone B), while the city above the tunnel is under Palestinian civilian and military control (zone A). Where infrastructure and territory become incompatible, sovereignty and jurisdiction are divided along the up/down axis of the vertical dimension. The bridge's columns rest within the Palestinian area, and the road is Israeli, with the "international border" running through the thermodynamic joint between them.

A new way of imagining territory has been developed in the context of the Israel-Palestine conflict. The region is no longer seen as the two-dimensional surface of a single territory, but as a large, "hollow" three-dimensional space, within which the West Bank can be physically partitioned into two separate but overlapping national geographies. Within this volume, separate security corridors, infrastructure, overground bridges, and underground tunnels are woven into an Escher-like structure.

This hollow, three-dimensional way of seeing territory was first proposed in the UN Partition Plan of 1947. At two locations within the geographical arrangement it proposed, the territories of Israel and Palestine were to cross over each other, causing the border to change from a single-dimension line into a nondimensional point. The chosen solution was to fully embrace the third dimension: over these so-called kissing points, Israel was to be connected by a bridge and Palestine by a tunnel. The connection of the two estranged Palestinian territories of Gaza and the West Bank—forty-seven kilometers as the crow flies—would, according to the Oslo Accords, be similarly connected into a single political unit. The so-called safe passage would, as

Eyal Weisman

OCHA

Top: The Israeli tunnel road spans over Palestinian fields and dives under a Palestinian city. The path of the wall is approximated from expropriation orders.

Bottom: The road above is Israeli—the underpass in Palestine connecting Habla and Qalqilyah.

Benjamin Netanyahu declared while prime minister and recent plans promoted by the Rand Corporation and the World Bank still insist, become a Palestinian sovereign bridge spanning over Israeli territory[47] and include six motor lanes, two railway lines, high-voltage electricity cables, and an oil pipe.[48] In 2000, the maps submitted at Camp David for the partition of Jerusalem necessitated numerous "kissing points" between estranged Israeli and Palestinian neighborhoods. According to the Clinton plan, Jerusalem would have had sixty-four kilometers of walls and forty bridges and tunnels spanning over alien sovereignty connecting the enclaves to each other.

Now, hand-in-hand with the planned completion of the barrier, other three-dimensional solutions are being employed to resolve the problems of connecting estranged territorial islands. Transport contiguity in a dual road network has been invented to bypass the inability to provide territorial contiguity. The two neighboring Palestinian towns of Habla and Qalqilyah have recently been connected by an Israeli-built tunnel running under the section of the barrier that cut them apart. Sixteen other subsurface passages are planned across the West Bank, mostly under the main Jewish-only traffic arteries or under the intrusive folds of the barrier.[49] The new railway line designed to connect Tel Aviv to Jerusalem will pass in tunnels when it goes through the West Bank and resurface at the center of west Jerusalem.[50] Plans are also under way to transform Route 60—the main north-south traffic artery linking all major Palestinian cities—into an elevated viaduct placed on columns within the areas where the Israeli east-west arteries pass underneath. In the context of this territorial conflict, bridges are no longer just devices engineered to overcome a natural boundary or connect impossible points. Rather, they become the boundary itself, separating the two national groups across the vertical dimension.

According to the Israeli official responsible for traffic infrastructure, the friction between the settlers and Palestinians "could be solved if certain interchanges enabled Palestinians to enter the area from one side [and settlers from another]. We would drive above and they would drive from below, and vice versa."[51] In August 2004 the government of Israel presented to the World Bank a detailed document requesting financing for more then a dozen of these new apparatuses of vertical separation, portraying them as essential for the maintenance of traffic contiguity between the Palestinian areas otherwise severed by the barrier. But, as Amira Hass suggested, such financing may paradoxically be subsidizing and sustaining the regime behind the barrier, by giving the impression that Palestinian transport and movement can be sustained in an arrangement that leaves the settlements and the barrier intact.[52] What is generally known as the "humanitarian paradox" presents here a sharp dilemma: Is it moral to ease the pain of the barrier? Would international aid not amount to accepting the barrier as a fait accompli, at a time when its very legality is still in question? Effectively, given the ICJ ruling, donor countries investing in infrastructure that serves the barrier's construction would themselves be in breach of international law.

The knotted condition of volumetric partitions originates in what I have previously called the "politics of verticality,"[53] a political process that describes the mental and physical partitioning of the West Bank not only in surface but in volume. Under the national regime of vertical sovereignty, theological transcendentalism is combined with territorial military strategy not only to effect topographical variations where the · hilltop settlements overlook the valleys, but also to sever the airspace from the ground (Israel would control the airspace and electromagnetic radiation over Palestinian areas) and the crust of the ground from its archaeological and mineral depth. This "volumetric politics" reflects the territorial overlap of the two different cognitive and physical environments that see each other as its negative opposite: one—the "biblical," upperland Israel—scattered across isolated but well-tended hilltop settlements and woven together by a modern Jewish-only matrix of infrastructure and over passes; and the other, lower, Palestine—of crowded cities, towns, and villages that generally inhabit the valleys between and underneath, cut apart by wide Israeli bypasses and military checkpoints and maintaining fragile connection on improvised dust-roads and underpasses. This laminar arrangement is reflected by the legal/bureaucratic one that defines the settlers as full citizens of a "master nation" and casts the Palestinians out as an inferior nation over which Israel can rule by right.

With the technologies and infrastructure required for the physical segregation of the two nations along complex volumetric borders, it furthermore appears as if this most complex geopolitical problem of the Middle East has gone through a scale shift and has taken on an architectural dimension. The West Bank appears to have been reassembled in the shape of a complex airport building with its closed-off security enclaves, checkpoints, complex bypasses, and exclusive security corridors.

The fortified islands and the volumetric web of over- and underpasses are the two interdependent and synergetic components in the topology of conflict. Their combination distorts the traditional space-time coordinates of simple Euclidian geometry: the barrier makes the near (the Palestinian village) far, while the three-dimensional bypasses make the far (Israeli employment centers) near. This compartmentalization of space and reorganization of time is a literal demonstration of Derek Gregory's assertion that imagined geographies "fold difference into distance." [54]

The untenable territorial legal and sovereign knot created by the politics of separation reveals another fundamental truth: although hundreds of proposals prepared by do-good cartographers from the time of the British mandate to the present have attempted to find a path along which Israel and Palestine could be separated, this path has repeatedly proven itself politically and geometrically impossible. This land, it seems, can not be partitioned.

Israel and Palestine are not two different places that can be imagined to coexist side by side, but are in effect different readings of the same place, with overlapping memories and national claims. Against the endless search for the form and mechanisms of "perfect" separation comes the realization that a viable solution does not exist within the realm of territorial design. Instead, a nonterritorial approach based on cooperation, mutuality, and equality must be taken to bring about a new politics of space sharing.

Notes

1. There is a multiperspective problem regarding the semantics of the project: Israelis prefer to use the term "fence," as in "separation fence" or "antiterrorist fence," hoping to minimize, at least in their eyes, the scale of a massive construction and make it appear more domestic and benign—along the lines of "good fences make good neighbors." The Israeli and Palestinian opposition prefer the term "wall," concentrating on the urban areas where the fence solidifies into a wall. Their campaign hopes to equate it in the Western imagination with the Berlin Wall, a barrier that was as well composed throughout most of its route as a fence. When talking to former Palestinian president Mahmoud Abbas, President George W. Bush called the barrier "a wall" and with Sharon, "a fence." It must be noted that from the military perspective, a fence is generally preferable. The transparency of the fence allows the security forces to see and shoot through it, while a wall may allow the enemy to assemble and prepare for crossing undetected. Walls are generally used in dense urban areas where the danger is that snipers may shoot into the Israeli side. In this article, following the terminology set by human rights organization B'tselem, I have used the term "barrier," which I find capable of integrating the changing material manifestations of such a set of fortifications.

2. According to the "Peace Index" survey from October 2004, published in *Ha'aretz* on November 4, 2004, despite the international criticism, the barrier still enjoys the massive support of the Israeli public, with 83 percent supporting it from the entire center of the political spectrum. With about 20 percent of the Israel population being Palestinians citizens, the percentage of support may practically include the entire Israeli-Jewish public.

3. The spectrum of Israeli opinion regarding the politics of separation extends from the Israel Communist Party, which calls for a complete evacuation of Israeli settlements and a return to the 1967 green line, to (1) advocates of the Geneva Accord, a proposed final status agreement initiated by former justice minister Yossi Beilin and former Palestinian minister of information Yasser Abed Rabbo, providing for an independent and demilitarized Palestine based on the 1967 lines with slight modifications and land swaps that would allow Israel to keep the Gush Etzion settlements, the Jewish neighborhoods in East Jerusalem, the Jewish quarter of the Old City, and the settlement of Ma'aleh Edumim; and (2) the *Yesha* Council of Jewish Communities in Judea, Samaria, and the Gaza Strip that asks for seven separated, landlocked Palestinian cantons in zone A around Palestinian population centers. Each of these political groups sees the hardening of the border as essential for its territorial compromise. At present the coalition agreement that brought the Labor Party into the government allows for the continuation of the barrier project.

4. The 2004 redeployment plan from Gaza promoted by Ariel Sharon has been presented as a necessary price Israel would have to pay for retaining the major settlement blocks in the West Bank. Sharon himself has made clear these intentions. In the Jewish New Year issue of the mass daily *Yedioth Ahronoth* he claimed that the disengagement "frees Israel from pressure to adopt one or another plan that would have been dangerous for it. I don't see the terror coming to an end. . . . It is very possible that after the evacuation, for a very long period there won't be anything else. . . . Israel will continue its campaign against terror and will remain in the territories after the execution of the disengagement." Quoted in: Amira Hass, "Disengagement: And still the occupation", *Ha'aretz*, September 22, 2004.

5. The barrier is composed of a sequence of fortifications measuring between 35 and 100 meters in width. The main component of the barrier is a touch-sensitive, "smart," three-meter-high electronic fence, placed on a 150-centimeter-deep concrete foundation (to prevent digging under it) and topped with barbed wire (to prevent climbing over it). Along it run two patrol roads, a trace road (where footprints of intruders are registered), a trench, and pyramid-section barbed-wire fences. Together with day- and night-vision video cameras and small radars, these instruments make sure nobody would ever be able to cross it. At some places, when the barrier nears a Palestinian town, the tactically required see-through (and shoot-through) fence solidifies into an eight-meter-high bulletproof wall. There are about sixty kilometers built or planned of solid wall through or around Palestinian cities. Other locations along the route utilize enhanced natural barriers, like fifty-meter-high artificial cliffs cut into the mountain rock. As these lines are written in October 2004, 255 kilometers of wall have already been constructed, and, according to the United Nations Office for the Coordination of Humanitarian Affairs (http://ochaonline.un.org/), a further 367 kilometers are planned.

6.   The Ministry of Defense provides some details on its Web site: more than ten million square meters of earth were relocated and three thousand kilometers of barbed wire were already laid out. The barrier has an estimated per-kilometer construction cost of $1.5 million and is the biggest (both in terms of size and price) national infrastructure project ever undertaken in Israel. See www.mod.gov.il, August 12, 2004.

7.   Sharon managed to placate the right-wing ministers of his coalition government when he promised that the barrier did not mean that "we are here and they are there," as the slogan of the Left has it, but that "we are here and we are there": that Israel would effectively control the two sides of the fortified line.

8.   Baruch Kimmerling claims that the primary goal of the Sharon government is the destruction of the Palestinian Authority in particular and of any Palestinian polity in general. He claims that in Sharon's political and strategic vision, the Palestinians are not a nation with national rights over their territory but a collection of individual communities that may at best enjoy a limited version of personal rights. According to this strategy, isolated territories would nourish—as they already did—local "gangs" and clans that would challenge a central Palestinian authority. The current policy of ignoring the PA on a diplomatic level as part of a unilateral separation plan from Gaza fulfills the conditions of this term. Baruch Kimmerling, *Politicide: Ariel Sharon's War Against the Palestinians* (London: Verso Press, 2003).

9.   The green line, which the Palestinian government would like to see as its border with Israel, is 350 kilometers long. Compare this to the first Sharon proposal for the barrier route, which would be more than 1,000 kilometers long.

10. In order to decide what kind of sovereignty could be handed over to the Palestinians on the isolated territorial shards allocated to them, the IDF (not the government!) has set up a special team within the International Law unit of the Military Advocate General's Office to examine existing models of limited and soft sovereign forms. Case studies researched include examples from present-day Puerto Rico to Germany under the occupation forces in the decade after World War II. Although it found none of these models completely suitable for straightforward emulation, a synthesis of these two has been recommended.

11. The estimated route was divided into subsections, each a few dozen kilometers long, and each implemented by one of twenty-two separate private contractors on government tenders who compete between themselves on quality, price, and speed. The fact that the construction of the barrier is incremental means that some sections are constructed immediately after they get government approval, while others are already implemented and others not yet planned. For security and diplomatic reasons, the Ministry of Defense does not provide complete information about the entire route along which it plans to run the barrier.

12. Michel de Certeau insisted on a difference between space and place. Place could be described as a stable material reality with a specific, definite location, dimension, and material characteristics. Space, by contrast, exists through action, and is defined by the intersection of the path of mobile elements. A place could be a building and the space defined by the party that takes place within it. Michel de Certeau, *The Practice of Everyday Life* (Berkeley: University of California Press, 1998).

     For Henri Lefebvre, the triadic components of space are based on the difference between what he calls *perceived*, *conceived*, and *lived* space. *Perceived* space is the space occupied by sensory phenomena—the physical, real, and tangible environment. *Conceived* space is that of mental representations, the planned and constructed terrain of engineers, city planners, and architects, expressed in drawings, figures, and statistics. *Lived* space is the space of social practice. Making the distinction implies separate domains and different spatial practices. See Henri Lefebvre, *The Production of Space* (Oxford: Blackwell, 1991), and Henri Lefebvre, *Writings on Cities* (London: Blackwell, 1996).

13. Another tactical consideration in the positioning of fortification lines is latitude. Unlike commonly perceived, a defensible line should not run on top of a mountain ridge but at about three quarters of its height, on the slope facing the "enemy" side. The reason for this is that the silhouette of infantry patrols and military vehicles driving along the line would appear against the background sky. Because fortifications and barriers include roads running their length (the West Bank barrier has three parallel roads along its length), their route must conform as well to the limitation of vehicular movements, one of which is a maximum ascent and descent angle no steeper than 9 percent. The Ministry of Defense claims that following

these principles, it has laid the path of the barrier such that it attempts to keep similar latitude by following as much as possible the contours of topographical lines. According to this claim, the topography of the western slopes of the West Bank has generated the path of the barrier.

14. The illegal outposts recently set up on the eastern slopes of the West Bank Mountains have been located there in order to connect between the proposed eastern barrier and the settlements around the city of Nablus. Similarly, the locations of the outposts erected east of the large urban settlement of Ariel are an attempt to create the settlement continuity that would make the barrier cut deeper into the West Bank.

15. A short case study I have been asked to examine for the human rights organization B'tselem demonstrated that, contrary to claims by the Ministry of Defense, the military logic of building by topography tends to be compromised when the state aims to include areas earmarked for the future expansion of settlements. In the case of the settlement of Zufin, north of Qalqilyah, the path was set two kilometers east of the settlement's built-up area with the purpose of encompassing some tracts of noncontiguous land that is included in the settlement's jurisdiction area. As a result, Palestinian residents of Jayyous were separated from their vineyards. In other words, the path of the barrier has compromised the military logic for the aim of supporting the settlement. See Shlomi Suissa, *Not All It Seems: Preventing Palestinians Access to Their Lands West of the Separation Barrier in the Tulkarm-Qalqilyah Area* (Jerusalem: B'tselem, June 2004).

16. Yehezkel Lein, *Behind the Barrier: Human Rights Violations as a Result of Israel's Separation Barrier* (Jerusalem: B'tselem, April 2003), www.btselem.org/Download/2003_Behind_The_Barrier_Eng.doc.

17. Ibid.

18. The Ariel loop is a particularly intrusive fold that stretches out deep into the heart of the West Bank in order to incorporate the settlement city of Ariel (population 17,000). It was announced in July 2003 and immediately faced severe public outrage. The region of Ariel houses the largest numbers of settlers in relatively expensive and high-density buildings. Wealthy suburban settlements are crowded against impoverished Palestinian villages and towns. With an Israeli per capita gross domestic product (GDP) twenty times larger than that of Palestinians, the economic disparity between the neighboring communities (articulated by the proposed path of the barrier) is higher than between any two other neighboring populations worldwide.

19. The International Court of Justice (ICJ) ruled that, in building the barrier, Israel had violated international humanitarian law by infringing on Palestinians' freedom of movement and freedom to seek employment, education, and health. It noted that "Israel . . . is under an obligation to cease forthwith the works of construction of the wall being built in the Occupied Palestinian Territory, including in and around East Jerusalem, to dismantle forthwith the structure therein situated." Following the ruling, the United Nations General Assembly adopted a resolution condemning the barrier. One hundred and fifty nations voted in favor of the draft, ten abstained, and six—including the United States, Micronesia, the Marshall Islands, and Australia—opposed it.

20. In February 2004, the Ministry of Defense began to change the barrier's route in the area of Baqa al-Sharqiya. This was the first case in which it officially decided to make changes and publicly announced its intention to do so. As a consequence of further international pressure and the legal defeats for the Israeli government at the HCJ and ICJ, other segments of the routes have recently been returned to the drawing board. Furthermore, in August 2004 the Israeli attorney general surprisingly announced that in response to the ICJ's ruling, the government should "thoroughly examine" the possibility of formally applying the Fourth Geneva Convention to the occupied territories—something that Israeli governments have been reluctant to do throughout the forty years of the occupation.

21. Azmi Bishara, "Sealing Their Fate: The Wall's Implications for Palestinian Life," lecture delivered at the School of Oriental and African Studies, University of London, January 23, 2005.

22. The settlers claim that the HCJ principle of "proportionality" must be applied to them as well. Nadav Shragai, "Settlers plan mass court petitions over revised fence route," *Ha'aretz*, August 26, 2004.

23. Following the reroutings demanded by the High Court of Justice northwest of Jerusalem, for example, a long segment of the Modi'in-Jerusalem road will remain east of the barrier. The Ministry of Defense claimed that, in order to secure this route for Israeli motorists, it would be fortified with concrete walls on both its sides. This will in effect turn the road itself into an impassable barrier that will completely separate the Palestinian villages on either side. To overcome that, a few tunnels will be cut under the road for Palestinian pedestrians and vehicles.

24. Aluf Benn, "New fence route to be presented to U.S. first, then cabinet," *Ha'aretz*, September 7, 2004.

25. After pressure from settlement councils, the IDF has so far approved seventeen "special security zones" (also called by the IDF mini-barriers) and has already constructed three of them in the northern part of the West Bank. Each special security zone was budgeted at about $2.5 million, and in total $20 million. See Nadav Shragai and Nathan Guttman, "IDF proposes 400-meter security zone around settlements," *Ha'aretz*, October 3, 2003.

26. Michael Romann, "On Fences and Bypass Roads: Spatial Aspects of a Conflicting Environment," lecture delivered at the geography department of Tel Aviv University, November 22, 2004.

27. Jabal Al-Diek is a small suburb of Beit Sahour in the Bethlehem region. This community had the misfortune to have the Israeli hillside settlement of Har Homa (within the boundaries of Jerusalem) built on the ridge above it. Because of this proximity, Jabal Al-Diek will be enveloped by the barriers on all sides. This community will be separated from all the services it previously enjoyed in Beit Sahour. Residents will face restricted access to their families, friends, schools, hospitals, and workplaces. See full report by the United Nations Office for the Coordination of Humanitarian Affairs, http://ochaon nine.un.org/.

28. Yehezkel Lein, *Forbidden Roads: The Discriminatory West Bank Road Regime* (Jerusalem: B'tselem, August 2004).

29. Lein, *Behind the Barrier: Human Rights Violations As a Result of Israel's Seperation Barrier.*

30. Giorgio Agamben, *Homo Sacer: Sovereign Power and the Bare Life* (Stanford: Stanford University Press, 1998). See especially chapter 1, "The Paradox of Sovereignty," 15–29. Also Carl Schmitt, *Political Theology: Four Chapters on the Concept of Sovereignty* (Cambridge, MA: MIT Press, 1985).

31. Adi Ophir, "A Time of Occupation," in *The Other Israel*, ed. Roane Carey and Jonathan Shainin, (New York: The New Press, 2003), 60; in Hebrew see Ariella Azoulay and Adi Ophir, *Bad Days* (Tel Aviv: Resling Press, 2002).

32. See especially: The Hague Convention on the Laws and Customs of War on Land, and its attached Hague Regulations of 1907, www.icrc.org/ihl.nsf, August 13, 2004. These conventions aim to diminish the suffering of civilians and noncombatants, as far as military requirements permit, in times of war. Under the terms of International Humanitarian Law, the laws of belligerent occupation come into effect as soon as the government of the occupied territory is no longer capable of exercising its authority and ends when another government is in a position to impose its authority and control over that area. Where the law states that "private property cannot be confiscated," it immediately qualifies this restriction by "unless such ... seizure be imperatively demanded by the necessities of war," but that only for the duration of hostilities (Article 46).

33. Benny Morris, *The Birth of the Palestinian Refugee Problem Revisited* (Cambridge: Cambridge University Press, 2001).

34. This is the standard formula that appears in the orders. During the first twelve years of the occupation, settlements were defined as temporary security assets because they were integrated into the IDF plans for regional defense and were assumed to have the capacity to participate in the defense of the West Bank in the case of a military invasion from the east. The government has also argued that settlements were useful in controlling the Palestinian population within the occupied areas. On the basis of these arguments, the HCJ rejected all petitions of Palestinian landowners and accepted the government interpretation of "military necessity." As for the issue of "temporariness," Israeli governments used to claim that the future of the Occupied Territories would be agreed upon in the context of political negotiations, until when all projects and transformations of the built environment are to be considered as "temporary."

35. In June 1979, two years after the turnabout of power in Israel, several Palestinians petitioned against the requisition of their land for the establishment of the settlement of Elon Moreh. Responding to the petition, the government claimed, as routinely before, that the settlement was established in order to meet "temporary military need." But in court several of the settlers belonging to Gush Emunim, feeling themselves strengthened by the political transformation, proudly claimed that their right to settle the land of Israel is biblical and does not depend on the current needs and interests of the army; they sought thus to "naturalize" their presence in areas outside the legal borders of the state. Menachem Felix, one of the witnesses in the trial, explained the difference between Gush Emunim's view of time and that of the military: "Basing the requisition orders on security grounds in their narrow, technical meaning ... can be construed only in one way: the settlement is temporary and replaceable. We reject this frightening conclusion outright." See *HCJ 390/79,Dweikat et al. v. Government of Israel et al., Piskei Din 34(1) 1 (Elon Moreh)*, 21-21. The land seizure for the settlement was not accepted by the court and the settlement was dismantled. However, a new rationale for settling was developed by the state to compensate for it. See Yehezkel Lein and Eyal Weizman, *Land Grab: Israel's Settlement Policy in the West Bank* (Jerusalem: B'tselem, May 2002), www.btselem.org.

36. Iain Scobbie, "Sealing Their Fate: The Wall's Implications for Palestinian Life," Panel lecture in the School of Oriental and African Studies, University of London, January 23, 2005.

37. Samera Esmeir, "Introduction: In the Name of Security," *Adala's Review*, volume 4, Spring 2004, 5. The concept of security, as Hanna Herzog and Ronen Shamir argue in the same volume, "does not only relates to basic notions of 'law and order,' to personal protection against harm, or to concrete threats of violence and war. In its deepest sense 'security' is associated with the ability of the Jewish state to remain sovereign." See as well the review of this volume: Jonathan Yovel, "Security—or insecurity?" *Ha'aretz*, November 15, 2004.

38. United Nations Office for the Coordination of Humanitarian Affairs, www.ochaonline.un.org.

39. Amira Hass, "Donating to apartheid", *Ha'aretz*, September 8, 2004.

40. Mike Davis, *City of Quartz* (New York: Vintage Books, 1990), 223.

41. Aryeh Dayan, "Wall-eyed," *Ha'aretz*, July 22, 2003.

42. In response to the government arguments that the disengagement plan from Gaza is based on a demographic problem, Finance Minister Benjamin Netanyahu mentioned that "the only demographic problem is with Israeli Arabs"—a demographic problem that he said could be countered by improving the economical environment to encourage Jewish immigration from overseas. Gil Hoffman, "Netanyahu: Demographic problem lies within Israel," *The Jerusalem Post*, December 17, 2003.

43. Adriana Kemp calls this: ". . . the ambivalent attitude of the nation-state towards its 'geobody.' The presence of the border as a Janus, always polyvalent, never complete, expresses the tension between the political space of the state and the cultural space of the nation, a tension often hidden by the hyphenated concept of 'nation-state.'" Adriana Kemp, "Border Space and National Identity in Israel," in *Theory and Criticism, Space, Land, Home*, ed. Yehuda Shenhav (Jerusalem and Tel Aviv: The Van Leer Jerusalem Institute and Hakibbutz Hameuchad Publishing House, Spring 2000) 282, Hebrew.

44. Zvi Efrat, *Borderline Disorder* (Tel Aviv and Jerusalem: Israeli Ministry of Education and Israeli Ministry of Foreign Affairs, 2002).

45. Aluf Benn, "PM says would allow contiguous Palestinian territory in W. Bank," *Ha'aretz*, December 5, 2002.

46. Meron Benvenisti, "An Engineering Wander," in *Ha'aretz*, June 5, 1996 (my translation from Hebrew). This editorial later appeared in French in *Pre/occupations d'espace/Jerusalem au Pluriel* (Marseille: Image En Manoeuvres Editions, 2001), 171–173.

47. In an interview given to the London *Daily Telegraph*, Prime Minister Benjamin Netanyahu addressed the interviewer directly: "You connected two states separated by water with a tunnel [the Channel Tunnel]; we have a problem of connecting two entities separated by land . . . a separate corridor would allow the Palestinians a free connection between Gaza and the West Bank and the Israeli people territory and security." Quoted in Eli Kamir, "Safe passage," *Maarive*, April 8, 1998.

48. Israeli and Palestinian engineers proposed a bewildering variety of possible solutions to that engineering fit. A tunnel, a ditch, a land road cut off from the landscape with dikes on either side, a viaduct. The political debate turned very quickly to the question of "who's on top?" Avoiding the integrative solution of a land road, Israel asked for the Palestinian sovereign road to run through a seven-meter-deep ditch, while Palestinians naturally preferred the bridge. Ministry of Regional Cooperation, "The Safe Passage," internal publication, 1999. Yoram Shimon, an engineer and bridge builder commissioned to provide a feasibility study of this solution, claimed that the bridge would be supported by columns centered at fifty to sixty meters apart and would cost about $1 billion to construct. A similar bridge built over water near New Orleans is fifty kilometers long. See Shai Elias, "An expensive solution, but still possible," *Maarive*, April 8, 1998. For similar present plans see, Doug Suisman, *The Arc: A Formal Structure for the Palestinian State* (Washington, D.C.: Rand, 2004).

49. One tunnel has been built in Qalqilyah-Habla, another is planned near Tulkarm, three west of Ramallah, three around Bethlehem, and five in the south around Hebron. Other tunnels are currently planned to connect the Palestinian villages on the two sides of the Modi'in-Jerusalem highway. See United Nations Office for the Coordination of Humanitarian Affairs, Humanitarian Briefing, December 2004.

50. The westernmost tunnel will pass under Canada Park, which was developed over the ruins of Palestinian villages destroyed after the 1967 Six-Day War. The tunnel near Mevasseret Zion will pass through only a small section beyond the green line. See Aluf Benn, "TA-Jerusalem railway to pass through sections of West Bank," *Ha'aretz*, December 31, 2004.

51. This unnamed Israeli official was quoted in Amira Hass, "Israel asks PA donors to fund new, upgraded West Bank roads," *Ha'aretz*, September 5, 2004.

52. Ibid.; also United Nations Office for the Coordination of Humanitarian Affairs, Humanitarian Briefing, December 2004.

53. *The Politics of Verticality* was first published on www.opendemocracy.net, April 2002. A later version was published in *Territories: Islands, Camps and Other States of Utopia*, ed. Anselm Franke, Rafi Segal, and Eyal Weizman (Cologne: Walther Koning Publishing, 2003).

54. Derek Gregory, *The Colonial Present: Afghanistan, Palestine, Iraq* (Oxford: Blackwell Publishing, 2004), 262.

In the Spirit of Activism
Terry Boullata

Terry Boullata

One day in late August 2002, I woke up to find a military checkpoint at the crossroad in front of my house.

Plastic barriers cut the street into two. The army started banning us from driving toward the city of Jerusalem and the neighbors and I had to fight for our right to travel freely. We had to carry our tax papers every minute and to shout to get in or out.

As the days went on, the plastic barriers were changed into concrete blocks about 1–1.5 meters high. The blocks started shifting toward the hill up to my house at the entrance of Abu-Dis. Every block added during the day or night forced people to walk longer to cross farther inside the towns of Abu-Dis and Ezariyeh/Bethany.

When the concrete blocks were totally obstructing the road between my house and Abu-Dis, I started to jump over them like everyone else. Children, women, and elderly—everyone had to jump in order to cross to the other side. Jumping became essential training for Palestinian citizens living in the east suburbs of Jerusalem of Abu-Dis, Bethany, and East Sawahreh.

Jumping was not the only skill needed to carry out our daily routine. Tear gassing and sound bombs became an essential part of the game. Children going to schools were tear-gassed. The elderly jumping to reach the market or the hospitals were tear-gassed.

Tear gas filled my house on the top of the hill. The neighbors became more terrified every day as their children had to be kept at home while the army was roaring around in the neighborhood. The garbage bin was taken by the municipality under the pretext that the garbage truck could not reach us anymore (although in May 2004, the truck started collecting trash at the Israeli settlement established behind our houses and from the military base in the confiscated Cliff Hotel next door!).

Daily fighting started with the army surrounding our house. When coming back home, we would be faced by an army ambush. My husband, an illegal West Bank ID card holder, had to stay in the house for days whenever the army checkpoint was near the house.

Something had to be done. But no one knew what to do.

One afternoon, on the way back from school, I started arguing with a soldier to convince him to let me enter my neighborhood. Suddenly, an Israeli woman approached me. She had a tag with the name "Machsom Watch." *Machsom* means "checkpoint" in Hebrew and I soon learned that it was an organization that sends Israeli volunteers into the West Bank to monitor the conditions at checkpoints.

She asked what was happening and I couldn't wait to tell the story of the neighborhood and our daily sufferings. More Machsom Watch women started visiting us to get to know the geopolitical problems in the neighborhood.

Friendship was the first connection with those women. They brought media to cover the humiliations we faced, and, accordingly, we in the neighborhood became part of the media shows. Sometimes I would come back home to find three or four TV stations waiting for interviews.

Some media agencies were interested in covering more details of our daily sufferings: how children were reaching their schools from the neighborhood; how our West Bank ID-card-holding men were managing to return back to their East Jerusalem houses; how our children were managing to stay in touch with their grandparents on the other side of the wall. Our daily routine was exposed before the TV cameras. We agreed to do this for the sake of exposing the real story of the occupation wall, a story that has nothing to do with security as Israel claims, and everything to do with enforcing the occupation.

By January 2004 the Israeli army started replacing the one-meter concrete blocks with nine-meter-high slabs. The whole neighborhood was declared a military closed zone. The army checkpoints moved literally to the foundation of my house.

The Machsom Watch women were put on emergency call whenever my children had to leave for school in the morning or returned home at the end of the day. The whole neighborhood started unconsciously defying the wall and the army by continuing their daily routine of work and schooling despite military orders. Every ten minutes a new fight with the army flared up around the neighborhood and at night the neighbors would gather to retell their stories and bravery.

In February 2004 the International Court of Justice began to examine the legality of the wall and the media intensified their reports around the neighborhood. Israeli activists and politicians became interested in learning about the wall and Palestinian life around it. Several Israeli tour groups arrived and for many it was their first direct encounter with ordinary Palestinian citizens.

I have to admit that it was very mind-opening for me; many of these Israelis became close friends. Some of them started sleeping over in our house in order to help us in special tasks such as taking the children at the school where I am headmistress on a trip to the zoo in West Jerusalem.

I will never forget the school trip day. It was on Saturday, March 20, 2004. The Israeli civil administration refused to provide me with special permits for my West Bank teachers to escort the children (the eldest among the children were ten years old) on the zoo trip.

The Machsom Watch women came to the rescue. One woman slept at my house overnight and six other Israeli women arrived at 7:00 and escorted our school buses through the bypass checkpoint at the Ma'ale Adumim settlement. When stopped by the army on the checkpoint, they made their telephone calls—a diplomatic intervention—and in one hour all my schoolchildren were at the West Jerusalem zoo. Hundreds of these children were visiting a zoo for the first time in their lives. The looks on their faces made me cry and laugh at the same time.

We women, both Israelis and Palestinians, were able to make a small difference in the lives of these children from the eastern ghetto of Jerusalem.

During the trial at The Hague, I received an invitation by PENGON (the Palestinian Environmental Network of NGOs) to participate in a forum organized by the

United Civilians for Peace in Holland. I accepted the invitation with the dream of being in The Hague for the decision of the ICJ. And I got what I wanted.

On Saturday morning, we attended the NGO forum against the wall and on Monday afternoon I participated in the popular march against the wall at The Hague organized by Palestinians. All Palestinians participating were hopeful that the court would decide positively against the wall. But this was not enough. I still thought that we Palestinians had to have the world cry with us against the wall. The world should sing with us against the wall. The world should draw the same pictures of the wall.

Upon my return, I quickly contacted some Palestinian artists in East Jerusalem. My friends at the Sabreen artistic group, together with artists Suleiman Mansour and Hayan Ju'beh, gathered their old Israeli artist friends. The group started growing with every meeting. We discussed the importance of working jointly with Israeli artists. Israeli and Palestinian artists gathered and the discussion started. We agreed that the occupation was not just a Palestinian issue, but an Israeli/Palestinian one. We also agreed that the wall is an icon for the occupation and therefore we called ourselves "Artists Without Walls."

On April 1, we decided to go public about our goals with an artistic event. We agreed to make the wall invisible by opening a window through it. Our Israeli artist friends brought two projectors. The Palestinian community around the wall brought us electric cables and chairs. People gathered to watch what was happening. When it was totally dark, the projectors screened people standing on one side of the wall to the people standing on the other side of the wall. My neighbors came down to salute their family members who came to the other side. After two hours of cheering and waving, the projectors were turned off. The Israeli and Palestinian artists came around to our neighborhood for tea and dancing. We felt we were victorious.

Later in the summer, two more artistic events took place. An American singer came with his music (invited by the Popular Art Center in Ramallah) and Simone Bitton screened her award-winning film about the wall on the concrete blocks of the wall itself.

The wall is a violent action, but it cannot be resisted with violence. Only with nonviolence can we fight the wall. With this slogan, Israeli Knesset member Azmi Bishara started his one-week hunger strike on July 2, 2004, together with members of the Palestinian legislative council, political parties, and NGO representatives. The strikers

were bringing attention with their own bodies to the devastating reality of the building of the Israeli wall in the middle of the Beit Hanina/Ram area in East Jerusalem.

As a followup to the nonviolent resistance, I assisted in the coordination of the visit of Arun Gandhi (the grandson of Mahatma Gandhi) to Palestine in late August 2004. The visit was initiated by Palestinians for Peace and Democracy (a U.S.-based organization)[1] and was locally hosted by the Palestinian Campaign for Freedom and Peace, which included Palestinian political parties and NGOs.[2] Nonviolence was his message to the Palestinian resistance against the occupation. Nonviolence worked in India against the British occupation. It worked in South Africa and in the civil rights movement in North America. Nonviolence is the best strategy we, the Palestinian people, can adopt in resisting the occupation.

This is my belief, and so I shall continue resisting the wall and the occupation with my people, starting with my close family members in the neighborhood and friends in Artists Without Walls and the Palestinian Campaign for Freedom and Peace.

Terry Boullata

Notes

1.   See their Web site at www.p4pd.org.

2.   The Fatah Party, The People's Party, Palestinian Agricultural Relief Committees (PARC), and others.

The Wall Game

Lebbeus Woods

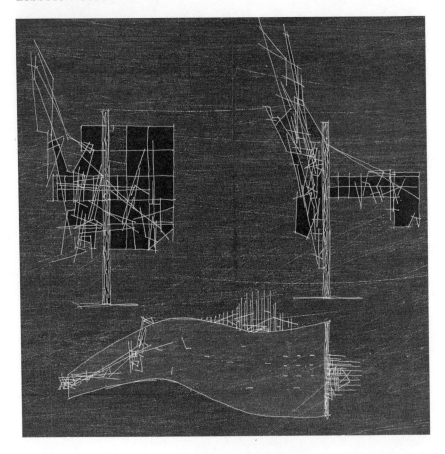

Israel, like any sovereign state, has the inherent right to defend itself, but not
by any means. If it flouts international law, as it is doing in continuing the construction
of the wall, it becomes a renegade state, outside the law and its protection. Whatever
Israel's power to get away with it for the moment, eventually it will come back to
haunt Israel, and in ways that may be unforeseen now, while it has the backing of the
United States and the tacit threat of its own nuclear weapons. Renegades eventually
isolate themselves, as the United States itself is learning from its own unilateral and

"preemptive" actions, and isolation ultimately threatens any nation's survival in a globally interdependent world.

The power of even the strongest nations can be wasted by their own misplaced exertions of power, even to the point where weaker, jealous, or vengeful nations can, by concerted effort, overcome them. It is in Israel's interest to stop building the wall, as a sign that it truly wants to be part of the international community of nations and is willing to abide by prevailing international law. In judging its position, Israel should recall that walls built to keep others out ultimately imprison those within. By continuing the construction of the wall, Israel is creating, in a grotesque historical twist, history's largest ghetto, separating and isolating its own people from the world upon which their survival, and that of the Jewish state, depends. But this need not be the case. There is still time. The wall is not yet completed. At this writing, only one-fourth of its planned extent is actually constructed. The rest weighs on the mind as though it already existed, but as yet it does not.

Let me be optimistic and imagine that the ruling powers in Israel come to, or are brought to, their senses and stop construction of the wall. The space for exchange, however tilted toward Israel by the existing imbalance of power, will remain open. But what should happen to the already constructed portions of the wall? Many will want to tear them down, and understandably so. They are ugly symbols, for many on the Israeli side and for most on the Palestinian side. Certainly, finished sections should be torn down to make the line more porous, so that Palestinians' direct access to their fields and jobs and villages is assured. But some sections of the wall could remain. If they were left as freestanding artifacts in a still-divided and yet still-negotiable land-scape, they might serve some useful purpose. One of these could be the Wall Game.

The Wall Game uses some sections of the wall as a two-sided playing field. Palestinians control one side, Israelis the other. Each side has a team of builders, architects, artists, and performers who make a construction on their side of the wall, using it as sole support. In other words, the new constructions cannot rest in any way directly on the ground, but only on the wall; they are cantilevered constructions. As such, the cantilever on one side must be balanced by the cantilever on the other side or else the wall will fall to one side or the other, and the game will be over.

It is a game only for two opposing sides. One side cannot play it alone, as unbalanced structural forces will bring the wall down very quickly. A one-sided game has no point—that is, no winner. The point of the Wall Game is to win.

There are three levels of "winning." The first level is to keep the game going. In this sense, both sides win against the improbability of their continuing to play and against the wall itself and the complex set of forces it activates. There is no time limit to the game. It ends only when one side wins over the other—the second level of winning—or they both lose. To understand how one side wins over the other, a little more must be known about the nature of the constructions they build.

It may be assumed that each team will build a different type of construction. Different materials, different configurations, different methods. This is because the

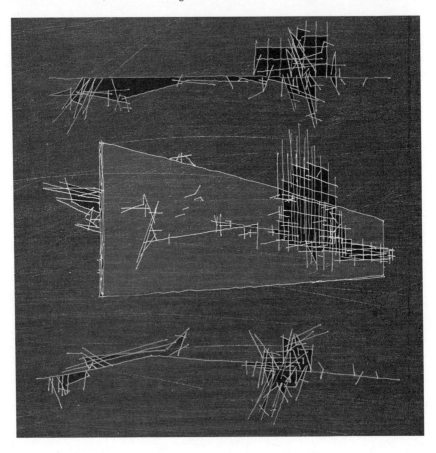

different teams represent different cultures, religions, histories, and aspirations. Even if both teams were to produce similar constructions, they could win on the first level only, because to win on the second level, one construction must convert the other.

Conversion of a construction occurs when its system of order—that is, its basic system of spatial reference—is transformed by the system of order of the opposing side. This occurs during predetermined time periods when the construction is left open to infiltration by the opposing construction, through the wall. During these time periods, the opposing team may build within the construction left open. Not every attempt to convert the opposing construction will be successful. If a construction left open to a conversion attempt is syntactically clear and strong, the attempt will have to be even clearer, stronger, and above all more succinct to reorder the open system of space and form in the time allowed.

The third level of winning is the most difficult to attain. It occurs when both constructions are converted, not according to the system of order of one side or another, but in such a way that an entirely new system of order is created. At this level, both sides win, because they transcend, together, their former states of opposition and enter a more complex, multivalent state. Resulting from the fusion of the former systems, their constructions achieve a new and hybrid system of order. They meet each other not as contenders but as co-inhabitants of a new spatial condition to which they have both contributed and which they must both work not only to maintain but to evolve further.

The Wall Game is designed to engage a new generation of Palestinian and Israeli players, who not only see the old games as destructive and self-defeating, but who want to create new and more productive modes of competition that may lead to new forms of cooperation. Because it is only a game, with neither territory nor lives at stake, winning and losing take on new meanings. As in any game, there is always next time to recoup pride and prestige—and thus the imperative to learn not only from failure but also from success. The winning team in any single game can be assured that the next time it plays, the opposing side will have not only learned their techniques, but also devised new tactics of their own. Neither victory nor defeat is ever final.

And there could be spin-offs. Certainly there will be in the development of new, computer-based technologies that oversee the conduct of the Wall Game. From monitoring the stresses in the wall that is the playing field, which gives both sides the information they need to continue construction, to judging the success or failure of a conversion attempt, computers—programmed to be as objective as possible—will rely on software that could bring new dimensions to ethical thinking. After all, in this situation, what does "objective" mean?

Even the most bitterly opposed adversaries who learn to play together find it difficult to kill each other. It is instructive to consider the impact of the famous table tennis matches between China and the United States in the seventies in ending open hostilities between these countries (such as the Korean War), or the role of the Olympics—and the United States's refusal to play in Moscow in 1980—in the rap-

prochement between the Soviet Union and the United States in the eighties. It can be argued that these games were only a sign that the opposing sides were ready to cooperate more openly and that the games were only symbolic, but that does nothing to diminish the importance of games as a method of approach. As cultural historian Johan Huizinga wrote in *Homo Ludens*,[1] "Play is a uniquely adaptive act, not subordinate to some other adaptive act, but with a special function of its own in human experience." This is an insight whose day of usefulness may, once again, be at hand.

Notes

1. Johan Huizinga, *Homo Ludens* (Boston: Beacon Press, 1971).

Contributors

Suad Amiry was born in Damascus in 1951. After studying in public schools in Damascus, Amman, and Cairo, she received her BSc (Architecture) at the American University of Beirut, an MSc in Urban Planning (University of Michigan), and her PhD in Architecture (University of Edinburgh). She has taught in the schools of architecture at the University of Jordan (Amman) and at Birzeit University (Palestine).

Amiry began her career in landscape architecture and published (with Jan Czecha) a manual on the "Trees and Shrubs of Jordan and the Holy Land for Landscape Planning." After the Madrid Peace Conference (1991) she joined the Palestinian Delegation in the Washington Peace Negotiations. When the Palestinian Authority was installed in 1996, she served as Deputy Minister of Culture in the first Palestinian Government, and represented Palestine frequently in various international cultural forums.

In 1990 Suad Amiry (with Professor Nazmi Jubeh) founded Riwaq, the Center for Architectural Conservation, in Ramallah-Bireh. The center, which she co-directs, has played a critical role in lobbying for legislation to protect Palestinian historical buildings and sites, and in establishing a database for the National Registry of Protected Buildings in Palestine. Riwaq has been the moving force in restoring a number of historical buildings in Hebron's old town (work which received the Aga Khan Award for Architectural Restoration in 2002), in Bethlehem, Nablus, Jerusalem, and Ramallah.

Amiry is the editor of Riwaq's Monograph Series, "History of Architecture in Palestine", and the author of several works on architecture and social history including *Traditional Floor Tiles of Palestine* (with Lina Subboh), *The Palestinian Village Home* (with Vera Tamari), *Throne Village Architecture*, *Earthquake in April* (with Mouhannad Hadid), and *Manateer: Watchtowers and Mansions of Jerusalem*. Her war diary, *Sharon and My Mother-in-Law*, has been translated into eleven languages and was a bestseller in Italy and France. In 2004, Amiry received the Viareggio Literary Award for International Writing.

Ariella Azoulay is a senior lecturer in the Program for Cultural Studies at Bar Ilan University, where she teaches Visual Culture and Contemporary Philosophy as part of the Program for Culture and Interpretation. She is the author of *Once Upon a*

Time: Photography following Walter Benjamin (2005, in Hebrew), *Death's Showcase* (2001), and *TRAining for ART* (2000, in Hebrew), as well the director of the documentary films *I Also Dwell Among Your Own People: Conversations with Azmi Bishara* (2004), *The Chain of Food* (2004), *The Angel of History* (2000), and *A Sign from Heaven* (1999).

Dalit Baum, PhD, is a feminist activist and teacher, working in a community school for disempowered women in Israel. She is an organizer with the Coalition of Women for a Just Peace and with Women in Black, and a co-founder of Black Laundry—Queers against the Occupation and for Social Justice. During the last two years she has been active in the popular resistance to the construction of the Separation Wall in Palestine.

Terry Boullata is head of the board of directors of the Women's Studies Center. Founded in 1989, the center strives for full social and political equality for Palestinian women and men and provides training and capacity-building programs to enhance women's ability to interact with governmental and nongovernmental bodies. The center works with the Palestinian Legislative Council, political parties, the Palestinian National Authority, and private and public institutions to advance the rights of women. A participant in the Geneva Accord initiative for peace among Palestinians and Israelis, Boullata attended the signing ceremony in December 2003, and continues her activity in the women's forum on behalf of a swift implementation of the initiative.

Boullata is founder and headmistress of the New Generation Kindergarten and School in Abu-Dis, an East Jerusalem suburb. The kindergarten was founded in 1999 as a private enterprise to provide children of a marginalized community with opportunities for quality education and has grown to become a private elementary school, adding an extra elementary class every year. With the construction of the peace-threatening Israeli occupation wall in the West Bank, Boullata became as antiwall activist.

Lindsay Bremner is a practicing architect and an Honorary Professorial Research Fellow in the Wits School of Arts at the University of the Witwatersrand, where she was formerly the chair of architecture. She has published and lectured widely on the transformation of the South African city, including her recent book *Johannesburg: One, City Colliding Worlds* (2004). In 2005, Bremner was visiting professor at the

Massachusetts Institute of Technology, where she ran a graduate level architectural studio on the city of Durban, South Africa, entitled "Liquid Durban".

Mike Davis is a San Diego-based agitator and the author of *City of Quartz*, *Ecology of Fear, Magical Urbanism, Late Victorian Holocausts, Dead Cities*, *Under the Perfect Sun* (with Jim Miller and Kelly Mayhew), and the forthcoming *Planet of Slums*.

Sari Hanafi is a sociologist and the director of the Palestinian Refugee and Diaspora Center, Shaml. His work focuses on economic sociology and network analysis of the Palestinian refugees; relationships between diaspora and center; returnees; local and international NGOs and donors, and conflict resolution on the post-war period. Hanafi is the author of numerous articles and books, including: *Here and Their: The Palestinian Diaspora from Social and Political Perspectives* (2001, in Arabic); *Between Two Worlds: Palestinian Businessmen in the Diaspora and the Construction of a Palestinian Entity* (1997, in Arabic and French); and *La Syrie des ingénieurs. Perspective comparée avec l'Egypte* (1997). He has been working on several books on Arab NGOs, most recently (in collaboration with Linda Taber) *Donors, International Organizations and Local NGO: The Emergence of Palestinian Globalized Elite* (2003). Hanafi holds a PhD in sociology from EHESS-Paris.

Dafna Kaplan, born and raised in Tel Aviv, is an independent photographer who works in documentary, portrait, studio and artistic photography, and is a regular contributor to leading Israeli publications, including *Ha'aretz* and *La-Ish*. She initiated, organized and led a seminar for the Jerusalem Municipality, "The Language of Photography as a Tool of Self-Expression and a Path to Societal Growth," is currently working on a project documenting graffiti in Israel and Palestine, and is in the final stages of research documenting political expressions in Rabin Square and other public spaces in Tel Aviv over the decade since the assassination of Prime Minister Yitzhak Rabin. Kaplan regularly exhibits her work in Israel and internationally. She is a graduate of the Department of Professional Photography, Hadassah College, Jerusalem, received a B.A. in photography from New York University, and completed the program in cultural studies at Alma College, Tel Aviv.

Tom Kay, an architect, was born in Palestine in 1935, where he was only to live for four months before returning to central Europe. He grew up in England with a brief stay in Canada as a toddler. After practicing from 1959 to 1961 in Tel Aviv with Dov Karmi, Kay sustained an architectural practice in London from 1964 to 2001. During this time he held teaching positions at the RCA, the AA, London University, and the PoW Institute. Since January 2002, Kay has been a resident of the West Bank, where he teaches full-time at Birzeit University, writes PAL notes, and takes photographs.

Stephanie Koury is a legal adviser to the PLO on the issue of settlements and the wall. She served as a member of the Palestinian delegation to the International Court of Justice on the Advisory Opinion on the Legal Consequences of Israel's Construction of a Wall in Occupied Palestinian Territory.

Miki Kratsman is a photographer for the Israeli daily *Ha'aretz* and for the weekly magazine *Ha'ir* as well as for numerous international publications. Born in Argentina in 1959, Kratsman began his professional career in 1984 as a photographer for the Israeli daily *Hadashot*, where he worked until 1994. In 1997 he won the Enrique Calvin Israel Museum Award and, in 2001, the national prize in photography from the Israeli Ministry of Education and Culture. In the same year, he received the British Multi-Exposure grant, designed to encourage exchange between English, Israeli, and Palestinian artists.

Kratsman's work has been exhibited widely, including shows at the Tel Aviv Museum of Art (1993 and 2000), the Israel Museum in Jerusalem (1999 and 2003), the Palazzo delle Papesse in Siena (2000), the Maison Robert Doisneau in Paris (2001), the Bezalel Academy of Art and Design (1996) and the Nelly Aman Gallery in Tel Aviv (2001 and 2003). His photographs have been published in numerous collections, including *Following the Missile Attack on Israel, A Day in the Life of Israel, 16 Cambio-16 Years of Photojournalism* (Spain), and *Documenta X—The Book.*

Kratsman has taught in Israel at the College of Photography (1996–1999), at the School for Geographic Photography (1998–2003), at the Vital School of Design (2001) and at Haifa University, where he was professor in the Department of Arts (2002–2003).

Dean MacCannell is professor of Environmental Design and Landscape Architecture at the University of California at Davis, where he teaches an advanced design studio on postmodern landscapes. He is author of *The Tourist: A New Theory of the Leisure Class, Empty Meeting Grounds*, and numerous papers and articles on social and psychoanalytic aspects of art, architecture, and design.

Dr. Ruchama Marton is a psychiatrist, feminist, and human rights activist, as well as the founder and president of Physicians for Human Rights-Israel (Tel Aviv), an organization of Israeli and Palestinian physicians active since 1988 in counteracting Israel's violations of human rights and in providing health care where it has otherwise been denied. Among her publications is *Torture: Human Rights, Medical Ethics and the Case of Israel* (ed. with Neve Gordon, 1995). Dr. Marton is the recipient of several peace and human rights awards, including the Emil Grunzweig Award for Human Rights, presented by the Association for Civil Rights, Israel, and the Jonathan Mann Award for Global Health and Human Rights, 2002.

Daniel Bertrand Monk is the George and Myra Cooley Professor of Peace Studies and director of the Peace Studies Program at Colgate University. He is the author of *An Aesthetic Occupation: the Immediacy of Architecture and the Palestine Conflict* (2002), as well as other writings on the Israel/Palestine conflict. Currently, he is at work on a study of Israel's "Era of Euphoria" following the June 1967 Arab-Israeli war. Monk co-coordinates the Virtual Security Project, an international research network focusing on peace, politics, and conflict in a postanalog world.

Adi Ophir is associate professor at the Cohn Institute for the History and Philosophy of Science and Ideas, Tel Aviv University, and the Shalom Hartman Institute for Advanced Judaic Studies. His work focuses on modern and contemporary continental philosophy in the domains of ethics, political philosophy, and critical studies. His most recent publications include "Moral Technologies: The Administration of Disaster and the Forsaking of Lives" (2002), "Life as Sacred and Forsaken: Introduction to Gorgio Agamben's *Homo Sacer*" (in Shay Lavie, ed., Technologies of Justice, 2003), "Evils, Evil, and the Question of Ethics" (in *Modernity and the Problem of Evil*, Alan Schrift, ed. , forthcoming). Books by Ophir include *Plato's Invisible Cities*

(1991), *Working for the Present: Essays on Comtemporary Israeli Culture* (2001); and, with Ariella Azoulay, *Terrible Days: Between Disaster and Utopia* (2002). Forthcoming is *The Order of Evils*. Ophir is the editor and founder of *Theory and Criticism*, an interdisciplinary journal for critical theory and cultural studies dedicated to Israeli culture and society.

Rebecca Solnit is a writer, art critic, and curator living in San Diego. She is the winner of the Lannen Award and a National Book Critic's Circle Award for criticism for *River of Shadows: Eadweard Muybridge and the Technological Wild West*. Other books include *Wanderlust*, *As Eve Said to the Serpent*, *Hope in the Dark: Untold Histories*, *Wild Possibilities*; and *Savage Dreams: A Journey into the Landscape Wars of the American West*. Solnit is a recent contributor to *The Nation* as well as to numerous other publications.

Michael Sorkin is the principal of the Michael Sorkin Studio in New York City, a design practice devoted to both practical and theoretical projects at all scales with a special interest in the city. The studio has undertaken numerous projects in the United States., Europe, Asia, and the Middle East. Sorkin's books include *Variations on A Theme Park, Exquisite Corpse, Local Code, Giving Ground* (ed. with Joan Copjec), *Wiggle, Some Assembly Required, Other Plans, The Next Jerusalem, After The World Trade Center* (ed. with Sharon Zukin), *Starting From Zero*, and *Analyzing Ambasz*. Forthcoming are *Twenty Minutes in Manhattan, Work on the City, Indefensible Space: The Architecture of the National Insecurity State*, and *All Over the Map*. Sorkin is the director of the Graduate Urban Design Program at the City College of New York.

Anita Vitullo is a writer and researcher based in East Jerusalem. She has been assistant editor of *The Journal of Palestine Studies* (1976–1980), contributing editor of *Middle East Report* (1982–1998), and director of research for the Palestinian Human Rights Information Project (1987–1994). Vitullo has served as program advisor for the World Food Program, researcher for the Palestinian National Poverty Report, special projects coordinator for the Palestinian Independent Commission on Citizens' Rights, and consultant to UNICEF and the Birzeit University Development Studies Program. Since 1998, she has worked with the Palestinian development organization, Welfare Association, in Jerusalem, where she is program development manager. A former radio journalist, Vitullo has published widely on Palestinian development and human rights issues.

Eyal Weizman is an architect based in London and director of the Goldsmiths College Centre for Architecture Research. Working in private practice in Israel, Weizman combined architectural projects with his research for the human rights organization B'tselem. Together with Rafi Segal he conceived the exhibition and publication *A Civilian Occupation: The Politics of Israeli Architecture*, projects that were subsequently banned by the Israeli Association of Architects, but later exhibited internationally. His PhD thesis on *The Politics of Verticality* is the basis for both a documentary film and a forthcoming book.

Lebbeus Woods is an architect and theoretician whose notable projects include Centricity (1987), Solohouse (1988), Berlin Free-Zone (1990), War and Architecture/Sarajevo projects (1993–94), Havana projects (1995), Terrain projects (1998–99), The Fall installation (2002), and System Wien (2005). Monographs on his work include *Anarchitecture: architecture is a political act* (1992), *Radical Reconstruction* (1997/2000), *Earthquake!* (2001), *The Storm and The Fall* (2004), and *System Wien* (2005). His works are in public collections including the Museum of Modern Art (New York), The Whitney Museum of American Art (New York), the San Francisco Museum of Modern Art, The Cooper-Hewitt Museum (New York), the Carnegie Museum of Art (Pittsburgh), the Museum of Applied Arts , MAK (Vienna), the Fondation Cartier pour l'art contemporain (Paris), and the Getty Research Institute for the Arts and Humanities (Los Angeles). He is the recipient of an American Institute of Architects Honors Award and the Chrysler Award for Innovation in Design. He has been a visiting professor at The Bartlett (London), SCI-ARC (Los Angeles), Columbia University and Harvard University. He is presently Professor of Architecture at The Cooper Union in New York City.

Haim Yacobi is an architect and planner. Currently, he is a post-doctoral fellow in the Department of Politics and Government at Ben Gurion University in Beer-Sheva, Israel. His academic research and publications focus on the politics of architecture, planning, and the notion of place.

Oren Yiftachel is professor of Geography and Public Policy at Ben-Gurion University in Beer-Sheva, Israel, where he served as department chair from 1999 to 2003. After studying geography, urban planning, and public policy in Australia and Israel, he taught at Curtin University, Australia; the Technion, Israel; Columbia University, and the University of Pennsylvania. Yiftachel has received research fellowships from RMIT, Melbourne; the U.S. Institute of Peace, Washington D.C.; and the Van Leer Institute in Jerusalem. He is the founding editor of the journal *Hagar/Hajer: International Social Science Review*, and is the author of numerous books, including *Planning a Mixed Region in Israel: The Political Geography of Galilee* (1992), *Planning as Control: Policy and Resistance in a Divided Society* (1995), *Ethnic Frontiers and Peripheries* (ed.with A. Meir, 1998), *The Power of Planning* (ed. with Hedgcock, Little and Alexander, 2001), *Hegemony and Challenges: Israelis in Conflict* (co-editor, 2004), and *Ethnocracy: Land, Politics, and Identities in Israel/Palestine* (2005).

Slavoj Zizek, philosopher and psychoanalyst, is senior researcher at the Department of Philosophy, University of Ljubljana and co-director of the Institute for Humanities, Birkbeck College, University of London. His latest book is *The Parallax View* (forthcoming, 2006).

Dafna Kaplan